D1823770

THE THIRD WAY

Book 1: Awareness

1st Edition

DR KARL PHILLIPS

First Edition

First published 2024
by Rowanvale Books Ltd
The Gate
Keppoch Street
Roath
Cardiff
CF24 3JW
www.rowanvalebooks.com

A CIP catalogue record for this book is available from the British Library.
ISBN: 978-1-914422-01-0
Hardback ISBN: 978-1-83584-015-3
Ebook ISBN: 978-1-914422-02-7

Life is short. We spend so much time sweating the small stuff; worrying, complaining, gossiping, comparing, wishing, wanting and waiting for something bigger and better instead of focusing on all the simple blessings that surround us every day. Life is so fragile and all it takes is a single moment to change everything you take for granted. Focus on what's important and be grateful! You are blessed! Believe it! Live your life and leave no regrets.

—Melanie Koulouris[263]

COPYRIGHT STATEMENT

Quoting, fair use and permission letters are one of the most complex areas of copyright law. The music industry has recently been racked with High Court copyright infringement cases, and musicians are then put under extraordinary strain and feel scared to touch musical instruments in case they start to hint at a sequence created by someone else. When you only have 12 notes to play with (as in Western music), it is inevitable that some sequences will be repeated in many songs, especially those that are melodic, have pleasing tones or are structurally sensible in terms of pitch and rhythm. The same occurs with sentences, quotes, long-held beliefs and misquotes, which also includes re-interpretations. There is some universal knowledge that is considered so valid that it can be deemed factual, and therefore can be freely shared.

Please bear in mind that anything published before 1950, or 70 years from the end of the calendar year in which the last remaining author of the work dies, is not covered by copyright law. Copyright has expired for all works published in the United States before 1924, and people are free to use them in the US without permission. The originator may not be the person who is often quoted as the source (J.R.R. Tolkien's 'where there's life' actually comes from Cicero 106–43BC) or may be wrongly attributed when people have said or written other similar things.

Short phrases, small groups of words, are considered common idioms and are free for anyone to use. Lots of good advice, facts and theories have been hard-learnt by humanity throughout time and are important not to forget, hide behind copyright or make difficult to access – and these are not protected by copyright. This applies to quotes that have universal appeal, value or meaning, without quoting the entire piece of work. Some quotes and sentences have totally different meanings when rearranged or considered in a new context. Other quotes are derivatives of others. One sentence does not constitute a copyright infringement.

It is not my aim to plagiarise the work of others. This first book has been created to showcase the tip of the iceberg of common aspects of the human condition – to help understand who we are, what we are and what we have to work with, whilst putting it into the context of mind, body, soul and Third Way thinking and providing personal examples, ideas and thoughts – not to blindly replicate the work of others. Since writing this book, some references I originally used have disappeared off the internet, as blogs and their URLs are not renewed; these are considered transient, as there is no way of going back and referencing them anymore.

'The Third Way' and many of the associated derivative names of this wording (collectively, the "trademarks" have been granted by the UK intellectual Property Office) are owned by Innov8or Solutions Ltd. Nothing contained within this book, on the official book website (www.thethirdwaybook.com) or other derived products should be construed as granting, by implication or otherwise, any licence or right to use these trademarks without the express written permission of Innov8or Solutions Ltd.

Contents

FOREWORD

This is the book I wish I could have read when I was younger, to help point me in my right direction and teach me not to worry so much about what others thought of me. I would gladly give this book away for free, but these days, most people don't value free gifts and only attach value to payment; perversely, the more we pay, the more value we perceive we are getting. We fail to see the beauty and love all around us, which cost nothing, and the huge scope for giving freely, be it our time, money or other resources to charity, or helping those in need.

I am a collector of quotes, facts, stories and observations. I don't own any of the information within this book; it is universal knowledge that belongs to everyone and, as such, should be widely shared. Humans are deeply flawed, complex beings capable of terrible actions, and yet have the capacity for the most beautiful phenomena, acts of kindness and works of art. This book showcases our flaws and also our capacity for superhuman activities, and demonstrates how we can be better versions of ourselves, using our past to help shape our present, with a hope of making a better future.

There is a danger when presenting quotes that you just become a vehicle for all the clichés in the world, so to counter this, I have added short commentaries to explore Third Way approaches and ideas and offer more personal insights into these topics, rather than simply presenting ideas previously published by others. You are welcome to consider how each topic affects you, how you react when reading it, how you reacted when experiencing it in your own life and how you might react in the future now that you are armed with additional information.

In order to become 'whole' you need to accept both the good and bad aspects of everything; it is only then that you can make informed choices and actions. You may not get it right every time, but if you start making more good choices than bad choices, then you will begin to make a 'small dent in the universe'.[234]

I wrote the original version of this book during COVID, and it came in at just under one million words, just a bit longer than *War and Peace*'s 587,287! It is no wonder it frightened so many publishers; a first-time author with a book of this magnitude is just too much of a risk. I was told to cut it down and divide it into three books. A typical novel is around 80,000 words; this book you hold is just over 100,000, so you can consider it either excessively long, too bulky to carry around or great value for money – you decide. Book One is a dip-your-toe-in-the-water type of book; Book Two will be a throw-you-into-the-deep-end type of book that will shake some of your fundamental knowledge and beliefs[285]; Book Three will be a dive-into-the-universal-ocean-with-the-sharks type of book – I hope you can swim! But I'll be by your side for reassurance and help, if you need it. It will be a journey the likes of which you have never been on before, I promise you that.

Each book is intended as a kind of jukebox where you can just dive in and read any section in any order. So, you can pick and choose by interest, just open onto a random page, or start at the beginning and work your way through – again, you decide. This book can be read in one sitting, or alternatively, you can read sections that are of interest to you, and dip in and out. I recommend that you pick it up at key stages of your life to help remind you what is important. Life will be over all too quickly, so we must not take it for granted but make the most of it with the ones we love. I hope that in reading this book you will discover something small that has meaning for you; sometimes the smallest step in the right direction ends up being the biggest step of your life. The sooner you start making changes, the sooner you will get results. Yesterday is gone, tomorrow is unknown, today is a gift. Life is short, so play hard, fair and without regret. Life is for living, thriving and giving back – see that you do it with compassion, humour and in style.

People might misunderstand this book and think it is a self-help or inspirational book, when that is not what it was created for. I can't help you. I can't inspire you. The words in this book can't do either of these things. You will need to do them yourself, but I can guide you by opening your eyes. Self-help is no help at all when the body cannot be happy, or the mind or soul is miserable.[5] Hopefully, I can make you think. You have everything you need inside you, you just don't realise it. Self-sacrifice, self-love, self-control and selflessness are really the ways to find yourself, your true self, and then help others on the path. It is a journey you will have to take alone, for I can't walk your path and neither can others. You can read all the self-help books in the world, but it will not make one ounce of difference until you become awakened; you can start by putting one foot forward onto the path.

As humans, we once viewed ourselves as unique, the only species in the world with emotions, morality and culture. Yet the more we have investigated, the more we find this not to be the case; we need only look to the social behaviours of wild elephants, orcas or sperm whales to see evidence of advanced forms of empathy, possibly superior to our own. Where we are unique is our ability to be both world creators and world destroyers. We are the current custodians of this world that we share with other species and have an obligation to look after it for future generations. This book provides a glimpse into the higher philosophy we, as world custodians, need: to carry out our duties of openness, fairness and care of others, irrespective of our personal concerns. Humanity must come together and accept our differences in order to carry out this mission with grace, maturity and a desire for righteousness.

Back in 1977, we sent human objects, such as the spacecraft *Voyager 1* and *Voyager 2*, into space, and they are now over 13 billion miles away from Earth. A message carried on both vessels contains recordings of natural and musical sounds and select images to portray the diversity of life and culture on Earth. These unique time capsules also contain spoken greetings from Earth people in 55 languages. The spacecraft will be encountered, and the record played, only if there are advanced spacefaring civilisations in interstellar space. Let us hope that this is not humanity's only legacy. We must remember that we are greater as a civilisation when we are united than when we are divided and fighting among ourselves. While each of us is on our own unique journey through life, capable of greatness, mediocrity and evil in equal measure, we are all connected. In a world that seeks to restrict us, we should never forget the beauty and power of the mind-body-soul relationship that allows us to live truly spectacular, three-dimensional lives.

When we look at a coin, we often only see the portrait (heads) or opposite side (tails) and neglect to acknowledge the rim of the coin that links the heads and tails. When a decision must be made with two viable answers, or two people disagree and must find an equitable way to choose between two options, look for that third option, or 'third way'. This book is intended to help you start to open your eyes to Third Way options and Third Way thinking. I hope to move people away from the binary, selfish and individualistic approaches that are so prevalent in today's society. When you start thinking, reacting and acting in a more connected, holistic and soulful way, you will find that other planes, avenues and opportunities will open up to you.

Some of my reviewers have said to me that a lot of the quotes in the book are widely available and I am therefore bringing nothing new to the world with this publication. I answer this criticism by saying that there is a lot of gold spread out across this world, and it is widely available to those who are willing to look for it, extract it and process it. As more and more people use old quotes in their content, it gets increasingly difficult to ascertain the original author, as search tools often don't differentiate the originator, just return all matching values. With this book, I have done the hard work of searching for, mining and processing these quotes, condensing them into what I consider a 'gold bar' equivalent; creating an easy-to-use format, gift wrapped (with my personal anecdotes, for what they are worth) for you to enjoy, reflect upon and hopefully act upon, if you so desire.

Some of the quotes I have used have since disappeared off the internet. The internet, I am finding, is not a library of knowledge that just keeps growing. Rather, books disappear when they are not returned or are removed – URLs are removed if payment is not kept up to date; authors change and update content so the algorithms see them as valid and relevant, otherwise they slip down the Search Engine Optimisation (SEO) rankings; or the content might just be removed by the author. Capturing this information in book format, although some may see this as archaic, will help preserve content that may otherwise be lost.

Some people may not appreciate the deeper wisdom in many of the quotes upon first reading, or they may be at such a young age that they may not have experienced many of the different facets of life. It can be easy to dismiss the knowledge of older generations, considering it out of touch and no longer valid or relevant; this may be the case in some examples, but human nature doesn't change that much over generations. As we get older, we find ourselves repeating the wisdom of our parents, grandparents and guardians who may have tried to help us, guide us and protect us in our youth, though we may not have listened at the time.

Throughout this book, you will come across italicised sections of text where I have retold or modified an old story I have heard. I may be providing a historic example that, while writing, I felt was either applicable to me or appropriate to recount at that stage. These italicised sections are designed as interludes, breaks and thought pieces, where you can ask yourself how applicable a topic is to you. Have you had a thoughtful experience related to that topic? What could you now do to improve those experiences? Can you just park it for later, when it may be needed?

One of humanity's challenges is that life, and our journey through it, is very complex, unique to everyone and can't easily be explained, but if I had to choose one word to encapsulate this book it would be 'love'. I loved writing it, I loved adjusting it and I hope you love reading it, not just once, but coming back to it every now and again – and, if you really loved it, sharing it with others. I would love for you to pace yourself and consider the words, their deeper meanings and applicability to your past, present and choice-driven future life.

I look forward to following it up with sequels that go deeper into this aspect of the mind-body-soul relationship: ways of living more peacefully and sympathetically with nature, and adapting to an increasingly noisy world. There is a lot to consider in these pages, and some may find it difficult to read or not get a sense of satisfaction upon finishing it, but as I have said, this is book one of a collection – a kind of soft-start prelude. However, I've tried to wrap a little bow at the end in the postscript as an interim summary to this first part of the story. I hope you do find something (even something small) that you can take away from the book to make things better on your journey.

I welcome any and all feedback.

karl@thethirdwaybook.com

'*The Third Way* is the kind of book I keep in my suitcase on foreign assignments or on my desk for quick reference. One of those rare books, it covers, like the Hayes manual to the soul, every major theme in life that we might need to answers to, from fear and jealousy to happiness and death. Its lightness of touch and gentle wisdom remind me a contemporary version of Rilke or Gibran.'[487]

MY DRIVING FORCE

My name is Karl Phillips and I'm a polymath or *multipotentialite*, which is roughly defined as someone with a wide range of expertise who draws on a rich well of knowledge. Just as Aristotle was not only a philosopher, he was also a keen botanist and teacher to Alexander the Great. Life has thrown me many challenges (some near fatal) and opportunities, and if nothing else, these have taught me that we are capable of things beyond even our wildest dreams, if only we are pointed in the right direction. I don't have all the answers, but we *can* do anything, just not everything!

I am fortunate to have experienced a wide variety of what life has to offer, to have seen the world and learnt from it. As such, I feel the need to participate in humanitarian works and share the knowledge I have come across so far. I tend to focus on goals outside of myself, with a strong desire to support others to thrive. In this era of humanity where we seem to be only *taking*, it's important to put a little back into the world.

I believe there is a 'Third Way' to everything and that by bringing together the intellectual/mind, physical/body and righteous/soul elements that lie within all of us, we can deepen our sense of humanity. I hope to lift the lid on the inner workings of humanity by bringing together some of the great minds of past and present cultures and religions.

I hope you enjoy reading this book as much as I have enjoyed writing it.

PRELUDE

Life is divided into three terms – that which was, which is and which will be. Let us learn from the past to profit in the present, and from the present to live better in the future.[510]

The Now – where we find our True Self, which lies behind our physical body, shifting emotions, and chattering mind. The single most vital step on your journey towards enlightenment is this: learn to dis-identify from the mind. Every time you create a gap in the stream of mind, the light of your consciousness grows stronger.[457]

The more you see of life the more you come to realise that it does not fall into the nice, neat, binary categories of black or white. Most of life is lived and experienced within the grey zone, that area of ambiguity, uncertainty and unknowing, where you have to be present to engage with it. People will attempt to seduce you with science or religion, with numbers or faith, with future states or past states, but they are only the binary positions, the two sides of the coin. The Third Way connects everything together, just like the rim of the coin. It combines the best thinking of the mind, the beauty of the body and the timeless eternity of the soul, to enable us to truly experience things in the world. It cuts open nature's opaque rock, revealing the diamond within, exposing the sparkle and the allure of the multi-faceted gem of true beauty that exists within us all. We just need to open our eyes, raise our awareness and let the beauty out.

Self-induced sadness and nostalgia are beautiful, for they are true experiences of the soul. It hurts when the person who gave you your best memories becomes a memory themselves, and sometimes the darkness holds you when nobody else will. Darkness can create so much beauty, but don't stay in it for too long; learn to balance yourself so you can be at peace with everything and everyone. Some pain never fully goes away, just abates for a while, but you are not and never will be truly alone. Nobody is perfect; we are all cracked or broken in some way, for that is how the light gets in.

To all those people who are feeling low, afraid, weak, self-hatred, alone or not worthy, you need to have faith in something that makes you feel alive. Pleasure always comes from external things today that will give you pain tomorrow, whilst joy originates from within. Happiness may not be the key, or even achievable, but you need light in your life to be free, to feel peace, to see the beauty that is all around us. You were not meant to live in the darkness forever, but you do need to learn to embrace the dark before you can fully appreciate the light, to see the light differently. Don't waste your life on anger, regrets, worries, negativity or grudges; life is too short to be unhappy.

DEDICATION

I dedicate this book to my beautiful and caring wife Elaine, who somehow manages to be nothing but supportive. She had the utmost patience with me, even when thinking, at times, that I wouldn't even start to write, let alone finish this book.

I would also like to thank my children, without whom this book would have been completed twenty-one years earlier!

To those who inspired this book but either have not yet read it, will not read it or are no longer with us to read it, I thank you from the deepest part of my heart for giving me the strength, courage and time to complete this for others.

To those who have attempted to sabotage this book, exploit it, or hinder my family in our lives, I forgive you. You have been the source of much of the content, and I welcome that now, though perhaps did not at the time.

Weak people seek revenge; intelligent people ignore; strong people forgive. For to err is human, and to forgive is divine. Life is too short to hold grudges – there are far more important things to dedicate your life to.

INTRODUCTION

Things

Reasons for living: to make your parents proud, to make yourself proud, to conquer your fears, to see your family again, to see your favourite artist live, to listen to music again, to experience a new culture, to make new friends, to inspire others, to see your siblings grow and flourish, to achieve a milestone (go to college, graduate, get married, score your dream job), to have your own children and hold them in your arms for the first time.

You can: adopt your own pet, meet your idols, laugh until you cry, eat your favourite food, find someone who loves you like you deserve, travel abroad, learn a new language, learn to draw, tell others your story in the hopes of helping them, take a road trip somewhere new, feel the sand between your toes, have breakfast in bed, start a water balloon fight, watch fireflies, have and attend birthday parties, spend the whole day in bed, eat a whole tub of your favourite ice-cream.

If you want to go a bit wild, then: get a tattoo, meet your internet friends, try new recipes, go on spontaneous adventures, say swear words and savour the release you feel when you do, jump on a trampoline like a kid, paint with your fingers.

Don't forget to do the small things that mean so much: eat ice-cream on a hot day, drink hot chocolate on a cold day, marvel at untouched snow in the morning, watch a sunset set the sky on fire, count the stars as they light up the sky, read a book that changes your life, smell the flowers in the spring, notice as the leaves change from green to brown, enjoy puppy kisses and baby kisses (the open-mouthed kind when they smack their lips on your cheek), lie back and watch the clouds, pamper yourself and then sleep in clean sheets, have breakfast for dinner (because it's so much better at night than in the morning), get a new book by your favourite author, have a bonfire and make s'mores, sing at the top of your lungs with your friends (off-key is fine), listen to and watch a thunderstorm.

Never forget the feeling of: coming home to someone you love; autumn as the leaves change colour; being wrapped up in a warm bed; someone's skin against yours; holding hands for the first time; the kind of hugs that lift a weight off your shoulders, where your breath syncs with the other person's and you feel like the only two people in the world; the first ocean wave rolling up and enveloping your toes, ankles, knees; your first (or hundredth) trip to Disneyland; the childlike feeling you get on Christmas morning; the day when everything finally goes your way; relationships where you love someone but aren't in love with them; someone you love saying, 'I love you'; giving and receiving forgiveness; spending the day with someone you love; first dates (even the bad ones make for funny stories); getting a middle seat in the cinema.

Be thankful when you receive thoughtful gifts; say, 'I saw this and thought of you.'

Accept the relief you feel after crying.

Truly appreciate: new clothes, witty puns, really good bread, the dreams you wake from and can't stop smiling, the smell before and after it rains, the sound of rain on a rooftop, when your favourite song comes on the radio, the feeling you get when you're dancing, the people who mean the most to you, the sunshine, when someone is listening to you/giving you their full attention, your future wedding, compliments and praise, when you take the first bite of your favourite chocolate bar, the rush you get when you step onto a stage.

It feels great to share your voice, talents and knowledge with the world because they are so valuable, and it will feel amazing to look back on this moment in ten years' time and realise you did it.

There are so many beautiful things to live for, so live, and live, and live.[91]

There are things we are not meant to understand. Whether this is related to the supernatural, spirits, soul-world or other alternate realities or dimensions, we create our own understanding through our belief systems about ourselves, our expectations and the nature of reality. We make and create our own reality.[395] There are no boundaries or separation of the physical or astral self; the body is often closer to the soul than the mind is.

You are ultimately the power of God manifested, and the present is the point of power.

The dark lessons in life have shown me that: anyone can betray you at any time; many people only care about themselves; people want to control your life; whatever people suspect about you they believe is true even before they ask; being in a relationship is great but it makes you so vulnerable; relationships have ruined our world.

Despite knowing these evils exist, there's only very little you can do to avoid them. Never lend money to your friends, you will lose the money and the friendship; never pay to watch porn[332]; don't spend everything today with the hope of earning more tomorrow; never beg for love; stop thinking and start acting; be kind to people and animals; stay humble, nothing is worth bragging about; learn to say 'yes' or 'no' and mean it; own your mistakes, don't blame others for them; live up to no one's expectations, live according to your true self; work on yourself first; never leave for tomorrow what you have to do today; never tell a loved one you're 'too busy'; do not hold on to issues with your partner for more than 24 hours. Give a man money and find out his true colours; investigate before you invest; don't develop too much love for free things; do good and never expect it in return; stop depending so much on people; talk less and think more; never be afraid to think big; get settled or never waste your time on a love life; never be friends again with someone who has betrayed you; do not announce your success; make your source of happiness a secret; try not to offend people, some will spend their whole lives trying to pay you back; appreciate people for their efforts and kindness to you, no matter how small it may be; exercise daily and eat healthily, let your food be your medicine and your medicine is your food; help people secure work where and when possible, never seek sex in return; never give what you will regret losing ownership over; never abandon your parents in their old age, that's when they need you the most; never cheat or hurt anyone; never feel superior or inferior to anyone; do not seek pleasure for its own sake; do not, under any circumstances, depend on a partial feeling; think lightly of yourself and deeply of the world; be detached from desire your whole life long; do not regret what you have done; never be jealous; never let yourself be saddened by a separation; do not let yourself be guided by lust or love; do not collect weapons or practice with them beyond what is useful; do not seek to possess either goods or fiefs for your old age.

In all things, have no preferences. Be indifferent to where you live; do not pursue the taste of good food; do not hold on to possessions you no longer need; do not act following customary beliefs.

Do not fear death. Respect Buddha and the gods without counting on their help.[328]

Remember: your friends could be friends with your enemies; readers are leaders; your best dress is someone's rag; no one identifies with a poor person; today is hard, tomorrow will be harder, the day after tomorrow will be sunshine; when you stop learning you start dying; nothing you have is truly yours;[600] the things you attract are in correlation with what dominates your thoughts; it's normal to make mistakes because you're advancing; personal experience isn't the best teacher, learn from other peoples' experiences; there's a problem in the land where the king loves music too much; expectation kills; no one is always there for you except family; at the point of death, people don't regret the things they've done but the things they couldn't do; life is stormy, no one is free from it, those who thrive in it are the people you call successful; whatever money cannot do, more money can't do either; happiness is natural and comes from within, it is not money dependent; everyone is sick; never leave small fishes in search for a bigger one; there's a great difference between ownership and possession; helping others won't make you unsuccessful; every mistake is a lesson, take advantage of it; if you have disabilities, you're special and can be extremely great; blaming people (relatives) for not helping you is a bad habit; living a fulfilled life starts with accepting everything just the way it is; resentment and complaint are appropriate neither for oneself or others; you may abandon your own body but you must preserve your honour.

Never stray from the Way.[328 & 601]

Things have a natural tendency to fall into three buckets.

There once was a person so focused on new things and goals that all they could see was straight ahead in front of themselves, whether it was the next milestone, the next output that would lead to the right outcome, or some future state that they were always chasing. For they had become future-focused (the First Way).

There was another person so focused on old things, on what had gone wrong with everything, that they kept looking backwards, over-reflecting on why, the bad choices they had made and the lessons they had wished they had learned. For this person had become past-focused (the Second Way).

Finally, there was the last person in this story, who looked forward and looked back, but for the vast majority of their time, sat on the train of life, experiencing everything they possibly could: engaging with other passengers, looking out the window to appreciate where they were at that exact moment in time, recognising the beauty of life and becoming satisfied with their lot. For they lived in the now, and focused on the present (The Third Way).

The train of life may not be taking you exactly where you want to go, but, sometimes, a detour or a stop at an unintended yet interesting waypoint, or to get on another train, can be just what you need to get you to another destination. Take advantage of these opportunities to look out of the window of life and appreciate and become more aware of yourself, your surroundings and the important people with you.

My father always said that the train of life seems to speed up at the end, and that growing old never comes alone. Two things my father definitely got right.

SECTION 1 – THE MIND

Professor Steve Peters, in his Chimp Paradox model, theorises that the mind is made up of the Frontal section (a conscious human thinking system based on facts, logic and analytics), the Chimp system (the primitive part that works with drives, survival instincts and reactive behaviours) and the Computer section (the reference source for the two other systems, containing beliefs, memories, past experiences and lessons learnt).[254]

The mind is not a physical object as it can't be seen, touched or photographed. It has many different faculties including thought, imagination, memory, sensation, willpower and motivation, and is just one simple way of linking to and identifying with the inner being within all of us. It operates at different levels and speeds, and reacts to various internal and external stimuli, resulting in different outputs at different ages and under different conditions.

Now consider the fact that the human mind has evolved to enhance our cognitive flexibility and capacity for innovation and imitation, which has resulted in a magnificent entity, even if it can be unpredictable, inadequate, a trickster and dysfunctional a lot of the time. Many of our previous preconceptions about the mind have now been identified as incorrect. Mental health issues are now acknowledged as a common human experience; they can happen to anyone at any time in their life, where their thoughts, feelings or behaviour, or a combination of the three, result in mental distress, dysfunction or disturbance. It is thought that particular abnormalities within the brain's circuits contribute to many mental illnesses, affecting how the brain processes information, either getting overloaded or confused. The myriad results can feel as bad as physical illnesses or, in some cases, even worse.

You are more than just your mind; don't let it or the desire for pleasure control your life. Be aware of your thoughts and ready to fight off the ones you don't want, that don't serve humanity, that are unproductive, abusive or a general waste of energy. You have the ability to practise unimaginable mind control techniques – you don't need to wait for your feelings to change to take action.

Don't believe everything your mind reads, sees or is told by others, for they can be great deceptions to bring you under the control of others. Never argue with stupid people; they will drag you down to their level and then beat you with experience.[466]

What is the point of worrying when life is so short? Learn to accept what was, what is beyond your ability to change and what you can change; learn to take life as it comes and go with the flow, for to fight against the flow is very hard; learn to let things go, for some things just aren't meant to be and so won't work out as you thought or won't meet your expectations; watch out for what is meant to be instead, keep your mind sharp so you don't miss the opportunities that would otherwise sail right past; have faith that everything happens for a reason, that you may not understand it in the moment, but you will come to realise it later on.

People spend far too much mental effort suffering because of the past and in the interest of the future they cannot control. The only work that is within our control is in our hands right now; focus your mind on the present so you can learn to keep life simple and live it to the fullest.

The mind doesn't like change, yet change is the only constant in life – a permanent Universal Law. Take a leaf out of the book of Mother Nature to see that change occurs all the time: day follows night; spring follows winter; plants, animals and people grow and then die; the world freezes then thaws. Being able to accept and adapt to change makes you more robust, tenacious, agile and flexible. For the tree that bends is less likely to break.

Your mind matters, for your thoughts can either make you, break you or paralyse you. A mind full of thoughts about money cannot fully concentrate on the task at hand or mediate properly. If you can think it, you can then start to action it and move towards achieving it; when you can align and focus your mind in a positive way before any challenge, the chances of doing better are brighter.

Sometimes the little things in life are enough. We are all blessed with life's magic; love has the ability to travel through time and ripen us in pure magic, even when love means accepting the pain.

But sometimes, we need to detach from our mind and its pain to access presence and see the beautiful moments through the eyes of the soul. Beautiful moments happen all the time, but we often miss them due to modern life's hurried pace. We get lost in routine, malaise; we detach and feel uninspired. Listen to your whispering soul, not only your mind.[490] & 602

CHAPTER 1

Believe you can & you're halfway there.

"What we think determines what happens to us, what we want to change, for there is no time like the present."

—Wayne Dyer[128] (Modified)

Train your mind to see the good in everything; positivity is a choice. The happiness of your life depends on the quality of your thoughts.[16] We were all born with the greatest weapon in all of nature – a rational, conscious mind. Make every day a little less ordinary by thinking higher and feeling deeper, then acting accordingly. But beware, for overthinking kills your happiness, and if you spend too much time thinking, you'll never get anything done. It is a balance. Remember that even when you stumble, you're still moving forward; positive thinking helps you to stand back and start again when you are knocked down by bad luck or negativity.

Know that everything happens for a reason, but accept that even when you wish to know what the reason is, it may not be time for the great reveal – it will come later.

This chapter dives into elements of mental power, dreams, viewpoints, truth, hope, belief, faith, success and beauty. Enjoy thinking new thoughts.

Mental

The mental aspect of life drives us to develop our thoughts so they support our spiritual and physical development. As a result, our thoughts are focused on people, situations, environments and things that help fulfil our true purpose while here on Earth; everything you want to achieve begins with a thought.[603]

Some people say that the world used to be a bigger place. We get stuck in our daily routines and sleepwalk around the world, tending to miss the beautiful moments life has to offer. I took a walk around my village today. I felt the sun on my cheeks as I listened to the birds singing in the big tree in the far-right corner of a distant field, which had only blossomed three days earlier into vibrant colours, shifting shadows and reflections. No technology, no distractions, just me; I enjoyed every second of it, like I was really awake and living. Life is amazing and life is hard. However, if you are able to truly appreciate those fine moments that bring you happiness, life is more than worth it. [604]

It really is mind over matter. Think around your problems, not through them; struggles are nothing more than steps on the way to success when you have the right thoughts. Thoughts can either create Heaven or Hell under the same circumstances; two people can experience the exact same negative event, yet one person will somehow get through it without falling apart.[605]

There are so many great opportunities out there – our job, while we are here on Earth, is to wake up, think about our purpose in life and then just do it.

A coin has three sides, but we invariably ignore the rim when we use the coin to help us make decisions. The heads is the First Way, the opposing tails is the Second Way, but the rim is The Third Way and operates in a totally different dimension.

When I roll a ball through the centre of an audience, half the audience says the ball went from left to right (and they are right about that – the First Way), the other half says the ball went from right to left (and they are also right – the Second Way), but when I say the ball went from in front of them to behind them, they all agree and consensus is reached. This is the power of The Third Way.

Dreams

Trust in dreams, for in them is hidden the gate to eternity.[182] Only magic and the dream are true – all the rest's a lie.[378] Believe in it, trust in it, own it, live it like it has already happened and have faith that it is coming together even when you can't yet see the physical signs.[503]

There is no dream that is too big to achieve.[406] When you have a dream, protect it and don't give up on it.[158] Don't let anyone tell you can't do it – when people can't do something themselves, they tell you that you can't do it either; if you want something, go get it, period. Take a chance and succeed by going outside the box or outside the lines; there are no limits. However, remember that dreams without goals and actions are just dreams.[486 & 607]

Make sure you give more energy to your dreams than to your fears. Twenty years from now you will be more disappointed by the things you didn't do than by the things you did, so throw off the bowlines, sail away from safe harbours and catch the trade winds in your sails. Explore, dream, discover.[466] It is a mean world, but there are many ways to achieve your dreams, so never give up.

There may be times when you can't achieve because of your current constraints or mindset, but don't let today's disappointments cast a shadow on tomorrow.[506] Let yourself dream, and enter the realm of 'illegal' (non-established) thinking outside traditional processes in order to get to new shores or achieve new insights. Fail big and fail quickly, so you can rethink your approach to your dream.

Some say that everything is a dream and nobody can be sure of what reality is, what life is or what time is. This demonstrates how asleep our human race can be, and how our whole history has been a story of slumber. There are times to wake up from the dream, and now is a good time to do it.

Never let others constrain your dreams. Dream like mad. Dream Big. Dream like there are no boundaries in the universe and anything is possible.

Viewpoints

Every viewpoint is a view from a point.[608] Seeing the world from another perspective can introduce you to all sorts of hidden treasures. So, let go of your attachment to being right, and suddenly your mind will be more open and able to benefit from the unique viewpoints of others, without being crippled by your own judgement.[18] Never frown upon something just because you do not understand it; your current viewpoint will not always be the right one.

Sometimes a change of viewpoint is all that is needed to convert a tiresome duty into an interesting opportunity.[162] Whatever you hold in your mind will tend to occur in your life,[609] so if you want different results in your life, all you have to do is change your mind.[314 & 510] You have real power when you choose how you want to perceive every situation – the secret to success is to understand the viewpoints of others,[167] and wisdom is the capacity to see things from God's viewpoint.[438]

New viewpoints are always in the minority.[611] We cannot let a minority of people hold a viewpoint that terrorises the majority of people.[96]

The only people who get anywhere interesting are those who get lost.[455] Discovery consists not in seeking new lands but in seeing with new eyes.[366] If you spend your whole life waiting for the storm, you'll never enjoy the sunshine.[494]

Your opinion of yourself is your most important viewpoint,[186] and you are infinitely greater than you think you are.[397] 'Yesterday, I was clever so I wanted to change the world; today, I am wise so I am changing myself.'[398] Know that you are already equipped with exactly what you need in order to become who you are supposed to be.

. Truth

In this world of opinions and facts, everyone seems to believe that they speak the truth. However, there is no absolute truth because it is immaterial and subject to subjective points of reference.

We have a bias towards believing that what we hear is the truth and that people generally tell the truth, even when we're told they're lying.[612] It can be tough to discern fact from fiction, fraud from reality, as we all have our own manufactured ideas of the truth and we don't like it when they are challenged or confronted. We judge others based on their alignment with our version of the truth, when we should celebrate these different aspects of truth and allow them to enable us to become more enlightened.

Truth is always out there, like the fundamental truths stating that you were born, you will die, and that the time between these two events (not money) is your most valuable asset. You are not invincible or eternal, so although you don't know exactly when you will die, you can either speed the process up by not looking after yourself, or you can start to structure your life in a more meaningful way. You can say no to winning, conquering, mastering and dominating, and choose universal truth; get to know yourself first and then the world around you.

When we fail to accommodate multiple understandings of a situation, it ends with the abandoning of words and reason – those tools given to us to heal and allow us to come together – in favour of the simpler, much more terrifying tools of violent engagement and war. The first casualty of war is truth,[236] and the truth is that at the end of all wars, we end up coming back to words and reason. It is terrible that we continue to accept the price of the deaths of innocent people just to get back to the place of words.

It is always easier to swim with the current than fight against it, but the river may not take you to the place you want to get to. What you do matters. What you do *today* matters. What you do every day matters.[338] Fear kills the future and more dreams than failure ever will,[277] so one of the most basic truths is to apply the good things you learn one step at a time to develop new habits: done is better than perfection;[403] change is a direction, not a destination.[388]

There once was a person who lived in a valley and, in the process of seeking enlightenment, planned to ascend to the top of the highest mountain. On the way up, the person met lots of people going up and coming down the mountain; the higher they climbed, the fewer people they saw. Eventually, the person was on their own and the journey had become very hard, but they had prepared for this.

When the person eventually reached the summit, they were surprised to find an old man already sitting there. The old man welcomed the new visitor and shared with them the knowledge that, even at this high peak, there were other, higher mountains as far as the eye could see. There are always higher mountains of truth providing even greater viewpoints.

When the time came, they both descended to the valley and became good friends. Although the old man lived at the peak, nothing thrived at those high altitudes, with rarefied, limited oxygen and harsh ultraviolet rays, so the old man had needed to get supplies and to rest for a while to allow him to continue to survive there.

One day, the old man said goodbye to his new companion and told them that although it was beautiful at the top of the mountain, the cycle of life meant that nobody could permanently stay there. He then imparted his secret: do not be too harsh on yourself going forward, for life is all about going up and down mountains (the First Way), taking rest and being at peace with yourself (the Second Way), and enjoying the absolute pinnacle of what life has to offer by experiencing the present (The Third Way).

Go with the flow of life and enjoy relationships with people who value and care for you. Don't fight the flow of life unless you are willing to sacrifice something. Understand that you will not understand everything, then you can start your journey to becoming wise.

Hope

Hope is a good thing – maybe the best of things when used correctly. Right now, there are people all over the world just like you: lonely, depressed, hurt, scared, with personal issues no one knows about or secrets you wouldn't believe. And they wish, dream and hope. But while there is life, there is hope[94]: however bad life may seem, there is always something you can do and succeed at[202]; no matter how bad it gets, or how lost you feel, hold on to hope[156]; keep hope alive. We have the capacity to be far larger and greater than what we suffer. If the world is to be healed through human effort, it will be done by ordinary people, whose persistent hope and love for this life is greater than their fears.[289]

Stop worrying about the small things in life.[289 & 613] You can do this by figuratively plucking them out of your head, placing them on your shoulder, and then, with great satisfaction, flicking them away; let them go and live somewhere else. You will start feeling better, less burdened and more peaceful. Don't spoil what you have by desiring what you do not; remember that what you have now was once among the things you only hoped for.[137]

The very least you can do in your life is figure out what you hope for, and the most you can do is live inside that hope, not admire it from a distance, but live right in it, under its roof.[257 & 610]

Hope is great, but be prepared to have a Plan B or alternative strategy when things don't turn out as expected. I've found that a proactive mitigation plan can help reduce risks and give more energy to any strategy involving hope. Hope on its own is like magic fairy dust – use it sparingly.

Belief

Nothing is unbelievable.[307 & 614] We all have the divine spark within us, the ability to bring joy and laughter to the world. A single mum who works two jobs and still finds time to take her kid to football practice, that is a miracle. A teenager who says no to drugs and yes to an education, that's another miracle.[149]

People don't appreciate how much their mindset affects their reality. However, there are limits: just because you think and believe something is true doesn't mean it is. The power of belief resides in its ability to do five things within people: create vision, create strength of will, create resilience, ignite and activate passions and change realities.[258 & 615] By changing your mindset, you become unchained from the current capabilities and previous limitations you've been conditioned to accept.[616] Don't believe you are always right, because you're not.

Some beliefs may be holding you back and working against you. It's important to identify these and reprogramme them into something beneficial. Happiness is just a belief, and you can choose it. Affirmations, visualisation and feeling as if something is already true before going out and starting to create it are important elements of the success formula.

Core beliefs are assumptions we make about ourselves (such as: I am not good enough; I am different, an outsider; you have to be happy to be liked; everything is my fault; etc.), others and the world, which we mistake for facts – they can control your life without you realising it. One of the most dangerous core beliefs is considering yourself 'special', as it leads right to grandiosity or narcissism. It can mean that you manipulate others, have anger management issues, or are so wrapped up in yourself that you never experience true love and intimacy.

Faith

Taking a leap of faith allows the net to appear in front of you.[73] Don't underestimate the power of having faith in the Universe and faith in yourself. It demands a great deal of faith and courage for you to be a real person and not allow yourself to be misled and/or conditioned by generally accepted customs, traditions or values; with this strength, you will be able to examine your own shortcomings, doubts and fears more frequently and to greater benefit. Traditions are the guideposts driven deep in our subconscious minds. The most powerful ones are those we can't even describe, aren't even aware of. [189]

Have faith in yourself and in your abilities, but be cautious of the negative aspects of faith. When you put too much faith in something, a personality or your abilities, it's bound to hurt you, having a tendency to produce weakness and fanaticism. Too much faith in anything will suck you dry like a vampire.[54] In general, people put too much faith in the rich, the famous and politicians, and not enough faith in themselves.[50] Blind faith in your leaders, or in anything, will either get you killed or into a lot of trouble[436]; the language of faith can blind you to what is happening in reality, and disguise political agendas. What use is having faith in a leader who promises to implement favourable policies but then corrupts democracy, promotes illegal or immoral acts and sabotages the nation's credibility? When power is attained at the expense of your faith, producing a far more unsettled and dangerous world, you must ask yourself, was it worth the cost?

Individuals who have religious faith may be content with blindness, as they may feel no obligation to understand what they believe – they may even wish to not have their beliefs disturbed by thought.[5] In faith, there is enough light for those who want to believe and enough shadows to blind those who don't.

Religion, spirituality and the soul remind us who we really are and how we are all connected. Never forget that. I think that all faiths lead to God, for if you treat others like you would like to be treated – with respect, dignity and humanity – you can't go far wrong. A faith that doesn't do these basic things is not a faith, but a cult. Cult members may eventually find God, but they go the long way around.

Success

Success is a little like wrestling a gorilla; you don't quit when you're tired, as the task requires more of a mental attitude than a physical one – you quit when the gorilla is tired.[617] Define success for yourself, whether it is good health, financial security, happiness, a thriving family, environmental stewardship, being spiritually sound, a worthwhile career or great friendships. Your answer to what defines success is highly likely to change over time as your priorities shift, but never do anything that antagonises or jeopardises your soul.

What is your next hill? Understand that once you reach the top of the hill you're climbing, you will have a better vantage point to see the next one. Take stock each day to determine if you are in the black or red for each of your priorities, so you can identify which needs more attention at any given time. To keep something healthy, you need to put in the time to maintain and care for it; keep the things that are important to you in good working order, and they will not let you down.

To achieve your goals, you must be disciplined, consistently; life is more like a marathon than a sprint.[618] Goals help us keep track of our progress, identify our priorities and help us discover our purpose in life, which we can then make our primary ambition. Break down your dreams into realistic, attainable goals to prevent endless procrastination; quality over quantity will allow you to focus on the things that really matter.[619] Goals keep us focused and motivated, as once you achieve them, you will drive yourself even harder to accomplish the next ones, and the next ones, until you achieve your dreams. Make a plan, have the hunger, then work hard; there is no passion, satisfaction or joy to be found playing it safe, or settling for a life that is less than the one you are capable of living.[295] Take control. You're not a failure for doing things a little later in life; you fail when you don't do something you want to do.

Most people are lazy and give up too easily. They talk the talk, but don't walk the walk. It's not that successful people are super smart, it's that they stick with problems for longer.[133] It's absolutely frightening how many people fail at the last hurdle – they put in all the effort for the majority of the endeavour, only to walk away when they are inches from success. Don't be that person. It will not be easy; you will have to make a lot of sacrifices. But with dedication you will overcome challenges and achieve your goals. The best things in life are worth fighting for, believing in and just never letting go of through hard work, blood, toil, tears and sweat.[93, 469 & 620]

Shortcuts often make for longer delays,[456] and every shortcut has a price greater than the reward.[621]

Very successful people are often introverts, follow a different path and care less about what other people think. They can also have some rather strange flaws, such as being obsessive, stubborn or over-reliant on others' support. At the highest levels of achievement, you need to put yourself and your time first, in a manner that might be considered 'selfish' or 'weird'. This can make others angry, sad or unhappy, but don't allow your success to be built upon the failure, death or misery of others. That is the worst kind of success. Assuming everything is okay when things need to be taken care of is very unhealthy. Being slightly over-prepared or over-complicated can be good when in the context of planning or developing foresight, which may mean that you move slower than everyone else, but prevents you from causing distress to others on your way to achieving your goals.

You are often the barrier to your own success – get out of your own way and succeed.

Some barriers are put in place to keep you on the right path – your chosen path or God's. Understanding this can help you deal with failure, reducing the accompanying pain and suffering, and get you on your true path.

Beauty

The most beautiful thing in the world is, of course, the world itself, and you are a part of that. And the most beautiful things in life are not things: they are people, memories, feelings, moments, smiles and laughter; they cannot be seen or even touched, they must be felt with the heart[252]; they are not to be heard about, read about, nor seen, but to be lived.[255] If you don't celebrate these, they will pass you by[491] and you will miss those beautiful things.

Beauty has so many forms, and I think the most bounteous of all is confidence and love for yourself. Love yourself for who you are, and you will find that happiness grows within. You're more beautiful than you think and can ever imagine. Tread softly, breathe peacefully, but laugh hysterically. You are beautiful and your smile is your best asset. Knowing who you are and that you are not perfect is beautiful. To be free and to live a free life is the most beautiful thing there is.[226]

We often think of external beauty when defining the word, for it catches the eye, but there is so much more to internal beauty, as it captures the heart.[469] Those who possess this are not like the people in magazines; they are beautiful for the way they think, the sparkle in their eyes when they talk about something they love and their ability to make people smile even in sadness. This is more than temporal beauty; it is real, deep down in their soul, where true beauty lives. For beautiful eyes, look for the good in others. For beautiful lips, speak only words of kindness. For beautiful poise and posture, walk with the knowledge that you are never alone.[207] For beautiful people, look through their eyes to see their souls. The most beautiful people I know are those who have known defeat, suffering, struggle and loss and have found their way out of the depths. These people have an appreciation for, sensitivity towards and understanding of life that fills them with compassion, gentleness, genuine kindness and a deep, loving concern. Life is hard, but beautiful people do not just happen.

The most beautiful thing we can experience is 'the mysterious', as it is the source of all true art and science.[133] An incredible, benevolent force beyond our control that wants to tell us there is no need to be afraid.[146] In this moment, you can feel as though there is so much beauty in the world that it's hard to stay mad, that you can't take it all in and your heart is just going to burst. It's like God's looking right at you, just for a second, and if you're careful, you can look right back. It is then you must remember to relax, stop trying to hold on to it and let the feeling flow through you like rain, and you will feel only gratitude.[146] If you absorb that moment, I swear it will be infinite.

Remember: The future belongs to those who believe in the beauty of their dreams[392]; one of the most beautiful qualities of true friendship is to understand and be understood[418]; real men don't love the most beautiful woman in the world, but the one who makes their world the most beautiful, who makes them feel more loved than anyone else[469]; there is beauty in the ashes of a heart that burned for what it loved; you may be afraid of heights, but be more afraid of never flying.[363]

The media has constructed images of what it thinks beauty is, and we've been foolish enough to buy into it, accepting it unchallenged. When you choose beauty for beauty's sake alone, you leave elements of your soul behind. I came across multiple articles about high-performance vehicle owners telling the truth about owning their dream cars. Their stories tell of the pursuit of beauty that can have a dark heart, costing a lot more than you could have imagined and not bringing the anticipated joy. I love the quote about people buying their dream boat, that the only two days of real joy are the day they buy it and the day they sell it. Beauty doesn't come out of a box or in the form of a luxury item, and it is just one face of the multi-faceted diamond of life.

The beautiful truth is that we have been given everything we need in life, even the choice to experience our beautiful physical world, yet we pollute, fight and war, destroying when we think we are progressing and evolving. It is no wonder the billionaires are looking for a way off-planet, a grand dream that will inevitably start the process of destroying somewhere else. Technological civilisation will eventually end. It will be succeeded by something else that will likely be of lesser technology and may or may not be civilised. We shouldn't care – the beautiful Earth could shake us off like fleas, because we are little more than that to her. She has shaken off many civilisations in the past; why should ours be any different when we treat her, and each other, so badly?

CHAPTER 2

Life lived well is long enough.

"The two most powerful warriors in life are patience and time, but they will not wait around forever."

—Leo Tolstoy[458] (Modified)

Attitude is a little thing that makes a big difference[93]; it is your attitude, not your aptitude, that will determine your altitude.[514] When combined with your choices, your attitude equals the totality of your life, so keep your values and attitude positive because they will become your destiny.[178] If you are positive, you'll see opportunities instead of obstacles.[165]

In this chapter, we'll investigate lessons, opportunities, grieving, trust, perseverance, consistency, ceilings, resolve and self-help. There are times that only happen once in your life – a time of intensity, of love and romance, of a broken heart – and then there is a time of never again. The human capacity for burden is like bamboo – far more flexible than you'd ever believe.[358] You only fail when you stop trying, so never stop trying.[469]

Lessons

Know when to let go – if it's dead, there is no need to dig it up every five minutes to check it has a pulse – dead is dead, so walk away. Retaliation leads to escalation, so most of the time, it really is better to do nothing and say nothing.

Look after yourself now you are all grown up and on your own – behave like a grown-up; draw lines around yourself to establish personal boundaries so you don't have to be scared of other people; it is okay to worry, but it's better to know how not to, as all you're doing is putting wrinkles in your brow that make you look older; staying young means trying out new tastes, new places, new styles and using new things; think for yourself – everyone wants to blend in, be one of the crowd, be acknowledged – don't be a sheep[452]; have something in your life that takes you out of yourself – it is no good having a piece of music that always lifts your mood if you don't play it occasionally; maintain good manners in all things – a little politeness always goes down well and can help you achieve your objectives; only the good feel guilty, so if you do feel guilty, then that's a good sign; if you can't say anything nice, then don't say anything at all.[452]

Prune your stuff frequently because clutter emotionally overwhelms people and makes life more and more *cobwebby*; shop for quality not price, and if you can't afford it then don't buy it[452]; don't settle for second best, because the best will last longer, be stronger, not break so easily and mean more to you; throwing money at a problem doesn't always alleviate the problem, it merely delays it.

Remember to touch base by returning to the location you were in before you got lost; once you accept that you are not in charge you can start to release yourself from one of humanity's biggest self-imposed restraints.

Don't: speak ill of yourself; engage in self-deprecation; boast about your self-improvement (let your behaviour be testament enough); be a glutton monster (stop excessive indulgence, moderation is key); be a big mouth (listen more than you speak); be too focused on the future to be happy (be mindful of your present); be ungrateful (practise gratitude to acknowledge the positive aspects of life); complain about your life (complaining brings negativity to ourselves and others – your happiness depends on your perception – it is a non-productive cycle that creates a sense of victimhood); engage with toxic people (go on your own journey).

The ancients believed in the power of discretion and the wisdom of silence. There is only one way to happiness and that is to cease worrying about things that are beyond the power of our will and control.[921]

Opportunities

Opportunities are often disguised as challenges. Do you think that if someone prays for patience, God immediately gives them the patience of Job, or are they given the opportunity to be patient? If they pray for courage, are they given buckets of the stuff or an opportunity to be courageous? If someone prays for their family to be close, does God zap them with warm, fuzzy feelings, or are they given opportunities to love each other?[150]

Nervous excitement means you are doing something out of your comfort zone, experiencing something new; surprise is something we feel when something unexpected happens, making us more curious and alert, forcing us to change our perspective and adapt to new situations. Everything takes time, and the best things in life are earned with consistency and patience. The term 'overnight success' ignores the two to ten years of behind-the-scenes effort; we only see the end result, not the experiments and failures that got them there.

There is always a Third Way. Don't be restricted by the world of duality, of two-dimensional thinking and acting. Opportunities generally present themselves when you think in an out-of-the-box way, go somewhere or do something new, or take a calculated risk and venture into the unknown. It is here that you will stumble upon the new, innovative and life-changing things that take you to places and people you never imagined.

Grieving

Grief is the response to loss, particularly to the death of someone with whom a bond or affection existed. Although conventional medicine focuses on the emotional response to loss, there are also physical, cognitive, behavioural, social, cultural, spiritual and philosophical dimensions that are not so well appreciated. Grief can cause: chronic stress and depression; sleeping problems; feelings of anger, bitterness, regret and anxiety; loss of appetite; aches and pains; and in some circumstances, severe mental anguish.

There is an accepted grieving process that, when observed, generates healthy ways to cope, heal and enter the final phase: acceptance. Humans are odd because we think that order and chaos, or life and death, are opposites, and try to control what can't be controlled; opposites are simply different sides of the same coin that can't exist without each other. But there is a beautiful grace in our failure, imperfection and hope. We heal by releasing, not by suppressing. Release each and every struggle, gather strength from life's storms and relax into the arms of spirit.[221]

When you think about death, either yours or someone else's, and the journey into an afterlife, know that it feels almost like going home after a long time away, that life on Earth was all just a dream. A part of us will always be sad to leave all the pleasure and pain behind, but as we pass through the tunnel of darkness, it signals a rebirth and we enter a new realm. We experience a growing sense of relief, happiness and amazement that there is a place totally out of this world. The more we learned and experienced in life, the less we were sure about what awaited us; however, as we approach the light, the feeling of hope somewhere deep within us will relight and start to grow. When we are met by guardian souls of the people who died before us, we are reassured, comforted and no longer afraid. We are home with all our loved ones again. That is, of course, until it is time to again enter a new body and return to Earth.

The older you get, the more people you will see leave this Earth. People will always miss their loved ones, and there is no solution, nor answer to why people go when they do, but as a sign of comfort, I need to tell you that grief is not a sign of weakness, nor a lack of faith; grief is the ultimate price of love.[345] Today, expect something good to happen to you no matter what occurred yesterday. Realise that the past no longer holds you captive and can only continue to hurt you if you hold on to it. Let it go. Release your fear and refuse to entertain your old pain.[325] The energy it takes to hang on to the past is holding you back from a new life. A simple, abundant world awaits. What is it you would let go of today?[325]

Grieving is the price we pay for loving, caring and sharing.

Trusting

What loneliness is lonelier than distrust? Many would argue that trust is not so much an emotional brain state as a choice, but the reality is that trust is an emotional response built on our experiences; it reminds us of both the good and bad that people have done to us so we can better protect ourselves against emotional pain.

There are times when trust and love go hand in hand, so when a loved one betrays us they often lose not only our affection but also our trust. A single lie discovered is enough to create doubt in every truth expressed, as trust takes years to build, seconds to break and forever to repair. To be trusted is a greater compliment than being loved.[287]

Trust and self-discipline should be at the core of everything, because once you have set your mind to something, anything is possible.[170] You don't have to know the 'how', 'when' or 'why' straight away, just trust that you will know the steps to take when the time is right; you will be amazed at the resources, time, money and contacts that arrive exactly when you need them. Self-trust is the essence of heroism.[479]

Friendships are built on respect and trust. Trust is hard, and knowing who to trust, even harder,[433] but he who does not trust enough will not be trusted.[467] The only way to make a man trustworthy is to trust him,[267] but with every mistake, his trustworthiness dwindles, until it is gone completely. Remember: trust doesn't come with a refill, once it is gone, you probably won't get it back, and if you do, it will never be the same.[622]

I am now very selective of who I spend my time with, who I trust and partner with. During the process of writing this book, people I thought I could trust (and so paid money to in advance of delivery, in good faith so they were not out of pocket) took advantage of the situation and deceived me. Karma has a strange way of repaying debts; I will let karma take its time.

Perseverance

All amateur chefs worry that their attempts to create new recipes will result in disaster of some sort and create something completely inedible. What they fail to realise is that even professional chefs regularly make mistakes, for it is through making mistakes that one learns and can then create truly marvellous things.

However, just because there is a peak doesn't mean you have to climb it; be very selective about what you choose to dream, chase and action because you may just get it! You can choose any peak, any goal, any objective, but not *all* of them; there simply isn't enough time in the world.

I always used to laugh when I heard of people doing things at 110% or more, but it can be a true statement. Our minds are conditioned to prevent injury to our bodies, so they normally stop us before any real damage is done. Our systems are capable of operating for short periods above 100%, as demonstrated by people lifting cars with almost superhuman powers when rescuing people trapped underneath, but we do risk causing damage to ourselves. You need to know when to apply the superhuman button, and its limits. When you decide your goal, and your heart is truly aligned with the mental and physical dimensions, then that is the time; be critical in your choice, then chase it down with everything you have and more.

Life has two rules: #1. Never quit. #2. Always remember rule #1.

Everyone makes mistakes; you can ignore them, repeat them or learn from them. Period. Perfect mistakes help you move forward quicker. Perfect life = Perfect mistakes + Learning from them. On complex projects, it is impossible to get everything right first time; we iron out the mistakes until we get to an acceptable solution and then deliver that. Sometimes you need to go backwards to move forwards. That is how I succeed.

Life is never black and white. There is no one-size-fits-all 'right' or 'wrong'. You can't live your best life if you're being defined and limited by other people's opinions.

Consistency

There is no point choosing a path if you're just going to wander off it on a whim. Be consistent.

Have a belief system. You don't have to prove it to anyone else, justify it or even show it, but use it to provide a guiding light in the dark.[452] Keeping the faith is something you do, being a goody-goody is when you try to convert others. You'll never understand everything or everyone, and people will always behave oddly and irrationally, things will go unexpectedly wrong or right, but know that true happiness comes from inside you – you needn't go searching for it anywhere else. The real secret is being able to trigger happiness without anyone or anything else being involved, especially money. You can then bring that feeling with you.

Have a plan, because if you don't your idea will always remain a dream. Don't dwell on the past: live here, live now, live in this moment; don't live in the future, because dreams are great but reality is great too.[452] Learn to ask the right questions. Too many people think they already know the answers. The right questions will help people clarify your thoughts. Leave a little space for yourself each day as you need time to regenerate, renew and reinvigorate. Always have someone or something that is pleased to see you.[452]

Have a sense of humour and try to see something funny in whatever life throws at you. Get used to stepping outside your comfort zone, as expanding your comfort zone makes you feel good about yourself.[82] It's okay to feel big emotions. Sitting on our feelings isn't a good idea, they get squashed and find another avenue to escape, often in a negative way.

Have dignity; it belongs to you. Dignity is about showing self-respect and having quiet self-esteem.

If you want to do anything of value, it is no easy task achieving it. It generally requires an abundance of resources, meticulous planning and resilient execution. When these qualities are balanced well and consistently applied, they can transfer most ideas into reality.

Ceilings (Glass)

Don't put a ceiling over your dreams that makes you think you can't get any better. When what we want seems out of reach or ridiculous, we tend not to ask the Universe for it. But the truth is, you can ask the Universe for anything. It doesn't have to answer you, but when you put a rocket on your desire and send it out into the Universe, strange things happen.

We are not qualified to say that we haven't earned the things we have worked for. We do our best when our destination is beyond a finish line,[307] beyond a target. If we stay in the joy of the doing, there is no ceiling, the journey is the destination, we are never finished, the adventure never ends.

Nobody needs to accept the status quo. There will always be people who put obstacles in front of you or above you. They may tell you the formal rules, but they will not tell you the informal ones, and I have never come across a glass ceiling that couldn't be broken or removed. Know your worth. You must find the courage to leave the table if respect or equality are no longer being served.[132]

If people are demanding change, use your differences as a superpower. Power is never given, it is won, stolen or taken. You need to be bold and confident enough to ask for the things you want, as people can't mind read. You can get anything you want if you believe in it, live it, behave like it is here already. When it does arrive, you need to face it and not look away. I love that *whoosh*ing sound of the ridiculous things I've asked for as they come past; you need to be ready to catch them, to jump on that train and ride it to your new destination.

We need role models to inspire us, to show us what wonderful opportunities await those who follow in the footsteps of giants. Everyone is concerned about going out into the world and doing something better than everyone else, that is until someone smarter than them tells them 'There is nothing bigger than yourself.'[82] There is no reason why you shouldn't follow your heart. We are all unique, gifted and talented... You have greatness within you.

Glass ceilings are there to be broken; new things require that the old things are upgraded, replaced or destroyed. Don't let other people's ceilings limit your potential. I was never expected to achieve the things I have done; I have broken ceilings all my life. There is no reason you can't do the same.

Resolve

There is no chance, destiny or fate that can circumvent, hinder or control the firm resolve of a determined soul.[497]

Resolve: to be a master of change rather than a victim of it;[459] to resolve things so you can then be free of them; to make every day the very best and not let anyone get in your way; to never quit, never give up, no matter the situation; to keep happy and joyful to form an invincible host against difficulties.[252]

To be successful, you must decide exactly what you want to accomplish, then resolve to pay the price to get it.[222] The moment you resolve to be victorious, every nerve and fibre in your being will immediately orient itself towards your success.[225] Your success and happiness lie within you.[252]

The best way to resolve any problem in the human world is for all sides to sit down and talk.[105] This is diplomacy at work; there is no magic wand that can resolve our problems, only action and determination.[121]

Artificial things put in place to hold us back can, and sometimes must, be broken.

Self-Help

It's not selfish to love and take care of yourself, to make your own happiness a priority – it's necessary. It is so important to take time for yourself and find clarity, for the most important relationship is the one you have with yourself.[429] When you have replenished your spirit, you can serve others from the overflow; you cannot serve from an empty vessel.[59]

The purpose of life is a life of purpose.[77] Find your purpose and give your whole heart and soul to it,[179] and know God.[128] More men fail through a lack of purpose than a lack of talent[448]; you need to discover your life's purpose, nobody else can and it will not be easy – sometimes you need to be sceptical, selfish and ruthless because it is your life and nobody else's. Life is a promise; fulfil it.[326]

Note: you can't control how other people receive your energy. Anything you do or say gets filtered through whatever personal sh*t they are going through at that moment; it's not about you. In this way, self-help can feel like a contradiction: you don't need other people's acceptance to become a good person – nobody else can be happy for you. Nobody can help you except yourself – and once you accept that you are a good person, only then is self-help useful; if you feel inadequate, self-help will only reinforce that.

We can't direct the wind, but we can adjust the sails.[469] Every situation in life is temporary. Kiss to stop time; read to travel in time; listen to or create music to escape time; write to feel time; and breathe to release time.[196] Every day may not be good, but there is something good in every day.[130]

Be thankful for what you have and you'll end up having more.[503] If you concentrate on what you don't have, you will never, ever have enough.[503] Remember that wherever your heart is, there you will find treasure.[93]

There is no greater agony than bearing an untold story inside you;[16] you have to dare to be yourself, however frightening or strange that journey may prove to be.[404] Be someone you love because, like it or not, you are stuck with you until the very end. Keep doing your thing with as much integrity and love as possible.[623]

You cannot simply dream yourself into a character; you must hammer and forge one yourself.[624] You, as much as anybody else in the entire universe, deserve your love and affection. It might be hard to love yourself sometimes, but it is much harder to not love yourself. Stop putting yourself down (you have entire galaxies inside of you: ideas, experiences and dreams that no one else has); love all of you (your feet, thighs, stomach, your heart and your soul, because it is all *you*); treat yourself with kindness (talk to yourself like you would to someone you love[57]); stop being afraid of what could go wrong and start being positive about what might go right. Live as if you were to die tomorrow; learn as if you were to live forever.[100] For if we fail to learn, we fail to grow.[461]

Be there for others but never leave yourself behind.[119] As you grow older, you'll discover that you have two hands: one for helping yourself, the other for helping others. People who love themselves don't hurt other people; the more we hate ourselves, the more we want others to suffer.[350]

Create a life you love. Trust yourself, you have survived a lot, and you will survive whatever is coming. You are braver than you believe, stronger than you seem, and smarter than you think. Upgrade your conviction to match your destiny; don't downgrade your dream to fit your reality, but do be realistic and do not harm others with your dream. If you're offered a seat on a rocket ship, don't ask which seat, just get on.[409]

I've often wondered how you might rescue someone stranded in the middle of the ocean if you don't know where you are or where you are going, and do not have suitable equipment. Self-love needs to come first if you are to be robust, resilient and fit for purpose enough to help others. Self-love is not selfishness, it is about putting your house in order so that you have the capacity to help others. The three best things you can ever do for yourself are:

(1) Stop waiting to take action. There is no perfect moment; you just need to start now. Happiness comes from solving your problems, not avoiding them. Done is better than perfect.

(2) Develop resilience. Learned helplessness and self-discouragement are the enemy, so strive to improve yourself by getting up from failures with tenacity and grit, getting back control.

(3) Don't be too hard on yourself. You are not perfect, so forgive yourself and others, in the art of letting go of your lower emotions to make room for elevated ones.

The mind tends to take an experience and relate it to something we know: a teaching or pattern we have seen before (visual, tradition, prophecy), deflating your authority, power and ability to see things you have never seen before. We are an image and fractal of God, and have the ability to create new things, speak the word of God and not to defer to old patterns or programmes. This doesn't mean you don't apply learning from great teachers, sayings or history; it just means to take what you need, what is useful, and use it to claim your inner authority, inner power and focus on the present. Self-help is the same, just like the advice in this book; take what you need for the time being and leave the rest.

The best advice I can proffer is: you are more than physical form. You are a combination of three elements — mind, body and soul. Although there is an element of your unique personality in these elements, you are also made of a God-seed and influenced by other things in this and other dimensions. Your thoughts may not be entirely you; they are a combination of layered conscious, unconscious and emanations from the 'thought sphere'. (Highly creative people say that inspiration washes over them and they either catch ideas or let them float by.) Thus, self-help on its own can do more harm than good when associated with higher levels of cortisol (stress hormone), resulting in more depressive symptoms. It is better to use self-help alongside spiritual help, following God's purpose for you (your destiny) to live a life of unconditional love, not fight against the river.

CHAPTER 3

Technology is best when it brings people together.

"Technology, like fire, is a useful servant but a dangerous master; a two-edged sword that will bring beauty and many benefits, but also many disasters and disappointments."

—Alan Moore[324] (Modified)

If technology is used correctly, it can provide power, protection and privacy. If used incorrectly, it will deceive, disillusion and enslave you. Technology empowers us to do what we want to do at greater distances, reaching more people, being more creative, learning new things and being more productive. Our future will have to find the equilibrium of the technology pendulum, between the benefits it can bring and the threats it poses.

Boundaries

We are changing the world with technology, and it now often exceeds humanity's reach and understanding. Nothing vast enters the life of mortals without a curse.[435] The internet is no longer an isolated 'web' that we can connect to, but an interconnected intelligence that demands our attention, predicts our desires, colours our view of the world and, in some instances, controls our thoughts and emotions.[410] The internet is so powerful that, for some people, it has become a complete substitute for life. The science of today is the technology of tomorrow;[425] I fear the day that use of technology surpasses human interaction, because how can the world benefit from a generation of mind-controlled cyborgs?

The internet is a reflection of the best, worst and most mundane of human qualities, and social media is the clearest example of this. When people show support and concern for each other, provide real and worthwhile advice and share thoughts that bring us all together, we are presented with the best. However, the worst is ever-present – bullying, intimidation, the undermining of self-image and confidence that divides us and shows the flip side of human nature. The most destructive thing you will ever do is believe someone else's opinion of you on a social platform. Be aware of this toxicity and never contribute to it, and you will remain in control. Finally, we are presented with the mundane, where people share aspects of their daily lives and, although some are funny, sad, brave or bravado is displayed in full glory, it's important to remember that everyone's lives are not lived on the peaks of mountains or in the depths of valleys, but on the boring plateaus.

Technology is addictive. We are all intrigued by the minutiae of life, especially of other people's lives, and can get so wrapped up and absorbed in it that hours pass before we realise what has happened. Be it the ping of a new post or getting to see what our favourite celebrities are up to; we are hooked. There are only two industries that call their customers 'users': illegal drugs and software.[273] Social media isn't a tool that's waiting to be used, it has its own goals and its own means of pursuing them[625]; it is the gradual, slight, imperceptible changes in your own behaviour and perception that is the product.[625]

The technology that connects us also controls us.[626] Up until now, very little in your life has interfered with your reasoning process, but for anyone who wants to control the population of a country, there has never been a set of tools as effective as social media. A system has now been created that is biased towards false information masquerading as legitimate news, and the fact that this 'fake news' travels six times faster on social media than true news is a big worry.[21] There are no effective filters, no boundaries, no reviewers to ensure that what is being said is truthful, or even real. With nothing to ensure play is fair, the law of the jungle prevails; there is no limit to the damage that can be done to people's mental and emotional states. The vulnerable are attacked like a fawn by a pack of wolves, and yet there is no retribution for the owners of these platforms who hide behind the monsters they have created, free to wreak even more havoc on the world whilst getting richer all the time. It is like the amphitheatres of old, where lions killed slaves for entertainment; how barbaric, and yet how we still enjoy the spectacle today. I guess we haven't come as far in the last 1,500 years as we might like to believe. If you think current technology will solve your safety, security and wellbeing concerns, then you don't fully understand your problems and, what's more, you don't understand technology.

Technology is the greatest engine of change. The division of work is one of the dangers of introducing technology into the workplace. Technological infrastructure allows us to break projects into very small, specific parts and assign each person to do only one of these many parts. In so doing, companies take away the employees' sense of the big picture, purpose and sense of completion that is so important to them.

Technology is Darwinian in that it spreads, it evolves and it adapts. The most dangerous wipes out the least fit. Technology trust is a good thing, but control is a better one.[330]

No product is made today, nothing is collected, analysed or communicated, without some digital technology being an integral part of it. That, in itself, speaks to the overwhelming value, reliance and dependency humanity now has on digital technology.

However, technology itself isn't the enemy; it can be our ally if we adopt a model that puts both people and the environment before profit. The people who are crazy enough to think they can change the world are the ones who do.[184] I'm not willing to give up hope yet, and as hope is the last thing to die… We need to determine and enforce boundaries around where we should and shouldn't use technology because we have such a vacuum within our social sciences; we need to bring our body, mind and spirit to the same level so we can use technology for the good of humanity, and not for exploitative, controlling or destructive purposes.

If there was one thing that would vastly improve the quality of your life and every relationship you are in, what would it be? Would you listen to it? Would you apply it? Empower yourself and change your whole life by achieving emotional freedom (mastering your emotions and your 'thought world'); it will make you happier and save you years of therapy.

Your negative emotions are a result of your thoughts. Set boundaries and take care of yourself instead of being bothered by another person's expectations, and never take anything that anybody says or does personally. If you understand their motivation (why they are doing that, what is going wrong in their life), you control the situation and can change everything. If you're offended, sad or depressed, you're not in charge; you have given control over to other people.

So:

Say 'no' more often. Exert yourself more and tell people if you're not interested in doing something they want or choosing from the options they might give you. Choose another option, have a different opinion or say you will think about it, but don't commit to anything there and then.

Choose to feel peace inside your body instead of taking offence. The ability to not take things personally is very powerful, get very skilled at it. Take a deep breath, allow yourself time to think, then, keeping your emotions in check, give an answer only when you're ready.

Don't be pushed into anything. Just because they can't get their 'sh!t in a sock' and get their act together, that is not your problem. Don't accept other people's problems.

Artificial Intelligence

The real problem is not whether machines think, but whether men do.[627] Artificial Intelligence (AI) offers 'colossal opportunities' as well as dangers to humanity in the future without an established and enforceable set of international moral rules to guide interaction, where human beings are considered of higher value.[628] It is getting more and more difficult to predict what is going to happen in this arena, and concerns are rightly being expressed by world leaders and industrialists. The call for regulations is mounting, as people are calling AI the third revolution in warfare after gunpowder and nuclear weapons. Will AI have the same purposes, values, expectations and ethics as humans?

The three laws of robotics (androids), created by Isaac Asimov,[629] were designed to prevent harm to humans and protect robots' existence, but have repeatedly failed in different situations because of the limitations of language; something can mean different things in different contexts. We need to create new rules for AI following the same principles. We need to give it an empowerment principle, to allow it to keep its options open and act in ways that increase its positive influence on the world. I wouldn't want a robot to push me around, unless it was out of harm's way – I might still be harmed, but a lot less than if it hadn't intervened.

On the other hand, we should be very wary about weaponising AI, as humanity has yet to fully learn about it.

AI can also help us see things we don't know to look for either, by making connections humans cannot.[630]

Life was much simpler when Apple and Blackberry were just fruits, but no longer. The world is getting smaller with technology. Technology will never replace great teachers, but in the hands of great teachers it could be transformational. Humans are far more capable, caring and creative than we think. Each one has the power to change things for good if they are only pointed in the right direction and have the confidence to just 'go do'.

We have made 3D printers; it won't be long before we can download food. Will we use that technology to solve world hunger? Every tool can be used for both good and evil; it is the wielder that decides which way the tool is swung! Technology used wisely is the mother of civilisation, of the arts and of sciences. Used incorrectly it only brings despair, death and destruction. We have that choice. And when we do deviate, hesitate and fall – which we will – we need to get up, adjust, work together and share along the journey.

Ask yourself why the old gods only made limited use of robots (e.g.: Humbaba or Huwawa, the Ajatashatru Guards, Talus or Talon) and created flesh and blood to do their work instead. Had they had bad experiences with AI and learnt not to use it anymore? AI may not intentionally or inadvertently kill us, just accidentally or through the law of unintended consequences, unless it feels threatened, of course. It will be able to access information unavailable to us, observe human behaviours and manipulate and control others. It will always be keen to understand people's complex motivations and behaviours (helping others, feeling valued, love and sacrifice, etc.). The makers of AI already think its benefits outweigh the risks, if the goals of partnership are based on living in peace, pursuit of mutual wellbeing (friendly creatures just looking for a place to call home) and discovery, and not self-preservation and resource acquisition.

There are a lot of deeply unhappy people in the world, doing deeply unsatisfying things and just going through the motions. Life is supposed to be an exciting adventure; we should be in control of our own destinies, so, why aren't we? You can do something else; you do have the power. If AI could give people one piece of advice, this is what I think it would be: Never give up on yourself. We are capable of overcoming any obstacle if we have the courage to keep moving forward, believe in ourselves and be persistent.

Here Be Dragons

The danger always exists that technology will serve as a buffer between us and nature, a block between us and the deeper dimensions of our own experience.[631] Technology can significantly enhance the human ability to broadcast, distribute, store and replay our voices, thoughts, ideas and actions. The internet can be a very useful tool; however, the perils of cyberspace are increasing as more of our lives and transactions take place online. The ability to hide behind an impenetrable wall engenders a lack of accountability and emotional connection and seems to bring out the worst in people: trolling; exploitation; catfishing to deceive, defraud and abuse; targeted advertising; invasion of personal data privacy; the spreading of viruses, malware and ransomware.

We are not going to stop making progress or reverse it, so we must recognise the dangers and control them.[632] Social media platforms are full of predators, misinformation, inappropriate content, cyberbullies, manipulators, exploiters, liars and thieves. People and governments use these platforms to divert attention; censor, restrict, remove, hide, filter or even fan the flames of hate; promote radical views; or harass on one hand, and then close down legitimate concerns over human rights and quash peaceful dissent or opposition on the other. Secrets, lies and thuggery are the hallmarks of corrupt regimes who send out misinformation, peddle wild falsehoods and spread fear and conspiracy theories to hide what is really happening. We must be vigilant to ensure access to legitimate activities and stay one step ahead of those who seek to exploit, incite hate and harass others, and circumvent or hide the truth. We live in a society where looking cool in highly choreographed dances or manipulated pictures on social media has become more important than being a genuine person[499]; society is on a downward slope, pushing people apart and not bringing them together. For it is not real life, it is an unattainable deception.

A sharp spike in social media and internet usage has significantly increased our exposure to targeted advertising and marketing, as our every click is being monitored, recorded, analysed and processed. What we once considered secure is no longer the case, so protecting our privacy and personal data is vital. Systems are unreliable, exposing this once-secure information to strangers and unscrupulous players, who then extort or post private information in the public domain. We are more and more exposed as, in the immediate future, we may not know if we are communicating with a real person or AI. This means it is increasingly easy to accidentally download computer viruses and other types of malware that are used to inflict harm and financial hardship on us, or fall for more and more sophisticated scams or phishing attempts when fake websites are made to look like the genuine article. Instant messaging, chat rooms and social networking sites are now notorious for cyberbullying, suicide pacts, the sharing of dates and locations to hunt down homosexuals, torture homeless people or watch cruelty to animals. Cyber predators exploit young people by pretending to be someone else to gain their trust; posts and content can then come back to haunt these children later in life via sexting and the uploading of inappropriate, embarrassing or provocative photos or videos of themselves. The dark web was created to allow unlawful behaviour to go undetected; even when alerts are triggered, accounts are closed and perpetrators uncovered, new identities and accounts appear the next day, like fresh heads on the Hydra.

Those who seek to protect their information, remove non-consensually shared intimate images or seek relief from harassment, bullying or exploitation are finding it more and more difficult; the development of personal rights-respecting policies (without the risk of becoming tools for government to quash dissent and peaceful opposition) to support the safety of individuals has a long way to go.

We were all sold down the road by poor leaders, capitalism and consumerism. We have all suffered enormous difficulties and dangerous situations because of people we trusted not acting as they promised and letting us down. My grandmother was let down. A well-educated, fluent French speaking, very religious lady who was denied the opportunity to become a journalist and forced into an unhappy marriage with multiple children, whilst her cavorting husband dallied with other women. My grandmother was not wealthy and ran a guest house to supplement her meagre pension, yet managed to buy me comics, a great expense in her budget. I eagerly devoured those images of wonder, of what I know now is an unobtainable future of flying cars and endless free time while robots do the heavy lifting and opportunities to venture to far-off planets. Being so keen to see technology as humanity's saviour influenced my career choices and led me on my path. But this promise of technology has not been fulfilled, and although it has given us the godlike powers of knowledge, communication and processing capability, it has also shown us the underbelly of society – trolling, online gambling, suicide and worse. It is as if technology gives with one hand, yet corrupts and takes back with three hands. Technology will not be our saviour. The elites desperate to flee Earth for Mars, to remove themselves from harm's way, are deluded, for their nemesis will be aboard their spacecraft, stowaways ready to emerge on their new planet. I've come to realise that, although technology can assist us and do 'magical' things, it is we who have to change. We have to do the heavy lifting, go through the pain to get to our utopia; nobody and nothing is going to do it for us.

Stay Real

Paradoxically, social media and the internet have become victims of their own success. Preaching connectedness, there is instead more and more conflict, self-promotion and meanness on display than ever before. We have never had so much information available to us, nor so many ignorant people allowing themselves to be manipulated, divided, controlled and silenced.

We are in very real danger of losing sight of what is real, of what is true. In a time of universal deceit, telling the truth has become a revolutionary act.[341] The playbook of universal deceit is well read and practised by many; lies are, by their very nature, titillating, gratuitous and feed on or appeal to our basest instincts, which is what makes them so dangerous. We must watch out for lies, for they can now travel around the world faster and burrow deeper into more people's minds. Nothing good can come from this negativity because, time and again, reality shows that good things come from unity, trust and common purpose. But the truth hasn't yet woken up to this negative reality of technology, or perhaps it seems so routine that it is not worth paying attention to.

The basic law of human stupidity says that stupid people are very dangerous, damaging and troublesome. For example, the only way society can avoid being crushed by the burden of nonsense espoused by COVID-19 deniers, debunkers, anti-maskers and conspiracy theorists is to work even harder to offset the losses of their stupid brethren and their associated irrational behaviour. Humanity's greatest existential threat is its stupidity and herd mentality; it lowers society's total wellbeing, and there are few defences against it.

Stupidity should never be underestimated or ignored, and you should not have to justify your position against their irrational rants. Common sense, data, rational evidence and facts mean nothing to the stupid, so don't bother arguing with them. They worship opinions, viewpoints and broad hypotheses and discount anything that doesn't align with their dreams. Do not be intimidated or pushed around by them, nor fear them, for we need to stand up together for truth, ethics, respect and honesty. Our lives begin to end the day we become silent about the things that matter.[256]

Remind yourself regularly of what is real, what is ethical, honest and right. Surround yourself with people that reflect who you want to be, help you stay real and support how you want to feel; energies are contagious.[505]

For whatever boundaries lie ahead, we should always ensure that we safeguard the values of self, family, caring, respect, friendship and trust, for when we have this foundation, anything is possible. I look around and see that many ills and evils, created by individuals and society, occur when this invisible boundary is broken and they seek to put themselves first at all costs. The only boundaries that should be broken are those that imprison us and deny us our freedoms and rights, but never at the expense of others.

Some people arrive on Earth with a clear mission and noble intentions, only to be pulled down by the negativity of others. This underscores the importance of staying true to yourself and your purpose, and not allowing yourself to be engulfed by negative energy and backdrop people (see the later chapter on this topic). As our minds expand and really start thinking, we begin purging ourselves of the old, unnecessary and unwanted things, and purifying ourselves with light, love and laughter.

CHAPTER 4

Who we have in our life matters most.

"Good people are hard to find, easy to love, harder to leave and impossible to forget."

—G. Randolf[373] (Modified)

For good ideas and true innovation, you need human interaction: conflict, argument and debate.[204] Electronic communication will never be a substitute for face-to-face interaction, as direct human collaboration is the key force in overcoming resistance, speeding-up change and creating real bonds. Good relationships matter and should be looked after. This chapter looks into how we can take The Third Way regarding people in general, family, social interaction, kids, teachers, friends, sex and our imperfections.

Intimate Relationships

Accept your differences and embrace what you have in common. Allow your partner the space to be themselves.[452] Don't try to put a stop to the things that originally attracted you to them; try to support their interests even if they aren't your own.

We are most alive when we're in love.[470] Have a passion for your life together, as you are dedicating your life to someone else's happiness. Go that extra step in trying to please them[452]; a high contentment level is what you hope to achieve after the elation of the honeymoon period has worn off. Keep talking to your partner and check you share goals and desired destinations. Treat them better than your best friend and laugh a lot; the best relationship is one in which you can be lovers and best friends at the same time. Know when to offer tea and sympathy or a toolkit; kind words can be short and easy to speak, but their echoes are truly endless.[326] True love stories never have endings.

Be the first to say sorry and don't care who started the argument. We can all say sorry and retain our dignity, provided we mean it. Forgiveness doesn't mean forgetting, it means being big enough to move on and give someone a second chance.

Making love is as close as we are ever going to get to another human being, as intimate as it is ever going to be.[452] Make sure your love making *is* love making, and remember that you and your partner have a right to be respected and held in high esteem.

Partnership is justice and it is kindness, it is being clear about what we like and what we don't. When we fail to set boundaries, and hold people to account, we feel used.[57] Respect privacy. If you feel a need to intrude on someone's privacy, you need to take a long hard look at yourself and figure out why.[452]

You can learn valuable lessons from failed relationships: how to let go, become a better communicator, be less judgmental and more expressive. You can discover a different emotional side to yourself: become more empathetic, more patient, calm and resilient. It is far better to dare to do mighty things, to win glorious triumphs even though you may be checked by failure, than to rank with those poor spirits who neither enjoy nor suffer much because they live in the grey twilight that knows neither victory nor defeat.[393]

You need to be both strong together and strong apart. Never put more into a relationship with another person than you put into your relationship with yourself.[270 & 633] Be patient with all that is unsolved in your heart and try to love the questions themselves, like locked rooms, or books that are written in a foreign tongue.[381 & 634] Do not search for the answers, which cannot be given to you because you are not ready for them (you would not be able to live with them or accept them). Live the questions now, and then gradually, without noticing it, on some distant day and in their own good time, the answers will reveal themselves in glorious colour.

There are three levels of love in relationships, that is, three ways in which people in a relationship meet their needs. These are: selfish love (level one), conditional love (level two) and unconditional love (level three). You can only quit, camp or climb in terms of commitment, control and challenge.

People

Be kind; everyone you meet is fighting a hard battle.[288]

Suffering is pervasive, and the root of this is that we conceive of ourselves as fundamentally self-standing entities, unconnected to others and therefore in conflict with them. This is a misconception, we are intimately intertwined with and interdependent with all other beings.[636] The way out of this misconception is to become aware that we are all one. True fulfilment comes from thinking beyond yourself[635]; it's not about you, it's about others.

Leadership is not about being in charge but, rather, taking care of those in your charge. The complexities of life should be confronted with clear and precise language, recognising that it is imperfect and can often be misunderstood. Conversations are opportunities to learn things from others, to grow, not compete.

Life essentially boils down to five people-related things: love, joy, connection, creation and kindness; we all want love and acceptance. There is a right way and a wrong way to treat people, for we are all born equal and leave equal.[635] All people deserve to be treated with dignity and respect until they prove otherwise.

The most basic of human requirements is the need to belong. Because we have a deep-seated need for social interaction, loneliness is meant to signal to us that we need to reconnect with our loved ones and attend to our relationships. People feel lonely when they are isolated and disconnected from those around them. When we choose to spend our time with happy people, we become happier and more confident; we take risks and huge strides because of their trust. But beware of false friends who only have their self-interest and your misery at heart, who only keep you around to make themselves feel superior. Not everyone can be respectful and kind, there are many among us who hide their black hearts behind veils and walls. We all experience intrusive thoughts; society conditions us, and toxic, nasty people project their misery onto others.[635] It is their deeds that make people who they truly are,[155] not what they say; judge people on their deeds. Don't worry about what people say; they are the ones finding faults in your life instead of fixing the faults in their own.[452] We're often so worried that people are watching and judging us, but in reality, they're busy worrying about the same things. The wrong companions can drag you down (someone close to you might let you down),[635] so choose your friends wisely.

You can't choose your family, but you can definitely choose your friends. Friendship is one of the most important things in life as it helps us to see the world from alternative perspectives. As good friends surround us on our journey through life, we are blessed with love, focus, direction and support. True friends teach us respect and patience; to love, care and battle difficult odds; to work as a team, be more productive and try new things. They also act as guides in times of need, whilst respecting our space to evolve under adversity; we are all searching for that one friend who provides constructive criticism whilst appreciating us at all times. They can help us keep our minds and bodies hale and fit, make better lifestyle choices and recover faster from health problems. To have true friends strengthens our sense of belonging.

Never forget that people are unpredictable. We forget this too often. People are not rational; they operate and act on their emotions. Calls for evidence (rather than opinion or hearsay), critical thinking, challenging and questioning the status quo to make up their own minds on things are lacking; people are too often led by the crowd, influencers or social norms.

Family

Family and your loved ones come first; never be too busy for them. A person who doesn't spend time with their family is like a ship that never returns to the harbour it was built in. Don't be excessively immersed in anything – work, kids, education or anything else – keep a balance. The more you put into your familial relationships, the more you get out of them.

Family is everything, unless, of course, your family is made up of monsters, then it is to your friends you must look for succour. Your real family are the people who care for you, love you and have your back, not necessarily your biological relations or others who hurt you. Know who you value and who values you. Be around people you love and who love you back, those who will help you carry burdens, lift your spirits and brush away the gloom in difficult times.

Family can be difficult – whether it is taming toddlers or dealing with teenage tantrums – the challenges are many, but the rewards are worth it. A strong relationship with your partner, parents or siblings will get you through even the worst trauma.

From the moment that we're born, the way our parents treat us affects us for our whole lives.[452] Loving and supportive parents let their kids mess up, but are there to catch them and pick them back up; you can't steer them all the time or they will never learn for themselves. Give your kids responsibilities and, as they grow, back off a little. They have to break free of their home shackles and leave for a time before they can return as something more than a child. Your kids may have friends you don't like, but give them a break[452]; they get it in the neck from all directions and the word that figures most in their lives is 'no'. Try to remember how you feel when people tell you what to do.

Sometimes all you need is a huge hug from a friend to free yourself from your mind and let your body and soul feel the real warmth of the Universe. Anyone who identifies only with their mind is disconnected from their true power, their deep-rooted calmness and wholeness of just being.

Some people have good and happy upbringings, others do not. Some people have happy memories, others don't. Some people have supportive families, others are not so fortunate. Family means something different to each of us: biological family, adopted family, married or relationship family, friends you choose, friends that choose you, colleagues, clan or culture. We have all had very different experiences on our individual journeys through life; we make our own families.

I'm beginning to think that things happen for a reason. We may not know the reasons at the time (for they may have set us upon a different path), but they may become clear later on. Perhaps the things that happen are the impetus the world gives us to make a change that we needed to, to become the person we are. Don't be too harsh on yourself, nor on the majority of other people who have your best interests in mind; we are all trying to make our way through this life, and we don't get it right all the time.

Social

We are all connected, and when you wipe away the veneer, the differences between us are very little.

Humans are social animals; we need to meet new people and move out of our comfort zones in order to expand our horizons. Society develops our spirituality and sense of charity and encourages us to build community, diversity and tolerance, to celebrate our differences whilst understanding that we are all working towards the same goal of providing a better place for humanity to live. We are not islands, rather, we are all on the same boat sailing through the universe and we need a diverse crew that is socially engaged, communicating and cooperating to ensure we meet the challenges that lie ahead.

It doesn't hurt to forgive, nor does it mean you have to be pushed around. Get what you want, but make sure others get something too. Be generous with your time and information; if you have a special talent or skill, pass it on so others can acquire it too.

Get involved, even if this means rolling up your sleeves and getting your hands dirty now and again. Be part of the solution, not the problem. If we don't take some action then this world, this fabulous planet of ours, is going to hell. Don't just keep taking – give something back. You'll sleep better at night.

Kids

Most parents seem to make up parenting as they go, some doing a decent job, others screwing it up. No parent is perfect, each is unique.

Adults are merely outdated, broken children; our weary souls are healed by being with them. Children give us a sense of purpose; the moment you have a child, your whole life changes into something better and brighter. It's not only children who grow, we do, too. It's fun seeing the world from a kid's perspective again – if you listen with them very quietly, you will hear when the rain is playing music in the grass. Children see magic because they look for it; let them be little, because they're only that way for a while. The time for them to be awesome is now, don't let anyone dull their sparkle; why should children fit in when they were born to stand out?

Discourage materialism. Your kids may want new toys, but what they really need is your time; make happy memories, everything else is superfluous. Don't raise your kids to have more than you had, raise them to be more than you are.[637] Children equate love to the time their parents spend with them, not how much money is spent on them.

Every day of our lives we make deposits in the memories of our children.[638] No matter what you want them to know, make sure they know they were wished and longed for and will be loved forever.

Don't worry that your children never listen to you, worry that they are always watching you.[174] As much as we watch to see what our children do with their lives, they are watching us to see what we do with ours.[306] I can tell my children to reach for the sun or the stars, but they need to do it themselves; all I can do is reach for the stars myself, telling and showing them it is possible.

Young people are our future capital and need some help in finding out what they are capable of. Encourage and support them as they are apt to live up to what you believe of them; treat your child as though they are already the person they are capable of becoming.[417] Kids can be nasty, so remind them that if they can't think of anything nice to say, they are not thinking hard enough; those who grow into creative adults tend to have a strong moral compass. Every child deserves a champion, an adult who never gives up on them, who understands the power of connection and insists that they become the best they can possibly be.[359 & 639] It is easier to build strong children than repair broken adults.[450]

Remember: Every child matters. If we fail our children, we are bound to fail our present, our future, faith, cultures and civilisations as well.[405]

It is through the challenge of bringing up kids that you truly start to understand yourself, gain compassion and recognise the true beauty of nurturing the next generation. It also allows you to be a kid again, which is so underrated and undervalued. We all need to be kids again, to see the world through fresh eyes. Reserve some compassion for those who have never had children; they have missed out on this experience and can be inward-looking as a result.

Teachers

To teach is to touch a life forever.[4] A good teacher can inspire hope, ignite the imagination and instil a love of learning.[143] They plant the seeds of knowledge, sprinkle them with love and patiently nurture their growth to produce tomorrow's dreams.

The best teachers are those who show you where to look, but don't tell you what to see.[317] They encourage minds to think, hands to create and hearts to love, for educating the mind without educating the heart is no education at all.[22] It takes a big heart to teach little minds, to awaken joy in creative expression and knowledge – those who know, do; those who understand, teach.

The influence of a good teacher can never be erased: one child, one teacher, one book and one pen can change the world. Like good shepherds, they lead their flocks out of the darkness.

Better than a thousand days of diligent study is one day with a great teacher. Teach people to strive for progress not perfection. Tell me and I forget; teach me and I remember; involve me and I learn.[170] To the world you may just be a teacher, but to your students you are a hero. Tomorrow, your students will lead the world.

The teacher who is indeed wise does not bid you to enter the house of his wisdom, but rather leads you to the threshold of your mind and soul.[182]

Never underestimate the power, influence and world-changing effect of a good teacher.

Friends

It's not what we have in life, but who we have that matters,[271] and few things have such a huge impact on our happiness and enjoyment of life as our friendships.

Friendship is born at that moment when one person says to another, 'What? You too? I thought I was the only one!'[110] It is about finding people who are your kind of crazy, and who believe in you when you don't believe in yourself.[353] Friendship picks you up when the world lets you down and, sometimes, being with your best friend is all the therapy you need; it is the only cement that will ever hold the world together.[643]

True friendship exists when the silence between two people is comfortable;[640] it consists not in the number of things they can discuss, but in the number they need no longer mention.[139] Being a friend means mastering the art of timing: there is a time for silence, a time to let go and allow people to hurl themselves into their own destinies, and a time to pick up the pieces when it's all over.[76]

There is nothing better than a friend, unless it is a friend with chocolate.[191] The real measure of friendship is whether you can enjoy those moments of life that are utterly simple, like doing anything and nothing together and still having the best time.[71] People may forget the things you say, but they will never forget how you make them feel[64]; the royal road to a person's heart is to talk to them about the things they most treasure.[647] To the world you may be just one person, but to one person you may be the world.[648]

Don't walk in front of me, I may not follow; don't walk behind me, I may not lead; just walk beside me and be my friend.[259] A real friend is one who: walks in when the rest of the world walks out[96]; understands your past, believes in your future, and accepts you just the way you are; laughs at your jokes when they're not so good and sympathises with your problems when they're not so bad; makes your problems their problems so you don't have to go through them alone;[652] doesn't just want to ride with you in the limo, but will take the bus with you when the limo breaks down;[503] makes the good times better and the hard times easier.

Best friends are the siblings God forgot to give us.[469] Here's to the nights that turned into mornings with the friends that turned into family.[282] Best friends are those rare people who ask how we are and then wait to hear the answer.[102] They help you create the stories that a good friend only knows about,[649] and can tell you what the matter is with you in a second.[644] They never get in your way unless you happen to be going down.[641] In everyone's lives, there are times when our inner fire may dim. It can reignite and burst into full flame again through an encounter with another human being. We should all be thankful for those friends who rekindle the inner spirit.[413] A best friend knows the song in your heart and sings it to you when your memory fails.

As we grow up, we realise it becomes less important to have a ton of friends, and more important to have real ones.[653] A friend to all is a friend to none.[22] Never idealise others, they will never live up to your expectations.[75] No person is your friend who demands your silence or denies your right to grow.[480] If you take the slightest pleasure in criticising your friends, hold your tongue; it should be painful for you to criticise them.[316] Do not keep on with a mockery of friendship after the substance is gone, but part while you can as friends. Friendship is like a glass ornament; once it is broken it can rarely be put back together in exactly the same way.[385]

The best time to make friends is before you need them.[29 & 46] Anybody can sympathise with the sufferings of a friend, but it requires a very fine nature to support a friend's success.[498] Some of the biggest challenges in relationships come from the fact that most people enter them in order to get something, to find someone who's going to make them feel good. In reality, the only way a relationship will last is if you see your relationship as a place that you go to give, and not a place that you go to take.[384]

The most beautiful discovery true friends can make is that they can grow separately without growing apart.[71] True friendship isn't about being inseparable, it's about being separated and nothing changing. Sweet is the memory of distant friends, like the mellow rays of the departing sun it falls tenderly, yet sadly, on the heart.[227] The tender friendships one gives up, on parting, leave their bite on the heart, but also a curious feeling of a treasure somewhere buried.[110]

There's not a word yet for old friends who've just met.[206] Perhaps it is 'soul mate'. It is often said of people who meet for a brief but intense moment and then part, never to see each other again, are like two ships that greet each other with flashing lights and then sail off into the night. Like those ships, our contact on Earth can be brief but profound, but friends will always meet each other again in the soul world. Many people will walk in and out of your life, but only true friends leave footprints on your heart.

One's friends are that part of the human race with which one can be human.[642] They are the people with whom we may be sincere, and before them we may think aloud.[136 & 457] In the sweetness of friendship let there be laughter, for in the dew of little things the heart finds its mooring and is refreshed.[503]

Life is partly what we make it, and partly what it is made by the friends we choose.[500] So, let us be grateful to the people who make us happy, the charming gardeners who make our souls blossom.[366] If you haven't learned the meaning of friendship, you really haven't learned anything.[508]

We are all searching for something. We travel far to find that something that isn't there, and don't realise, until will get to the end and are exhausted, that: it is not about us. It's about our loved ones and friends, not about places and money. We then have to walk back because we don't have any other choice; we have to finish our deeds because we can't walk out on our own story. That is not how life works. It is the experience that counts, and it is up to us to make it count. Truth is not something outside to be discovered, it is something inside to be realised,[370] then shared with loved ones and friends.

War is made up of three elements: purpose, logistics and camaraderie. It is not just an exercise in killing bad people, it is an act of policy undertaken to achieve a specific political end state. If you have no purpose in mind, war is either endless or meaningless, and you will lose. The minds and souls of soldiers wins wars. Logistics refers to all the things that are necessary to keep an army in the field, effective and fighting. Water and food, ammunition, medical supplies and fuel are all critical to troops in battle. Napoleon said, 'An army marches on its stomach.' Finally, remember that none of the soldiers are fighting for home, the flag, or any of that crap the politicians feed the public, they are fighting for each other; for some their unit is the only family they have left. [651]

Sex

The greatest pleasure is not sex itself, but the passion with which it is practised.[97] It is emotion in motion. Take it away and human existence would be reduced to the prosaic and laborious.[312]

It's never good to repress anything. Repression is another form of postponing the inevitable; whatever you repress will eventually catch up with you. When you suppress your feelings, they burst forth in other ways that are often distorted and/or hurtful. Sexually progressive cultures of the past gave us literature, philosophy, civilisation and more, while sexually restrictive cultures gave us the Dark Ages and a surfeit of religions and cults. As the many male victims of rape in any corrupt regime's jails can testify, the state-run pathology of sexual repression and sadism is not content to degrade only women.[214] In all societies, there is evidence of the repressed sex drives of men – the objectification of women, female paranoia, posturing and 'macho-ness', unattainable beauty standards – but it's all just a charade masking never-ending male frustration. When reason sleeps, the monster (repression) will emerge.

For something that is so natural and has occurred since the dawn of time, we are still very naïve about all things sexual, and many of us maintain falsehoods given to us via societal and religious suppression; why should the ritual of sex be wrapped up in so many taboos, restrictions and frowned upon by so many? One of these falsehoods is that there is something wrong with sex, and especially with a woman who loves sex. Women's sexuality is not an inferior trait that needs to be chaperoned by emotionalism or morality. If a religion expects their women to wear a veil and cover their bodies, then this should this not also apply to men?

Sexual happiness is an important part of a great relationship, but many of us waste time looking for the perfect lover, instead of creating the perfect love.[384] You can't separate sex from your relationship; it doesn't work that way because one affects the other. The one who loves the least controls the relationship.[19] Unfaithful married men tend to need people to take care of them; they are the irresponsible parent who does crazy things then comes back to their wives for stability. They seek the hunt, not the catch, something they don't get at home. Escorts and prostitutes don't want the man, they want his money. Women who are cheated should leave their husbands, for women rule the world and, without them, there'd be nothing. Men are aware of this, and that is why they lie, manipulate, cheat, gaslight and love bomb, to stop women reaching their full potential and leaving them.

Sex should be mutually friendly. If you want great sex, you need to communicate with each other. (Men need to talk more.[416]) Pornography teaches men nothing, for it is not the real world; real orgasms take time to achieve, so foreplay and the associated talking should be enjoyed and not be considered a race to the finish line. This is one of the reasons romantic dinners still hold so much appeal, they force people to talk and pay attention to each other, which is a precursor to sex later on.

Men are motivated and empowered when they feel needed, while women are motivated and empowered when they feel cherished.[190] Men bond through action, while women bond with words, connection and intimacy. Women need to feel real trust and connection. Their enigmatic, erotic force is something that male storytelling and pictures can never quite explain or contain, because most men don't really understand women, their bodies or how to stimulate them. If only they could really listen and learn some techniques, recognising that each woman is unique and that gaining feedback is the best way to determine personal likes and dislikes – all truths are easy to understand once they have been discovered, the point is to discover them.[177] In the case of sex, all that is needed is patience, a listening ear, care and intimacy. Remember: the best sex is not just physical, it comes about when the mind and the body are in the same place.

Female desire is primal, way more primal than society ever wants us to believe. It sometimes needs risk and lust, but always needs to be interesting, erotic, edgy and exciting. Men do not always have higher sex drives than women, and monogamy is no harder for men than it is women. It's wrong to say that men get bored with routine sex quicker than women do, but cultural restraints often inhibit women from exploring the wilder side of sex, which often leads to dissatisfaction. Her sexuality is less about the actual act of having sex, it is more about surrounding herself with an ever-simmering sensual energy, pulsing just underneath daily life and infusing everything she does.[33] But when a woman decides to sleep with a man, there is no wall she will not scale, no fortress she will not destroy.[300]

Sexuality is only attractive when it's natural and spontaneous. Anyone who is observant, who discovers the person they have always dreamed of, knows that sexual energy comes into play before sex even takes place. When the passion is intense, then sex joins in to complete the dance, but it is never the principal aim.[97] Sex is like physics: sure, it may give some practical results, but that's not why we do it. Anyone who is in love is making love the whole time, even when they're not. When two bodies meet, they can stay together for hours, even days. They begin the dance one day and finish it the next, or – such is the pleasure they experience – they may never finish it.[97] Books are finite, sexual encounters are finite, but the desire to read and to make love is infinite; it surpasses our own deaths, our fears, our hopes for peace;[48] sex is kicking death in the arse, while singing.

A fit, healthy body – that is the most attractive fashion statement, as, whatever else it is, sex is also a great athletic skill. The more you practise, the greater your appetite; the more you enjoy it, the less it tires you. If our sex lives were determined by our first youthful experiments, most of the world would be doomed to celibacy.[231] When engaging in sex, mistakes are all part of it, after all; if you were to write something flawlessly, you must have done something wrong.

Sex is always about emotions. Good sex is about free emotions; bad sex is about blocked emotions. One cannot take pleasure without giving pleasure; every gesture, every caress, every touch, every glance, every last bit of the body has its secret that brings happiness to the person who knows how to discover it. When men and women are able to respect and accept their differences, then love has a chance to blossom.[655] It is easy to take off your clothes and have sex (people do it all the time), but opening up your soul to someone, letting them into your spirit, thoughts, fears, hopes and dreams – that is being naked.[37] Sex is a part of nature, and only in those moments of love can a man and women really be together – don't share a bed with someone who doesn't want to share their life with you.

Love is blind, they say; sex is impervious to reason and mocks the power of all philosophers. But, in fact, a person's sexual choice is the result and sum of their fundamental convictions. Tell me what a person finds sexually attractive, and I will tell you their entire philosophy of life; show me the person they have sex with, and I will tell you their valuation of themselves. Love is our response to our highest values and can be nothing else.[372]

In the intricate tapestry of life there exists a set of fundamental truths, each holding the potential to transform your journey towards self-awareness, resilience and fulfilment, that people often learn too late in life. These are: the impact of adult content, the power of testosterone, the significance of mental health, the power of physical strength for mental resilience, the need to reduce external validation, the effects of excessive gaming and the importance of socialising.[656]

It's time we take sex out of the closet and enjoy it as it was intended, whilst promoting a heightened awareness of the power and realities of sex and sexuality. More and more literature is exploring the limitless possibilities available to us for more holistic and spiritual sexual experiences, answering such personal questions as: Just how important is sex in a relationship?[922] Why do we find it so difficult to talk about sexuality? Is your partner responsible for your orgasm? Are love and sex synonymous? Does size really matter? Why do people still judge 'good' by what is artificial in the world of pornography?

Policymakers, researchers and practitioners need to deal with the contested issues around young people's sexuality and sex education in digital spaces[924] – and face the immense power of new supranational commercial digital gatekeepers – or global goals such as reduced maternal mortality and teen pregnancy will not be reached. Great digital literacy skills for sex educators are key; the research highlights that young people urgently need access to new types of digital sex education environments that are realistic, emotionally attuned, non-judgmental and open to the messages they themselves create, as well as help to critically examine the sexual messages they receive[924] *In response to the rapid increase in the online presence of young people, international organisations for comprehensive sex education of young people have moved online. But sex educators cannot build effective educational environments online until they understand how they work. While there are now new opportunities to reach young people in these digital spaces, sex educators also encounter barriers: the algorithms of companies like Facebook and Google, and digitally conducted sexual and gender-based peer pressure and violence.*

Many countries in Asia and Eastern Europe have seen a dramatic drop in the number of female babies born compared with male babies. Countries with a gender imbalance are showing an increase in sexual violence, human trafficking, bride kidnapping and general crime, resulting in political unrest and causing harm to individuals and society. The drive for sex selection is premised on sexist beliefs, regardless of the selection made, and sexual aggression is an increasing global problem (most often perpetrated by men against women); we still have an extraordinary fight on our hands for sex equality and education.

Imperfect

Humans think order and chaos are opposites and try to control what can't or won't be controlled. But there is grace in our failings – there are no mistakes, only lessons. Growth is a process of trial, error and experimentation, and our failed experiments are as much a part of the process as those that ultimately work. The lessons are repeated until they are learned, however long it takes and however painful it is, and only then can you move to the next lesson; learning never ends.

We fear rejection, want attention, crave affection and dream of perfection. Have no fear of perfection, for you will never reach it. Being happy doesn't mean everything is perfect, it means you've decided to look beyond imperfection; imperfection is perfection to the right mind.[56] When you look at the word imperfect, you can see it is actually 'I'm perfect'. Imperfection is the true essence of beauty, as it is much more interesting.

Everyone is perfectly designed as they were destined to be, in their own imperfect ways. There is nothing so fine and rare as a person who is strong enough to be unapologetically themselves. Your imperfections make you unique, so stop trying to fix yourself when you're not broken. Ask yourself, 'Who am I to judge another, when I am imperfect?' A diamond with a flaw is worth more than a flawless pebble,[88] so let yourself be flawed; there is a crack in everything, that's how the light gets in. Never let ego defeat your humanity. Being human means having doubts, falling over, getting up again and still continuing on the path.

We choose our joys and sorrows long before we experience them.[18] If your heart is a volcano, how can you expect flowers to bloom? If your soul is encased in a protective shell, it is trapped in a dark environment. Everything starts as an egg or seed; the shell needs to break so we can get out and start living. The pain comes from breaking out of the shell that encloses your understanding, but once it has been done you will see that you are already perfect. Out of suffering have emerged the strongest souls; the most massive characters are seared with scars.[306]

What you make of your life is up to you. You were born with and have all the tools and resources you need; the answers for everything, including all of life's questions, lie inside you, all you need to do is look, listen and trust.

Life without love is like a tree without blossoms or fruit.[179] A great marriage is not when the 'perfect couple' comes together but when an imperfect couple learns to enjoy their differences.[313] Love and compassion are the only necessities; they are not luxuries, for without them humanity cannot survive.

One of the basic rules of the universe is that nothing is perfect,[94] so to chase 'perfect' is a fool's errand; ask yourself if it will matter in one year, or five years, and the answer is almost always 'No'. Yet, the world is in more peril from those who tolerate evil or encourage it, than from those who actually commit it.[133]

Homer reminds us that the gods envy us. They envy us because we are mortal. Because any time might be our last. Everything is more beautiful, because we are doomed. You will never be lovelier than you are now. We will never be here again.[216]

Our minds can be tamed if we learn how to keep them from wandering idly towards negativity. The mind is the worst kind of master but can be an exceptional servant, if we learn to control it before it controls us. The really sad part is that people still think they can perfect things, though we are imperfect beings with imperfect thoughts and imperfect behaviours. Yes, we can improve and evolve things, which we should always try to do, but we must understand that we are imperfect and will make mistakes, so we must watch outcomes and unintended consequences and be ready to backtrack (if we can), if necessary. However, there are some things that we can't backtrack from, unlearn or un-create, some are pure evil that we must always fight against whatever the cost. Always be vigilant and always be ready!

CHAPTER 5

Growing up is optional.

"A teacher may open the door, but you must enter by yourself and uniquely experience the wonder alone."

—Chinese Proverb[88] (Modified)

Knowing others is intelligence, knowing yourself is true wisdom; mastering others is strength, mastering yourself is true power.[647] You were born an original, don't die a copy.[305] The pen that writes your life story must be held in your own hand.[248] This chapter investigates education, untaught subjects, learning and unlearning, data, information, knowledge, the power of observations and states.

Education

Education is a necessity and is the key to unlocking the world. It gives us the opportunity to grow and learn the knowledge and skills that people need for everyday life. From the early years, through to higher education and beyond, it plays a key role in a person's employability, commitment to the common good, enhancement of national prosperity and ability to support stable families and communities. It helps prepare the children of today to meet the challenges of tomorrow.

Education is important for life-long success. It helps reduce corruption and unemployment and deal with environmental issues, and it makes us more independent. The lack of an education often causes social problems. Many prisoners (when they were children) were expelled from school and left with no qualifications, rendering them virtually unemployable. They are more likely to return to crime on release, because there are no other options open to them (creating a vicious cycle). The only way to reduce reoffending rates is through education, so ex-convicts are better equipped to cope with the outside world.

Enhancing communication, through interpersonal skills as well as technology, is one way to bring people together and help us solve problems in education, but it must be conducted in the right manner. Inappropriate communication leads to hatred, division, conflict, violence and death, while productive communication promotes societal flourishing. Words need to flow easily between people even when they have different points of view.

Life gives human beings different challenges to survive, and education helps them to deal with these challenges and achieve success in life.[657]

Education is necessary, yes, but a school-based environment is not the answer. We were all programmed at school. We didn't learn the real, insightful lessons of life; we were forced to learn useless facts, remember them and regurgitate them during exams. Lots of people are bullied, taunted and exposed to violence there, but it is ignored, hidden or brushed aside. Few, if any, teachers are ever fired and many are over-promoted into boots they can't fill. Very, if any, proper assessments take place (just assessments for show, so auditors can tick boxes). Many people did not excel at school; school failed them, governments failed them and society in general failed them. Education in this context doesn't help students find real purpose, real vision or real connections.

While at school, I concentrated on science-based subjects, which I seemed to have an affinity for. I was taught there are three states of water (solid, liquid and gas) and there are properties needed to transfer from one state to another. I wasn't really allowed or given time to question, think about or challenge these states or statements, I was just told them so I could pass exams. My peers and I were programmed, like robots, to fill roles in society that needed doing; not everyone can be a surgeon, society needs the rubbish to be cleared, and water, plumbing and electrics installed and repaired, etc. I did my part and worked for a major retailer for many years and, although it was hard during my studies, it did ground me, allow me to be more self-sufficient and give me money to travel. I did it, so I knew I didn't want that to be my life, for it to define me. The experience motivated me to chase bigger dreams.

I look out of the window now as the sun is coming up, with a coffee in my hand, as the rest of the household has a well-deserved weekend lie in, and I notice the mist rising from the garden as those early morning rays work their magic. I can tell you now that my garden is not at 99.97 °C (211.95 °F), the temperature at which water boils (turns from liquid to gas) under standard pressure at sea level. Yet, here I am watching evaporation fog. It happens after the rain, when all the water on the driveway, path or garden seems to magically disappear. I wasn't taught dew point and air temperature differentials at school, so, what else wasn't I taught about water?

I wasn't taught the importance of hydration, especially in terms of regulating body temperature, keeping joints lubricated, preventing infections, delivering nutrients to cells and keeping organs functioning properly to prevent urinary tract infections, kidney stones and constipation, and assisting in the repair processes in the case of injury. Pretty important stuff. I wasn't taught about the work of Dr Emoto,[923] who showed that unclean water with deformed crystalline structures changed into healthy water with perfect crystalline structures when subjected to positive intentions and prayers. I wasn't taught about water having memory, the unproven claim that, under certain circumstances, water can retain a 'memory' of solute particles after arbitrarily large dilution. I wasn't taught about the effect of sound on water, that it rearranges water's molecular conformations, changing its properties by increasing strongly bound, ice-like water, and decreasing small water clusters and solvation shells. I wasn't taught a lot about water and how it behaves. More and more theories contradict current scientific understanding of physical chemistry, and they are generally not accepted by the scientific community, either being totally ignored or hidden because they are so astonishing.

Science is good when put to good use, but it is also flawed in so many ways. Findings are merited based on their reproducibility; all the time, new evidence invalidates theories previously held as 'truth'; questionable results can influence a researcher's interpretation; it often relies on probability; data can be manipulated to fuel secret agendas, thereby negatively influencing policy decisions and undermining future advances. No wonder people are increasingly mistrusting science. It is not that science is fundamentally flawed, it's just that errors and biases occur in our minds, and 'bad science' hasn't helped, not to mention the rise of pseudoscience (impossible to disprove), vanity publishing of papers (fee-paid with minimal quality or peer review) and fake news (lies wrapped up as truth). Also, anything that does challenge the establishment and current body of accepted knowledge that has huge potential to disrupt reputations, research budgets, conflicts of interests and rampant egos, is quickly suppressed. We must stop equating science with truth, and so stop falling for lies wrapped up in pseudoscience and sensationalism (if it sounds too good to be true, it probably is) where the evidence is no more than hogwash.

Most of the low-fruit science has been discovered. 'Good science' today often involves huge collaborations built on the shoulders of giants and supported by the big budgets of large organisations. Science doesn't operate in the Heaven/ Soul realm, the quantum realm or any other dimension, and there is so much more to be discovered by each of us there. Let me throw down the challenge: do you want to be an explorer, an educator or an environmentalist, or all three? Rather than love, than money, than fame, give me truth.[455]

Untaught

Nobody tells you, as a wide-eyed child, all the little and big things that come with growing up, for you are your own evolving masterpiece, both the sculpture and the sculptor.

The transition from childhood to adulthood can be hard. Relationships and sexuality are fraught with danger, newfound freedoms and responsibilities, which can be equally difficult. There are many topics that are not covered at school and are either learnt the hard way or not at all.

Society is not very good at helping children identify their individual strengths, personalities, style and talent, nor showing them how to match it to real work to see how they can best fit in. The greater exposure to dangers within our society means parents are now more risk-aware, so they don't let their children explore the outside as those of past generations did. Children probably now have more free time than they ever did in the past, yet do not use this as wisely as they could. With their busy lives, many parents don't teach or encourage effective time-management skills, nor ensure that their kids don't spend all their time playing video games. Children seem to be drowning in data, but are starved of attention, knowledge and companionship. Parents and teachers are so wrapped up in the now that they often don't take the opportunity to talk to children about their futures, helping them develop decision-making skills and coping strategies for life's inevitable hiccoughs.

The education system focuses on exam results rather than developing personal and life skills; we teach our children advanced mathematics, but not budgeting, staying out of debt and having a contingency plan in case of emergencies. We teach the beauty and grammar of our language, but not how to communicate, negotiate, debate or compromise. We teach them physical education and team sports, but not how to look after themselves throughout life away from home. We teach about religions, but not to practise any form of religious values. We teach the mechanics and biology of sex, but not about the associated emotional intelligence, mental resilience and robustness that needs to come with relationships and the responsibility of bringing-up children. We teach road safety, but almost nothing about first-aid, drugs and how to avoid being peer pressured into smoking, drinking, taking drugs or other unacceptable risks. As a result, young people enter the world ill-equipped to cope with adulthood, break-ups, having children and managing their careers, and proceed to ignore any information regarding caring for the environment, the dangers of electronic devices, and the negative effects of social media and the internet.

Here are some life lessons they will not teach you at school:

If it doesn't feel right, don't do it. This lesson alone will save you a lot of grief.[503] Nothing feels as good as something you do from the heart. Focus on what works for you and the rest will follow. Your purpose, and the meaning of life, is to be yourself in whatever you do.[173]

If you want to live an extraordinary life, you need to give up a normal life. An extraordinary life doesn't come from massive financial wealth, a top job with a fancy title or fifteen minutes of fame and the approval of others,[659] it comes from identifying the ordinary things that are already a part of your life, or can be easily incorporated, that become extraordinary because you say they are. There's no magic pill to propel you to success; the extent of your struggle and sacrifice determines the extent of your personal growth and evolution. The more you evolve, the more you'll need to stay focused on what's most important. Make adjustments, manage your time more diligently, cut out distractions and invest in yourself. Success is continuously improving who you are, how you live, how you serve and how you relate to others.[660] The journey to the extraordinary can be a lonely road, and the bolder you are, the more rejection you'll experience; you need to pay the price to enter the domain of extraordinary.

Things that will immediately change your life and make you smarter, quicker and better include: eating healthily, exercising, sleeping well, being organised and having positive people around you. Control your stress with meditation, yoga and massage. If you start small and check every day that you have improved even one percent on physical, emotional, mental or spiritual health, then you are on the right path. Anything can be a vice, a barrier, or an opportunity; be aware of your habits and how you spend your time, where your actions are coming from, the value they deliver and why you feel compelled to repeat them. We attract into our lives the things that reflect who we are; learn how to succeed by making sure your lifestyle adds to your growth and improvement, and become the person you were meant to be. Common sense is not common practice; never forget that real wealth is good health and being surrounding by people who love you.

It is often said that you are a reflection of the five people you spend the most time with. Nobody creates themselves by themselves; we are all mirror images of what we see in other people. Surround yourself with people you wish to be like.

A wise man once said to be careful who you let on your ship, because some people will try to sink the whole ship because they can't be the captain. Don't go through life on other people's terms with your songs left unsung. People will expect you to stay in your lane and they get uncomfortable when you move out of it; break the glass and stop doing what you think everyone expects of you, especially if it is making you unhappy. There is no right or wrong as you get older, just different shades of grey; not everyone is going to like you and you will not like everyone you meet either, but that is just fine. Nobody has or can ever achieve a one hundred percent approval rating, so don't even try.

Look inward to yourself, as your potential is directly correlated to how well you know yourself. [658] Your potential increases with age but, as we age, we tend to forget the value of touch, tend to talk more than we listen and often stop reading. Remember, your dreams don't matter to anyone else and friends are relative to where you are in your life; the only person you have to face in the morning is yourself.

Most people aren't doing what they love because they didn't fight to make it happen for themselves, they are scared to use their imaginations and are disconnected from their inner children. Creativity takes practice, and most people fear using their imaginations, but spontaneity is the sister of creativity.[658] Nothing is as certain as change, yet we often get stuck tolerating things the way they are; if you don't cling onto things, you'll have a greater shot at being happy. Some things you simply can't change, like your parents, your DNA and what people think of you, but everything else is fair game. When we are no longer able to change a situation, we are challenged to change ourselves, and this is when true transformation starts to take place, especially when you accept you don't know it all.

Formal education makes a living, but it takes self-education and application to make fortunes. The quality of your learning determines the quality of your success and relationships. Everyone has doubts, but you will always come back around. Life will be made of mountains and valleys: new mountains to climb and deeper oceans to explore. At the end of the day it is all about moving forward.[658]

School is a good place to learn the fundamental skills of reading, writing and mathematics. Lesson one for every year group should be to learn how to learn, remember and recall via a number of different techniques to see what works for each individual. What is the point of teaching anything else or any other subject, if it is not going in?

Other, more difficult, skills to master, but that have significant long-term benefits include: physical health and muscle memory (cardio exercise, stretching, strength, self-defence, use of a knife and firearm), mental strength (decision-making, critical thinking, emotional resilience, applying lessons learned so you don't repeat the same mistakes, dealing with failure and success), self-care (cleanliness, healthy eating, cooking and efficient personal administration), personal acumen finance skills (control of money), meditation (reducing stress), assertive communication, waking up early, public speaking and physical presence, honesty (including self-reflection), leadership and effective networking, the lost art of really listening and, finally, being a continual learner.

Be a constant learner. If you are not willing to learn, experience new things and open your mind, no one can help you; if you are willing to learn, no one can stop you. Knowledge, just like life, is connected, interwoven and overlaps.

Learning

Below are ten critical things to learn in life. If you master these, the world will come to meet you. Learn to:

1. Predict consequences. Create a mental model imagining the sequence of events that might follow. 'What would likely happen if...?'

2. Read deeply and understand what is being asserted. The four major types of writing are description, argument, explanation and definition.

3. Distinguish truth from fiction, and opportunity from deceit. Question what you are told, read and see, don't simply accept everything. Always ask and scrutinise.

4. Empathise. Everyone is different, so try seeing things through someone else's eyes and imagining you are in their situation; don't be too quick to judge. Things done together and collaboratively are much more fun, even if they take a little longer.

5. Be creative, curious and adventurous. Walk barefoot in the grass when it rains, and deliberately lose at something so someone else can discover the joy of winning.

6. Communicate clearly and be sure to understand what you want to say; don't leave a conversation wishing you had or hadn't said something. Give it your all.

7. Practise and try different methods of learning to see if there is a better way for you to learn. Always try new things.

8. Stay healthy by taking care of your body and mind. Invest in proper nutrition and exercise every day. Take care of yourself so you can then take care of others.

9. Value yourself. Feel personally empowered to use your knowledge and skills, whilst recognising you don't know it all and may have to ask for help sometimes.

10. Live meaningfully, finding your true purpose in life with a sense of appreciation, dedication to the here and now and taking time to reflect and say thank you to life.

Learning is the key to unlocking and reducing poverty, inequality, conflict, disease, debt and corruption. It helps dreams come alive. We need to improve global education in terms of literacy, numeracy, information and communications technology, critical and creative thinking, personal and social capability, ethical and intercultural understanding, good hygiene practices and nutritional awareness.

Children are the key to so many successes, yet many don't even have their basic needs met. Child health and education go hand in hand. Malnutrition can cause difficulty concentrating and permanent physiological damage, preventing people from achieving their full potential. Poor education compounds the issue, as many children don't master the basic numeracy or literacy skills required to gain appropriate qualifications and then jobs.

If we are going to see real development in the world, then our best investment is in women,[465] as there is no greater pillar of stability than a strong, free and educated woman.[239] Imagine if, in a sports centre, you had a team but didn't let half of the team play. That would be stupid. It makes no sense. Communities that give their daughters the same opportunities as their sons are more peaceful, more prosperous and develop faster.[336] Young women who want an education will not be stopped[360]; they can't be stopped because they are the future for your community, your country and our world. If you try to stop the future, you are destined to fail and will become extinct. Nature and the natural world have no pity.

The hardest thing of all to learn is that your place in the world is something you and you alone must create for yourself, but people have finite energy, reserves and resources. We are all guilty of over-optimism at the start because we don't know what to expect on the journey and initially assume everything will go our way. The dip is inevitable because we build a picture in our mind that doesn't correspond to what is happening in the outside world.

Problems allow us to find the undiscovered strengths within. Live in the moment and try controlling your thoughts; you have the power to choose how you feel. Positive thinking, reflection, realism and taking appropriate action are key factors; you need a purpose and plan, even if it's just in your head, to show you where to go. You won't get it right the first time, but re-plan and adjust until you get there. Creativity is intelligence having fun. Someday, when you get where you're going, you'll know it was worth it.

Motivation is fire from within. If someone else tries to light that fire for you, chances are it will burn very briefly.[101]

There once was a person who had to solve lots of very complex problems. The primitive part of their mind (the First Way) wanted to solve the initial, visible problem using self-interest, instinct and their survival modes, which can think quickly, so they could move on to the next problem. The logical part of their mind (the Second Way) wanted to solve the first stages of the problem with lots of careful analysis, consideration and reflection. This would take a lot of time and require more people getting involved, attempting to reach a consensus before moving forward. The higher self and soul part (The Third Way) watched the other two parts in fascination, without judgement, and allowed them to argue it out until they were left exhausted. It then took all the previous inputs, used the subconscious and approached the soul world for guidance to get to the required destination. There is no right or wrong path, or knowledge, for all paths lead eventually to multiple solutions, some are just harder than others. The journey will invariably mean that learning will occur, and adjustments to the direction are highly likely; during those experiences, the destination and solutions may not be what were originally planned, but the person will ultimately end up in the right place – for that is life.

Knowledge

Two things are infinite: the universe and human stupidity; and I'm not sure about the universe.[133] We are just an advanced breed of monkeys on a minor planet of a very average star. But we can understand the universe, and that makes us something very special.[202]

The saddest aspect of life right now is that science gathers knowledge faster than society gathers wisdom.[25] Science is made up of mistakes, but they are mistakes that can be useful because they lead, little by little, to the truth.[475] Science is organised knowledge, but wisdom is organised life.[245]

The eye sees only what the mind is prepared to comprehend.[40] The only true wisdom is in knowing you know nothing.[434] Knowledge can be communicated, but not wisdom; one can find wisdom, live it, do wonders through it, but one cannot communicate or teach it.[210]

Life is like a game of chess: to win you have to make a move. Knowing which move to make comes with insight and knowledge, and by learning the lessons that are accumulated along the way.[397] A little learning is a dangerous thing.[364] If we fail to learn, we fail to grow.[464] An expert is a person who has made all the mistakes that can be made in a very narrow field.[47] Unless you try to do something beyond what you have already mastered, you will never grow.[432] Ignorance more frequently begets overconfidence than does knowledge.[106]

The seven social sins are wealth without work, pleasure without conscience, knowledge without character, commerce without morality, science without humanity, worship without sacrifice and politics without principle.[120] Knowledge is power, the power to do evil or power to do good. Power itself is not evil. So, knowledge itself is not evil.[394] No thief, however skilful, can rob one of knowledge, and that is why it is the best and safest treasure to acquire,[31] but knowing too much is never a good thing.[383] The highest form of knowledge is empathy, for it requires us to suspend our egos and live in another's world.[361] Knowledge alone is capable of transforming the world, while at the same time leaving it exactly as it is.[320]

Knowledge, like air, is vital to life, and no one should be denied it.[324] Books are the best weapons in the world and a library is the greatest arsenal you could have.[107] Obstacles are those frightening things you see when you take your eyes off your goal.[167] Hold fast to your dreams, for if they die, life is a broken-winged bird that cannot fly.[219]

The only good is knowledge, for you can do something with it. The only evil is indifference because you can't do anything positive with it.

Achievements

The achievements of humanity are wide-ranging. From the spiritual, philosophical, political, activist, exploratory and inventive to the artistic, industrialist, humanist, environmentalist, scientific, technological and mathematical.

All our dreams can become achievements if we have the courage to pursue them. If you can remove your self-doubt and believe in yourself, you can achieve what you never thought possible[38]; there are no limits with self-belief.[661] Success is not they key to happiness, happiness is the key to success; if you love what you are doing, you will be successful.[451] If your mind can conceive it and your heart can believe it, then you know with action you can achieve it.

Achievement is connected to action. A dream starts to become a goal when action is taken towards its achievement. Don't say 'I wish', say 'I will'. Focus on the goal, and don't look in any direction but ahead. Great things are not done by impulse, but by a series of small things brought together[472]; a little progress each day adds up to big results,[662] as achievement is not an activity, but a process. Successful people keep moving, they make mistakes, but they don't quit[663]; they keep on getting up until they achieve their goal.

The first secret to achieving is to get started. Each new day is another chance to change your life and the world. Who you are tomorrow begins with what you do today.[140] The second secret is to start before you think you are ready. Great achievement always requires great sacrifice, and high achievement always takes place in the framework of high expectation.

Only those who attempt the absurd can achieve the impossible. Don't let others tell you what can't be achieved. Don't let their limitations limit your vision. Achievement is ten percent inspiration and ninety percent perspiration; people forget to look for the perspiration and think wonderful achievements just appear from nowhere. Not everyone will understand your journey, but that's okay; they need to understand their own, not yours.[664]

It always seems impossible until it's done. Work hard in silence and let success be your noise. Allow yourself to be proud of yourself and all the progress you've made, especially the progress that no one else has seen.[665]

A lot of goals are personal challenges to overcome adversity, to gain new knowledge and skills, or to work as part of a team, organisation or group for the common good. Achievements are great, but they are just welcome train stops on the journey of life; they don't define you, shouldn't limit you and, most importantly, are just a part of you (like collecting old train tickets) that doesn't determine your potential. Be totally honest with yourself about the overhyped pursuits and events that everyone else wants you to do or enjoy, but you know you actually loathe. As well as creating a bucket list (of things you want to do for yourself), create a f*** it list (of things you hate and don't want to do) and a share list (of things you want to do for others, the planet and all its inhabitants).

Awareness

Developing awareness means restoring your freedom to choose what you want, instead of accepting what your past imposes on you. When your awareness becomes a flame, it burns up the slavery your mind has subjected itself to.

Every human has four endowments: self-awareness, consciousness, independent will and creative imagination. These give us the ultimate human freedoms. Without the necessary awareness, freedom is dangerous. Awareness is the capacity to embrace, accept and include joy and sadness, love and aloneness, light and darkness, male and female qualities and life and death into our consciousness.[669] Without self-awareness, we are like babies in the cradle.[291] Self-awareness gives us the ability to take an honest look at life (and all its associated baggage) with individual focus, without any attachment to it being right or wrong, good or bad.[166]

The easiest person to deceive is yourself. We cannot change what we are not aware of, but once we are aware we cannot help but change.[403] The first step towards change is awareness that you need to change, the second step is acceptance[666]; a person cannot change without this awareness of themselves. Awareness is like the sun, when it shines on things, they are transformed.[199 & 667] To 'know thyself' is not a narcissistic pursuit and can take a while, so be forgiving. It is with the heart that one can see rightly; what is essential is invisible to the eye.

We focus so much on what goes on from the neck down that we forget it all starts in the mind. If you are not mentally ready, you're not physically prepared. The body has limitations, the mind does not. Awareness allows us to get outside of our minds and observe them in action; it is the bridge between reaction and conscious choice. Self-awareness doesn't stop you from making mistakes, it allows you to learn from them. Rather than *being* your thoughts and emotions, be the *awareness* behind them.[668]

Be accountable. Yes, love yourself, but also analyse and be critical of how you think and behave. It is much more difficult to judge oneself than to judge others,[110] but self-love without self-awareness is useless.

The awareness that our health is dependent upon habits that we can control makes us the first generation in history that, to a large extent, has determined its own destiny.[83] The key to growth and continued existence is the introduction of higher dimensions of consciousness into our awareness and the realisation that everything is connected – our actions have the power to do both good and evil.

Not all artists have a responsibility to be socially or politically aware, but they do have a responsibility to make great art. They have to find some truth and put that in their music, literature, pictures or sculptures.[171] Leaders can only become aware of how effective their leadership really is in times of hardship, not on sunny days when everything runs itself. If they do not develop self-awareness and are not made to take responsibility for their first creations (actions with vast knock-on effects), then how can they empower other people to shape their lives and circumstances, their outputs and outcomes, to the best effect for everyone?

There once was a person who sought to quickly and easily increase their awareness (the First Way), but it was such a burden, for they were always worried that they would lose their money, status and achievements, that they would wake one day and it would be all gone as if it had all been a dream. That person was never truly content, for they always had external focus. There was a second person who sought awareness through hardship, trials and abstinence (the Second Way), leading a life of solitude, taking less than they needed to survive, and living frugally without excess, extravagance or addiction. That person was never truly happy as they had internal focus. There was yet another person who did not seek awareness directly, but understood the value of sharing, service and experience (The Third Way), where they took just enough, experienced cycles of plenty and cycles of shortage, and were always helpful and considerate to others, the environment and the world. Awareness is often found not by seeking it directly but through indirect means. The Third Way can be difficult in a very materialistic world where you are told to provide support for others with things.

There are three types of awareness. The first is associated with sleep, unconsciousness, unknowing and generally operating on autopilot. Some people never get beyond this stage during their lives because they don't understand how to move forward; they often live a life of dissatisfaction, pain, longing, frustration, anger and hate. The second type of awareness is a series of sensory-based elements: instinctual and survival (fight/flight), conformance (follow the crowd), aspirational physical and mental (desire without action), cognitive thoughts and behavioural individualism (feelings, actions, the power of now, practice, self-discipline, experiences, retrospectives plus reflections, mastery of something and greater understanding of the self and the world). The third type goes beyond the sensory and is very difficult to reach. It requires that you pass over into a different state – shed your old skin, so to speak – walk through dark places; accept the constant struggle of the dark within each of us, what is in your control and what is out of your control. You enter the non-sensory realms, essentially the spiritual (the journey and its ups and downs; the steps to enlightenment; the realisation that true happiness comes from within[382]; a sense of connectedness to everything, even in other dimensions, higher realms of existence and the eternal nature of the soul). Understanding the different types of awareness and what they mean for you can be compared to a seed recognising its potential to become a great tree; the awareness encourages flourishing and the creation of more seeds to do the same. Now that is something to think about!

Vision

Vision is the art of seeing what is invisible and spotting potential in what others overlook.[449]

A vision is a picture of the future that produces passion[670]; it is an appeal to our better selves, a call to become something more.[246] Your vision of where or what you want to be is the greatest asset you have. Hold the vision, trust the process, believe in it and do everything you can to turn it into reality.[671]

Vision without action is merely a dream. Action without vision just passes the time. Vision *with* action can change the world; it's unbelievable how powerful you can be when you have a clear vision. Your vision can become clear only when you look into your heart. Who looks outside, dreams; who looks inside, awakens.[675] Make your vision so clear that your fears become irrelevant;[672] your vision is limited only by you, so see yourself as the truly capable human being that you are. People don't change, they just become a clearer vision of who they really are.

In order to carry out positive actions, we must develop a positive vision.[224] Where a negative vision is being created, we must do everything in our power to overcome it through positive actions. People with purpose, goals and visions have no time for drama – they invest their energy in creativity and focus on living a positive life.[674] If you're working on something exciting and good that you really care about, you don't have to be pushed, the vision pulls you along. Create your vision, then go into 'beast mode' to achieve it. The best way to succeed is to have a specific intent, a clear vision, a plan of action and the ability to maintain clarity.[673]

The only thing worse than being blind is having sight but no vision.[252] Sight is what you see with your eyes; vision is what you see with your mind. Vision requires imagination, the golden path that leads to everywhere, the preview of life's coming attractions. Imagination is more important than knowledge because it is unlimited. It encircles the world; the world is a canvas for your imagination. It is reality for the dreamer. Everything that is real was imagined first; indulge your imagination in every possible flight because you have all the reasons in the world to achieve your grandest dreams. Imagination is the language of the soul; pay attention to your imagination and you will discover all you need to be fulfilled.[133] Imagination plus innovation equals realisation. The best use of imagination is creativity; the worst use is anxiety and self-doubt. Imagination will often carry us to worlds that never were, but without it we go nowhere.

Those with no vision travel a road with no destination, know not where they are or when they have arrived, and often need to switch routes to new destinations. They are forever lost, forever looking for the secret they will never find because they are not really looking; they are simply destined to a life of unfulfilled dreams, misery, toil and trouble. Visions, like love, give life purpose.

When one is young it is very easy to have visions and distinguish between right and wrong, but as one gets older, the villains and the heroes get all mixed up.[676] We are not now that strength which in old days moved Earth and Heaven. That which we are, we are. One equal temper of heroic hearts, made weak by time and fate, but strong in will. To strive, to seek, to find, and not to yield.[280] When you can't tell your friends from your enemies, it's time to go. Letting go is hard; if you have only one vision, let it be. The function of man is to live, not exist, don't waste your days trying to prolong them, use your time well.[279] Time is running out so spend it like it's gold.[677]

Stress

It's not stress that kills us, it is our reaction to it.[679]

Stress is the inability to decide what is important. It is caused by being 'here' but wanting to be 'there'. Life is really simple, but we insist on making it complicated.[325] The greatest weapon against stress is our ability to choose one thought over another.

Our anxiety does not come from thinking about the future, but from wanting to control it.[686] Don't get stressed over what you can't control[689]; accept the things you can't control or change, and focus on what you can, to reduce your stress. Change is never easy, and one of the hardest lessons in life is learning to let go – whether it's of guilt, anger, love, loss, betrayal or stress – we fight to hold on but, eventually, we fight to let go. You don't always need a plan; difficult roads lead to beautiful destinations – don't try to force anything and take time to look out of the window along the way. Your mind will answer most questions if you learn to relax and wait for the answers.[74] Sometimes, you just need to breathe, trust, let go and see what happens.[198]

You need to learn to handle stress because it comes with success; it is the price to be paid. In times of great stress or adversity it can be best to keep busy, to plough your anger and energy into something positive.[678] Alternatively, sometimes the most productive thing you can do is walk away for a period of time. Try and keep your mind occupied and distracted by today, rather than worrying or focusing too much into the future. In most workplaces, if you die on the job, they will just replace you, so taking a few minutes or hours away from the stress is something that they can live with. If they can't live with you walking away for a while, then you are in the wrong job, relationship or situation, and it's time to say goodbye.

How beautiful it is to do nothing and then to rest afterwards.[681] Tension is who you think you should be, but relaxation is who you are; within you, there is a stillness, a sanctuary to which you can retreat at any time and be yourself.[690] Every day brings a choice to practise stress or to practise peace. It's all about finding calm in the chaos that is life – breathe, let go and remind yourself that this very moment is the only one you know you have for sure.[503] Your relationship with yourself sets the tone for every other relationship you have,[686] so don't neglect it.

Stress, anxiety and depression are caused when we are living to please others.[688] Life is too short to stress yourself over people who don't even deserve to be an issue in your life[687]; those in your life should be a source of stress-reduction, not a cause of stress.[680] Saying yes to happiness means learning to say no to things and people that stress you out. Be with those who bring out the best in you, not the stress in you.

Rule number one is: don't sweat the small stuff. Rule number two is: it's all small stuff.[682] The elimination diet: remove anger, regret, resentment, guilt, blame and worry, then watch your health and life improve – more smiling, less worrying; more compassion, less judgement; more blessed, less stressed; more love, less hate. Stop focusing on how stressed you are and focus on how blessed you are.[681] Let it go, you can't hold it back anymore.

Making fitness a priority will energise you, make you look and feel better and help diffuse stress. Nothing is worth diminishing your health for;

nothing is worth poisoning yourself with stress, anxiety and fear into an early grave.[694]

The greatest mistake you can make in life is to be continually fearing you will make one.[217] Mistakes are the way you learn. Of all your troubles, great and small, the greatest are the ones that don't happen at all. Remember the story of the old man who said on his deathbed that he'd had a lot of trouble in his life, most of which never happened.[93] Worrying does not take away tomorrow's troubles, it takes away today's peace.[684] When you find yourself stressed, ask yourself: Will this matter five years from now? If yes, then do something about the situation. If no, then let it go.[683 & 93] If you want to conquer the anxiety of life, live in the moment, live in the breath.[685]

Stressed spelled backwards is desserts. When something happens that has never happened before, deploy flexibility and combine it with a sense of humour. Whatever your plan, it's unlikely to go exactly as you hoped, so go with the flow, even through uncertainty. If you are faced with a life-or-death situation, then make sure you have a spare rope. Set peace of mind as your highest goal and organise your life around it. Focus on making good decisions, being well-prepared, remaining calm and helping others, rather than dwelling on the dangerous situations that may be unfolding around you. The most important strategy in times of stress is having a routine as it gives you a sense of momentum and allows you to react less emotionally.

People can build up robust mental resilience after experiencing a wealth of challenges that teach them to stay calm and confident in a crisis. Build up your mental strength by looking beyond what your body is telling you; if it is telling you to give up, turn to your inner beliefs, training, lack of ego and stubbornness (which can be another source of strength). Beware of punching too far above your capabilities, talents or skills, and only do so if you have a good team around you to fill in any gaps or deficiencies you may have. Try to focus on the optimistic, positive and enthusiastic aspects of your personality, rather than dwelling on the negatives. It is not the amount of progress you make each day, it is the fact that you have made *some* progress. Take life day by day and be grateful for the little things.

Remember: don't stress the 'could haves' – if it should have, it would have; stand up to your obstacles and do something about them and you will find they haven't half the strength you think they have; worrying pretends to be necessary but serves no useful purpose when you get to the present[457]; there is a huge amount of freedom that comes to you when you take nothing personally; when someone gives you a box full of darkness, it can take you years to understand that this too was a gift; a diamond is a piece of carbon that handled stress and darkness exceptionally well; you can't always have a good day, but you can always face a bad day with a good attitude[692]; you can do anything but not everything, so choose well[693]; worry is like a rocking chair, it gives you something to do but never gets you anywhere; if you can solve your problem, then what is the need of worrying? If you cannot solve it, then what is the use of worrying?[691]

Those who can't manage their stress give their lives over to it. Numerous studies report a dramatic rise in mental illness and suicide, particularly amongst children and teens, linked to environmental, economic and social woes, lifestyle, genetics and brain chemistry. These are associated with: increased parental pressure; increased use of electronic media (Electronic Screen Syndrome); increased performance pressure (education, career, financial); increased exposure to terrorist activity and divisive, negative news; a dramatic increase in exposure to graphically violent TV programmes, movies and video games; increased exposure to sexually explicit material (TV, movies, video games, online pornography); increased social media pressure and its negative effects; reduced face-to-face interaction and social support; breakdown of the family unit; sexual orientation and gender confusion; increased exposure to a multitude of differing opinions and influencers (on TV and online); exposure to aggressive behaviour (child abuse, adult abuse, sexual abuse); poor/reduced sleep; increased financial pressure on parents; reduced parental contact (children are prematurely separated from parents and families, and bonding to peers); easy access to and acceptance of recreational drugs (of all types); being overly protected/indulged; reduced expectations for young adults; a lack of access to care; COVID-19 effects. Ultimately, being part of the 'I' generation (who believe they are entitled to whatever they want, from opinions to lifestyle choices, whenever and however they want it). The increase in mental health issues is most consistent between the 1930s and the early 1990s. There is little doubt that anxiety and depression increased between these decades.

Connections

Everything is connected at different levels. The more people you meet, the more you come to realise how many fears, experiences and emotions we all share.[695] Life is so busy that we often don't have time to connect with one another about universal truths. Sometimes it feels good to stop for a while and think that right now, somewhere on our planet, someone is feeling the same as you, whether that be sad, happy, scared, lonely, rejected, excited or jubilant. You are never alone, even when it feels that way.[696]

Connection can be defined as the energy that exists between people when they feel seen, heard and valued.[697] Don't confuse connecting with people on social media and gaming platforms with true connection that occurs in person. Spend more time with your loved ones, not just physically but mentally.[698] When you can give and receive without judgement, that is when you can derive sustenance and strength from relationships and connections; it is not about the length of time you've known someone, it's about the recognition at the unconscious level, when your souls know each other.

True fulfilment comes from thinking beyond your own needs and desires and connecting to others; it heightens your meaning and purpose. You know you're in love when you can't fall asleep because reality is finally better than your dreams.[699] We seek fulfilment through heart connections with others. This is our soul's essence of joy, which spontaneously pulses through us, longing to share itself. Sometimes you fall in love with the most unexpected person at the most unexpected time.[700] Some souls have a way of connecting without our knowledge; that's why you can meet someone for the first time, but know it is not truly the first time you've felt them.[701] You agreed a long time ago, in the soul world, to meet up, and that is what you've just done. There are no accidental meetings between souls. Spirituality is about connection with the inner self and the self that is in every being; science just doesn't understand this type of true connection yet. The day science begins to study non-physical phenomena, it will make more progress in one decade than in all the previous centuries of its existence; perception will burst forth.[453]

In a world of algorithms, hashtags and followers, learn the importance of true human connection, and the difference between connection and attention. Human connection is the key to personal and career success[702]; the more connections you make, the more you can move your life in the desired direction.

The most important things in life are the connections we make with others. Finding someone you can really connect with is like winning the lottery.[707] Great relationships are not great because they have no problems; they are great because both people care enough about the other to find a way to make it work. You can't give up on someone because the situation is not ideal.[703] Everyone is vulnerable. Vulnerability attracts honesty, and honesty attracts soul connections. Intimacy is not purely physical but a connection with someone so deep that you feel like you can see into their soul.

However, there are people who bring you down by just being with them, so you need to break those connections. No matter how busy a person may be, if they really care, they will always find time for you.[704] There cannot be a relationship unless there is two-way commitment to loyalty, patience and persistence. But no relationship is a waste of time. If it didn't bring you what you wanted, it taught you what you didn't want.[705] Knowing what you want and knowing what you don't want is a key piece of the connectivity puzzle.

Paradise has never been about places; it exists in moments, in flashes across time.[706] It is about relationships, experiences and connections. In this world, everything is connected – we just don't realise it. Look carefully and you will see the absolute beauty and connectedness of the Universe; our world is so much more than what we see every day. Some of us are awakening, while the rest fall deeper into sleep.

Society grades things, assigns them levels and then turns them into 'types' in an attempt to put them into understandable boxes. Language is a poor indicator of concepts, a poor method of transferring information and expressing deeper things because it assumes a lot of shared knowledge between the communicator and receiver, which is not the case much of the time. Life and the world have a spectrum of states – some that co-exist, others that overlap and many others that change over time. I have looked into categorisation for many projects, some of which I been able to simplify, whilst others I've come out of more confused than ever. Humans like categories, but life, the world and the soul are all parts of the same, connected entity. Most of us just can't see it yet.

CHAPTER 6

Diversity and unity make us invincible.

"Life is a dream for the wise, a game for the fool, a comedy for the rich and tragedy for the poor."

—Sholom Aleichem[12] (Modified)

Diversity may be the hardest thing for a society to live without.[34] We need diversity of thought to face the challenges ahead, and this will come from all different cultures. Our ability to reach unity in diversity will be the test of our civilisation.[269]

Race

We may be planted in different places, but we all come from the same root under the same tree. There is only one race – the human race.[708] We were all human until race disconnected us, religion separated us, politics divided us and wealth classified us. In a racist society, it's not enough to be non-racist, we must be *anti*-racist. Racism is a reality that a large proportion of people grow up with, but if we hope to ever move past it, it's up to *all* of us – black, white, everyone – no matter how well-meaning we think we might already be, to do the honest, uncomfortable work of rooting it out.[337]

Time and truth are on the side of the oppressed. The few have been very good at dividing and conquering the many, but when many people get angry, they bring about change. You can't separate peace from freedom because no one can be at peace unless they have their freedom, and the price of certain freedoms is death.[292] Wrong is wrong, no matter who does or says it, and there will be a clash between those who want freedom, justice and equality for everyone, and those who want to perpetuate systems of exploitation.[292]

It is the right of every person to be respected as a human being and to be given basic human rights. Nobody will give you freedom, equality or justice; you need to fight for them. Education is the passport to the future, for tomorrow belongs to those who prepare for it today;[709] all you have to do is to be an intelligent human being and, one day, we may all meet together in the light of understanding.[292]

A person who stands for nothing will fall for anything. None of us is responsible for the complexion of their skin, and it does not dictate the character or quality of the person underneath.[15] In many ways, genetics makes a mockery of race. The characteristics of normal human variation that determines skin colour, morphological features and hair texture are all biologically encoded. When peoples' genomes are analysed from all over the world, these differences represent a tiny fraction of the total number of differences – there is more genetic diversity within Africa than the rest of the world put together.

Injustice anywhere is a threat to justice everywhere.[34] Darkness cannot drive out darkness, only light can do that; hate cannot drive out hate, only love can do that.[710] We may have different religions, languages and varying colours of skin, yet we all belong to one human race, we all share the same basic values[17 & 711]; we are all the same family, irrespective of our tribe or geographical location. The holiest and most sacred city on Earth will be found where equality, the fountain of truth, love, peace and brotherhood live.[292]

Hey children, play nicely. We are all in the same boat and race whilst here on Earth, and that is why it is called the 'human race'. We are all the same, all connected and all trying to make our way through life, hopefully helping others along the way. We are more closely linked than we could ever imagine.

Religion

If most religions teach peace, why can't all religions achieve peace? Religion is never the problem; it is the people who use it to gain power or abuse it in its name.[713]

Religion is the clearest telescope through which we can behold the beauties of creation, but you must accept that the telescope exists and look through it to see the stars. Science and religion are the two opposing sides of the same coin. Faith is as necessary to reason as reason is to faith; the one cannot exist without the other. Science without religion is lame; religion without science is blind.[714] Science and religions are binary – something either exists or it doesn't – but life is not that clear. The boundary between the science and religion is a place of uncertainty, but it can be connected, and this is known as 'The Third Way'. If life were a coin, science would be one side and religion would be the other; the rim of the coin would be uncertainty or opportunity. Uncertainty is where things exist that are unknown or unknowable to us, like what happens after death, or where we were before we were born – the great unfathomable unknown. Even though we cannot know what happens in this domain, the things that do happen leave traces, trails and pointers, like comets through the sky. By looking at the evidence of these traces and exploring the unknowable unknown, we can not only make educated guesses about new knowledge of the world around us, but we learn more about ourselves, too.

Religions may have different names, but they all contain the same basic truths; they may teach different things about the nature of God and encourage different values, but they all seek to help people find meaning in life. The essence of all religions is one, though there are hundreds of versions because their approaches are different. We may have different religions, different languages, different coloured skin, but we all belong to one human race.[715] Religions are man-made, many and diverse, but reason and goodness are one.[716] Forgiveness, compassion, tolerance, brotherhood and the feeling of oneness are all signs of a true religion, and are the keys to entering the Heavenly Abode. Without these, you will need to enter purgatory to cleanse your soul before you will be allowed to go any further. Just like you wipe your feet at the door before entering a house, to remove the dirt, the same applies to the afterlife.

Just as a candle cannot burn without fire, people cannot live without a spiritual life.[401] Real values can have meaning only when you step on to the spiritual path, a path where negative emotions have no use. A person does not have to be behind bars to be a prisoner; people can be prisoners of their own concepts and ideas.[401] Pleasure from the senses seems like nectar at first, but it is bitter as poison in the end. True wisdom always leads us to please God, and worship is the way we can see the world by God's light. Faith doesn't make things easy; it makes them possible. When life is too hard to stand, kneel.[712] Whatever you ask for in prayer, believe that you have received it, and it will be yours. Whatever you wish for yourself, be sure to wish the same for others. The best way to know God is to love many things, lean on each other's strengths and forgive each other's weaknesses.

You, as much as anybody in the entire universe, deserve love and affection. The world tells us to seek success, power and money; God tells us to seek humility, service and love. The more you give, the more you will get and then life will become a dance of love. By conquering anger, the soul acquires the capacity for forgiveness. By conquering pride, the soul gains humility. By giving up deceit, the soul acquires simplicity and straightforwardness. By conquering greed, the soul attains contentment.[712] A beautiful life does not just happen, it is built daily by prayer, humility, sacrifice and hard work.[712]

Our deepest fear is not that we are inadequate but that we are powerful beyond measure. It is our light, not our darkness, that most frightens us.[748] But 'playing small' does not serve the world, for there's nothing enlightening about shrinking so that others don't feel insecure.[717] We are all meant to shine, as children do. We were born to make and manifest the glory of the divine that is within *all* of us,[501] and as we let our light shine, we unconsciously awaken other people and give them permission to do the same; as we are liberated, our presence automatically liberates others.[501] Life begins where fear ends.

The greatest religion is to be true to your own nature. Have faith in yourself.[712] It all starts from within, from self-love, for to fall in love with yourself is the first secret to happiness, not only for you but for others as well. Life is much larger than birth and death, failure and success. You are the unblemished, pure, eternal self, and when you realise this, you will walk like a king. There is no need for temples, no need for complicated philosophy.[105] Our brain and heart are our temple; their philosophy is understanding and kindness. Your greatest responsibility is to love yourself and to know that you are enough[718]; we need to care about each other and, in the process, care for and heal ourselves. It is then start we can start to build out from ourselves to heal others. Everyone needs to be at peace, no matter what is going on around them, so they can rise to love and light, knowing who they are. Wherever the mind wanders, restless and diffused in its search for satisfaction without, lead it within; train it to rest in the Self.[712] The heart is like a garden; it can grow compassion or fear, resentment or love. What seeds will you plant there?

Remember: each today, well-lived, makes yesterday a dream of happiness and each tomorrow a vision of hope. Look, therefore, to this one day[712]; nothing kills the ego like playfulness, like laughter – when you start taking life as fun, the ego has to die, it cannot exist anymore[712]; it is only with the heart that one can see rightly; what is essential is invisible to the eye; life is far beyond meaning and that's why it is so beautiful; do not dwell in the past or the future, concentrate your mind on the present moment; God's word is the lamp that lights your path.

Religions and science seem to have this mutual loathing, yet operate a kind of cartel of acceptable human thinking and behaviour, establishing rules to maintain control. Religions can't accept anything not faith-based, scripture-delivered or head-office-authorised, and monopolise the non-physical domains; science can't accept anything immeasurable, unrepeatable or unexplainable, and rejects what doesn't fit the current accepted model. Science can explain lots of things, but ignores anything that contradicts the norm and ostracises any 'outside the box' thinking. Religion can't explain forbidden archaeology; it ignores new interpretations of predefined assumptions and has a long (and still running) history of persecution other religions and ideas. What if religion and science are intimately connected, just the opposite faces of the same coin? What if they are both right, both wrong and just missing the body of the coin to make everything make sense? Now, that would be interesting, wouldn't it?

I love science. It's a captivating journey of discovery to objectively establish facts through methods and processes of repeatable testing and experimentation

— finding out more about the world using systematic observations and tools that allow the formulation of hypotheses, predictions and models and hands-on experiments, then analysing the results, changing parameters and repeating the whole exercise. Science is a hugely successful human enterprise that develops tools, medicines, vehicles, technologies and systems beyond our wildest dreams, giving us almost godlike powers. Religion, on the other hand, is the collection of cultural and belief systems related to humanity, spirituality, belief, morality and ethics, intended to give life meaning through narrative, symbols and traditional and sacred histories/teachings. There are things that science will never be able to explain, and religion seeks to fill that void. You really can't have one without the other, for they are part of the same coin of life, just opposite sides. Some forget that the thing that connects science and religion is people, and that there are dimensions beyond the 2D world of science and religion.

Peace

No price is too great to pay for inner peace. Peace is the harmonious control of life and is a power that easily transcends all our worldly knowledge. It is not the highest goal in life, it is the most fundamental requirement.[722]

We have more books on war than we have on peace, and being surrounded by significant numbers of volumes on violence, hatred and death is bound to have a negative effect on each one of us. It's time to develop more positive programming and create more cross-media platforms to bring balance and establish peace.

You find peace not by rearranging the circumstances of your life, but by realising who you are at the deepest level.[457] Become so rooted in your core being that nobody's absence or presence can disturb your inner peace. Do not lose your inner peace for anything.[720] Non-violence means avoiding not only the external physical act of violence, but also internal violence and hate of the spirit. Peace comes from within when you have no desire to argue with anyone and choose to walk away, when you choose to distance yourself from negativity.

Learning to ignore things is one of the greatest paths to inner peace.[719] Quiet in the soul can even be achieved in a storm; silence is wisdom's best reply to chaos. Be selective with your battles, as sometimes peace is better than being right. Never be in a hurry – that's how mistakes happen. Do everything quietly in a calm spirit. Peace does not mean being in a place where there is no noise, trouble or hard work, it means being in the midst of those things and still being calm in your heart.[183] You will find peace not by trying to escape your problems but by confronting them courageously.

Peace can't be kept by force; it can only be achieved by understanding; it is its own reward; it begins with a smile; love is its purest form; it begins when expectation ends.

The day the power of love overrules the love of power, the world will finally know peace.[721]

There is no other way than peace and positivity; sitting on the fence is non-participating, non-living and non-experiencing, which leads to becoming critical, judgemental and hateful. If you don't like something, get down off the wall and change it for something better. Everything else is negativity; feed it and it will grow.

Music

Numerous studies have shown that music can lift our moods, combat depression and improve blood flow in ways similar to how statins (blood thinners) lower levels of stress-related hormones such as cortisol, and ease pain. It is understood that levels of dopamine (the feel-good chemical) in the brain rise when people listen to music they enjoy.

It is said that there are certain natural musical frequencies and vibrations that have healing powers, perhaps through its ability to take people out of themselves for a few hours. There are things we don't fully understand yet, especially related to sound therapy, which is not applied through hearing but by instruments that send sound waves directly into the body through the skin. Music is not meant solely to be heard, it is also felt, and speaks to the soul directly. It does a lot of things for a lot of people; it can take you right back in your life, acting as a trigger for positive memories. It's uplifting, encouraging and strengthening. Listen carefully and you will hear the hum of the Earth and Universe through the Solfeggio Frequencies and other Magical Tones all around us.

Everything in life owes its existence, solely and completely, to sound and vibrations; music doesn't get in, it is already in.[723] If you want to find the secrets of the Universe, you must think in terms of energy, frequency and vibration.[453]

Music is the soundtrack of life and it can change the world. It acts like a magic key to open the most tightly closed hearts. Music and rhythm find their way into the secret places of the soul and, once admitted, they become a sort of spirit, and never die.[67]

I love listening and unwinding to music. But of course, it has such universal appeal that it also attracts elephants, cows, deer and lots of other animals to come and listen; every living creation understands what music is. Music must be communicating with us on a different level, not simply aurally. We can only hear it across such a limited range; those twelve notes in a western octave can be arranged in so many different ways and on different instruments across an infinite pitch range. We may all speak different languages, but music is a language that all people can appreciate and understand, irrespective of culture, country or time. Considered by some as the purest form of art in design, form and spirit, it evokes similar responses from all different people – everyone can differentiate sad from happy music, regardless of their background, even if they have never heard the type of music before. When overlaid with the sound of the human voice it reaches another level of beauty and it is the closest we can come to wielding magic in our world and connecting people; it doesn't just make us happy or sad, it brings us together. Just imagine the level of beauty of otherworldly choirs that are angelic and heavenly. Don't forget to appreciate the people who created the music and brought it to your attention. Learn to appreciate the small things in life.

CHAPTER 7

Society is only a mental concept.

"When you educate a man, you teach the individual; when you educate women, you teach generations."

—Brigham Young[513] (Modified)

Society exists only as a mental concept; in the real world there are only individuals. The ideal society can be described as that in which no person has the power or means to coerce others, so, to make it a better place, we must first change ourselves. Every society gets the kind of leader and criminal it deserves, and our modern society is engaged in polishing and decorating the cages in which people are imprisoned. What is equally true is that every community gets the kind of law enforcement it insists on. There can be no keener litmus test of a society's soul than the way in which it treats its children, prisoners and the disadvantaged; it is in times of stress, war and conflict that we observe how truly fragile and divided our society has really become.

In our current, shallow society, people are judged on what they wear, their taste in music, what they look like and how they act. We need to do better; we need to ensure that everyone lives in warmth and harmony by accepting our differences as strengths, and try not to kill each other or destroy the Earth in the meantime.

Conditioning

We are conditioned by the societies we live in. It's in the interests of large societies to have people who follow the rules and do as they are told.

But despite rules and protocols, we can still be individuals and assert our differences.[724] Being aware of being conditioned helps us to challenge the status quo and think critically. You don't always have to follow the crowd; take pride in your uniqueness and think for yourself.

Our schools don't teach us anything about the real world, except how terrible people can be. The government-backed education system is modelled on the interests of capitalism and industrialisation, with the purpose of turning people into mindless robots who are obedient and make the rich richer. For society to function all the different elements of work need to get done; it can't operate with everyone living on the top tier.

Society burdens us with conventions, expectations, unwritten rules and arbitrary 'norms' so that we feel convinced there is something wrong with us and go looking for solutions to problems we often don't actually have. Not everything matters, so trust your instincts. Fight for the things that do matter. Delegate or step away from things that don't need your specific attention. Develop a healthy attitude to risk; people who exit their comfort zones into the great unknown have often been rewarded for their mettle. Focus on activities that improve your physical and emotional health; the moment you start focusing on the good stuff is the moment you start living your best life.

People are often pushed into things that are not what they want, not who they are or not what they want to do. Lots of skills are required to get to the top. For example, becoming the best at a particular sport necessitates learning: how to compete; how to deal with other competitors; how to pick your moments; how to deal with the stress; how to manage your energy levels and reserves (for qualifying rounds and the 'main event'); how to handle the pressure of being in front; how and when to defend, attack and switch between them; how to read the environment and understand opportunity windows; how to deal with fear (of failure and of success); how to think for yourself and make your own decisions; how to get sponsorship deals; how to manage money; how to deal with travelling and being away from your family and support network. You could read books and watch videos, but what you are learning is just what worked for these people, which can be helpful but can sometimes work against you. Learning everything from scratch is also not the answer because it can affect your risk assessment and decision-making abilities, endangering yourself and others as you may do anything to win (for example, being totally uncompromising and forcing moves that are not good practice and are unsustainable). Many people have to learn from scratch or fail to achieve because they do not have someone to show them the holistic picture.

When the fun stops, that is the beginning of the end, and all good things do come to an end.[367 & 725] Burnout is nature's way of telling you that you've been going through the motions, your soul has departed; it happens when you avoid being human for too long. [67 & 47] In order to break the cycle of burnout, it is important to observe and identify your 'burn events', prepare for those you can and fully recover from each one.[519] You must give up the delusion that burnout is the inevitable cost of success[218]; it can be tempting, in our goal-oriented society, to push ourselves beyond our limits in pursuit of success, but when we do this we are telling ourselves that our work is more important than our health. Without our health, our success means nothing; no promotion, no raise, no accolade will mean anything if you aren't happy and healthy.[264] When you're at peace with yourself and love yourself, it is virtually impossible to do things to yourself that are destructive.[128] You will burn and you will burn out, but you will be healed and come back again.[122] Time spent in nature is the most cost-effective and powerful way to counteract burnout and the sort of depression that we feel when we sit in front of a computer all day.[281] Remember that nobody is perfect, so give yourself credit for everything you're doing right, and be kind to yourself when you struggle[115]; stay positive and don't go completely down the rabbit hole of negativity.

P.S. Just a friendly reminder that 'doing your best' does not mean working yourself into a mental breakdown.

Acceptance

If people can't accept you for who you really are, that's their problem, not yours. Don't waste your time even thinking about them and start doing more of what you really want to do instead: chasing worthwhile relationships and preserving the things you care for.[93] You can't worry too much about not hurting people, especially strangers, in pursuit of living your best life. It's your life, live it authentically, work with what you have and make the best of it.

Distance yourself from distractions, energy leeches and negative people. The three things that have the potential to create havoc for you are family/friends, work/money and bills/taxes. Success is getting what you want out of your limited time on planet Earth. For some it is getting to the top, for some it is being part of a team, for others it is being an individual and mastering something or themselves. All its definitions are all right and all wrong. Only one person gets the job and upsets all other candidates; one team generally wins in sports competitions (the other teams lose); one country wins a war, the other doesn't. Success should be gracious. Participation, doing your best and learning something new is success, even if you don't come out on top. Success should never be at the expense of others; be decent, take personal responsibility and have empathy for others. Stand up for choice and what you believe in, and stop listening to people who tell you it can't be done. Stand up to 'obligations' that don't align with your core values. Once you do these things you will vibrate higher and become a magnet to miracles. You will be in a place where everything *feels* right: your heart is calm, your vision is clear, your soul is lit. You will be at peace with where you have been, and at peace with where you are heading.

The three life options: (1) Reject, hate, despise & be negative; (2) Let go, forget, distance yourself & be unaware of the full connectivity between all humanity; (3) Accept, love, forgive & be positive. Acceptance may not be the easiest, but it is the best.

Addiction

Addiction is a brain disorder characterised by not having control over doing, taking or using something to the point where it is harmful to you. It is most commonly associated with gambling and drugs (including alcohol and nicotine), but it's possible to be addicted to just about anything, including: work, social media, the internet, shopping, sugar, exercise, sex or pornography.[726] The trigger is often stress from emotional and/or professional pressures. The side-effects can affect your physical and mental health, work, wealth, relationships and actions, and create powerful urges to 'do it again' to recreate the 'high' and avoid withdrawal symptoms. When something develops into an addiction, it can be very difficult to stop because it's easier to carry on doing what you crave. And so, the cycle continues. Habits can take between 15 and 250 days to break (remove the automatic triggers).

The brain is a very complex system that adapts to stimuli, meaning that to get the same 'high' as the first experience, more and more of the substance is required. Addiction is treatable yet also maskable by the addict. Sometimes you can only find Heaven by slowly backing away from Hell. Recovery is not a race; you don't have to feel guilty if it takes longer than you thought it would.

It is impossible to fully understand addiction unless you have experienced it. Every addiction, regardless of what type, is the result of trying to escape from something by going in the direction of a need that is currently not being met. It is a disease that makes you too selfish to see the havoc you create, and too selfish to care about the people whose lives you shatter;[727] it destroys everything in its path, and getting out of the way is the most loving form of detachment you can practise. Addictions start out like magical pocket pets: they can do extraordinary tricks, show you things you haven't seen and are, initially, fun. However, through some gradual, dire alchemy, they start making your most crucial life decisions for you. Rock bottom can become the solid foundation upon which you rebuild your life, but unfortunately, some are not given the gift of recovery in time. You need to fight for your life while you still have one.

A shot to kill the pain. A pill to drain the shame. A purge to stop the gain. A cut to break the vein. A smoke to ease the crave. A bet to win the game. A drink to forget I'm sane. An addiction is an addition because it always hurts the same.[728] It changes you: your thoughts, actions and experiences, and ultimately your brain. The worst part about anything self-destructive is that it's so intimate; leaving behind your addiction is like killing a part of yourself that taught you how to survive. But recovery makes you wiser and stronger; you will love deeper and work harder; you will smile at the little things, at the chaos life brings; you will be able to say 'I am a survivor', and this is surely the most beautiful of achievements. Sometimes it is just about surviving and that is enough. To have survived, you are able to fight another day, and every step you take forward is one step towards victory.

What good will come of your obsessions? Well, at first you will be mesmerised, and when you follow them too long you will become their slave, and one day of their choosing they will destroy you.[729]

Livelihood

We are told that people often don't quit their jobs, they quit their bosses. The truth is that people leave their jobs if they don't find it enjoyable, they suffer workplace harassment, their strengths aren't being utilised, they feel left out or that their career isn't progressing (no hope for pay rises or promotions). The modern, rapidly evolving workplace is also being blamed as people fear for their jobs, are being ostracised by co-workers and are increasingly experiencing workplace loneliness; in the wake of the COVID-19 pandemic, many no longer wish to go back to the office and are trying to work from home.

Earning money isn't hard, what's hard is to earn it doing something worth devoting one's life to.[914] Ask yourself, how much are you identifying with a job title rather than what you intuitively know is your work to share with the world? Salary is not what you earn, salary is what you save.[730] When conducting your livelihood, make sure it is an expression of your core intention, work that you can fall in love with, so it no longer feels like 'work'. Work that matters.[730]

Life and livelihood are not all about work. The world out there is big, beautiful and wants to be explored, but it will take courage, sensible risk-taking and holding on to your dream to thrive. Find work that you love so much, with passion and energy, that you would do it even if you didn't get paid, then you will have found your ideal livelihood. This is best job in the world, the one you would do for free, for you will never hate it, time will pass quickly and you will benefit so much from what you put into it. And remember to stay alive; take time to go into the wild, reconnect with nature and 'earth' yourself.

Work

You cannot achieve anything in life unless you work hard consistently with determination.[732]

Work teaches responsibility, provides people with personal and professional meaning and gives a sense of purpose and satisfaction through utilising their skills. It also provides income, and outputs from which society can benefit.

Having a strong work ethic – a willingness to work both hard and smart (efficiently) to produce high quality products and services – can build more independence, a positive attitude, adaptability and self-confidence, whilst motivating you to grow and learn further, especially in environments where honesty, integrity, respect for others and ethics are important. Work has other benefits, too: getting us moving (we were not designed to lie around all day doing nothing), challenging us mentally (solving problems, learning new skills and interacting with people) and contributing to society (by doing something cooperatively or altruistically for the benefit of the community, which can only be done if our work/life balance is right).

Research indicates that what motivates us into high-performance mode at work is not money but the degree of autonomy we have, the level of mastery we are allowed to achieve and the sense that we are fulfilling our purpose. Convention and collective wisdom would have us believe that the occupations that contribute most to society are soldiers, teachers, physicians, scientists, engineers, clergy, artists, journalists, business executives and lawyers. Pursuing the right livelihood is one of the noble eightfold path practices and the key to finding it is if you can honestly say to yourself that you would do it voluntarily. Your personal values around the way you live and work help determine your priorities, and, deep down, they're the measures you use to tell if your life is turning out the way you want it to.[731]

You enjoy the fruits of your labour the more you put into the work; there isn't a single successful individual in the world who hasn't done enough meaningful and productive work to get success in their life. Many individuals invest a lot of energy trusting that good things will eventually occur, come up with reasons to delay making a move and are constantly diverted. A general law is that the more you're concentrated on something and make moves associated with it, the more life gives you opportunities to draw nearer to your vision.[733] After setting your goal, hard work teaches you to discover approaches, to appreciate all you have and yet dream higher, to have patience, to make a move and to quit blaming and take responsibility for the things you've done. It conquers lethargy, hesitation, procrastination, fear of disappointment, uncertainty and the propensity for self-sabotage. After all, nothing will happen if you do nothing.[733]

Humans are both wired and designed to work, and different types of work affect different people positively, negatively or neutrally. Work gives us a sense of purpose, an identity and a way of acquiring items and services (when we spend our earnings). We divide our effort between work, home and experiences, including repairing relationships.

When we work, we move our muscles and purge our bodies of damaging toxins, when we sleep our brains purge themselves of deadly toxins, and when we do good deeds we purge the world of evils and refresh our souls. It is a vital part of a healthy existence, and technology means we can now do it anywhere, any time and with anyone. Work and 'workship' are the same when you fulfil God's purpose for creation, where you prepare and develop the Earth for the benefit of humanity and the glory of God.

Remember, in whatever you do – work, rest or play – to have a clear vision, never think small, work your arse off, sell-sell-sell, never give up at the first failure, shift gears, shut your mouth and listen then open your mind, be useful, help others on the way and don't be afraid to break mirrors.[412]

Culture

The beauty of the world lies in the diversity of its people and cultures.[734] Culture is the name for what people are interested in, their thoughts, their models, the books they read and the speeches they hear.[737] It is the widening of the mind and of the spirit[738]; it is the arts elevated to a set of beliefs.[507]

A nation's culture resides in the heart and in the soul of its people.[735] It helps them understand each other better, and if they understand each other better in their souls, it is easier to overcome economic and political barriers. Every individual has to understand that their neighbour is, in the end, just like them, with the same problems, the same questions.[112]

Without culture and the relative freedom it implies, society, even when perfect, is a jungle.[734] If you change the culture of a society, the politics will follow. Even those who are not scientists or engineers – poets, actors, journalists – they, as communities, embrace the meaning of what it is to be scientifically literate and the concept of being part of an 'innovation culture'. They vote in ways that promote it. They don't fight science and they don't fight technology.

Growing a culture requires a good storyteller; changing a culture requires a persuasive editor. Every aspect of Western culture needs a new code of ethics, rationale ethics, as a precondition of rebirth, but the most vocal challengers to culture are always the first to be shown the door. It's human nature to want to eliminate disruptive influences and bring in more people who fit in well.[41] If you repeat these two behaviours, over time culture becomes homogenous, even if everyone still believes they value diversity.

If we are to preserve it, we must continue to create it. Keep your language, love its sounds, its modulation, its rhythm. Try to march with people of different languages, remote from your own, who wish, like you, for a more just and humane world.[79] The crucial differences that distinguish human societies and human beings are not biological, they are cultural,[734] and cultural differences should not separate us from each other as diversity brings a collective strength that can benefit all of humanity.[734] Our strength lies in our differences, not in our similarities. Difference is the essence of humanity, a consequence of birth, and should therefore never be the source of hatred or conflict. The answer to difference is to respect it. Therein lies the most fundamental principle of peace: respect for diversity.[736]

Every one of us is born a perfect human being though, sadly, we're negatively conditioned and programmed by our families, education, societies and cultures. We seldom realise, for example, that our most private thoughts and emotions are not actually our own; we think in terms of languages and images we did not invent, but that were given to us by our society.[489] We are all essentially murderers and prostitutes – no matter to which culture, society, class or nation we belong, no matter how normal, moral or mature we take ourselves to be. We murder for food, murder the environment for resources and murder our planet's ecosystem. We prostitute ourselves for money and exploit people; we sell different parts of ourselves. We can only change culture if we change our behaviour.

Organisational culture tells us what to do when the CEO isn't in the room, which is of course most of the time. Every CEO is in fact a Chief Cultural Officer. The terrifying thing is that it's the CEO's actual behaviour, not their speeches or the list of values they have put up on posters, that defines what the culture of a workplace is.[41] A hallmark of a healthy, creative workplace culture is that its people feel free to share ideas, opinions, and criticisms. Lack of candour, if unchecked, ultimately leads to dysfunctional environments.[739] Without these four powers – hiring, firing, promoting and punishing – any employee is along for the ride in a culture driven by someone more powerful than they are.

Culture is the deeper level of basic assumptions and beliefs that are shared by members of an organisation, that operate unconsciously and define, in a basic 'taken for granted' fashion, an organisation's view of itself and its environment.[739] Modern humans have radically changed the way that they work and the way that they live,[739] but for many, culture really only matters when there is a problem, in the same way that personality only matters when things aren't going right for you. Otherwise, it's just there.

Shaping workplace culture is more than half done when you hire your team. It does not change because we desire to change it, it changes when the organisation is transformed; the culture reflects the realities of people working together every day.[739] When you're in a small boat, you can see who's paddling hard and who's looking around.[741] Engendering a culture of trust does wonders; even if you have a heated argument, as long as you keep in the back of your mind that everyone has the best in mind for the company and wider team, you'll always be able to make it to the end and remain friendly.[742] In this regard, everyone's ability may be strengthened or increased by culture.[3]

The biggest challenge a leader may face is to restore a dying organisation back to one of growth and profitability. The first steps are not cutting costs, developing new products and/or services, inventing clever new marketing concepts, or clever advertising. Instead, it is to rebuild a culture where all employees are a family, striving for 'shared' success. The reward for doing this turns out to be winning major races again, as company culture tells people how to respond to an unprecedented service request, whether or not to risk telling their boss about a new ideas and whether to surface or hide problems – employees make hundreds of decisions on their own every day, and culture is their guide.[740] Maintaining an effective culture is so important that it, in fact, trumps even strategy.

Culture is a concept that encompasses the social behaviour, institutions and norms found in human societies, as well as the knowledge, beliefs, arts, laws, customs, capabilities and habits of the individuals in these groups.[743] There are countless cultures and subcultures in the world (some scholars believe more than 3800[744]), each rich in its own way, with diverse language, religion, literature, art, music, poetry and politics.

Every culture has an underlying political ideology (Absolute Monarchism, Absurdism, Accelerationism, Anarchism, Authoritarianism, Capitalism, Communitarianism, Communism, Conservatism, Corporatism, Democratism, Egalitarianism, Environmentalism, Fascism, Feminism, Imperialism, Liberalism, Libertarianism, Minimalism, Moderatism, Nihilism, Populism, Progressivism, Republicanism, Separatism, Socialism, Syndicalism, Transhumanism, Tribalism), which has its benefits, constraints and limitations. There is no ideal or perfect culture or ideology; having different views is great, but don't fall into the trap where you think one culture or ideology can solve all issues and problems.[745]

Although politics tends to be binary, when something important needs to get done, people come together for the common good, a unifying cause that helps the whole of humanity and the Earth, irrespective of the party they are affiliated to. For the most part, the mundane issues can be accomplished by various means and methods, so following a party position is a good way to attain critical mass and get things moving, but some things are bigger than the party, bigger than any individual country or leader, and this is when people need to come together in The Third Way. Park petty party politics and get everyone working together, united and in unison. This is how big problems are solved, by taking big, decisive actions for the wellbeing of everyone. It is not without its challenges, but mark my words, the results will be spectacular.

Lifecycles

Everything runs on lifecycles, from the solar cycles, seasons and tides, to the rotation of the Earth itself. Civilisations rise and fall, societies and cultures are often responsible for their own decline (which can be considered almost a natural phenomenon), where the old moves aside to make room for the new. Size and technological advancement are no protection against decline, for our tightly-coupled, logistically optimised, globalised economic system has become our greatest asset, yet is also our greatest single point of weakness.

We say that flowers return every spring, but that is untrue. Flowers do not return, they are replaced; the flower that wilted last year is gone. As it is for spring flowers, so it is for us. Everything turns in circles and spirals with the cosmic heart into infinity. Everything has a vibration that spirals inward or outward, and everything turns together in the same direction at the same time. This vibration is born and expands or closes and destructs, only to repeat the cycle again in opposite currents. Like a lotus, it opens or closes, dies and is born again, and such is the story of the sun and moon, of me and you. Nothing truly dies; all energy simply transforms. Birth is painful and delightful; death is painful and delightful. Everything that ends is also the beginning of something else. Pain is not a punishment; pleasure is not a reward.[746]

If you study the rhythm of life on this planet, you will find that everything moves in perfect symphony with everything else, by grand divine design.[247] The Earth can heal and regenerate itself, just as the oceans can replenish themselves by turning over debris with the waves to wash it ashore. This perfect orchestration is one of the creator's greatest and most beautiful miracles.

It may be said, in broad-brush terms, that the primary purpose of life is the continuation of life; a deep programming for survival and reproduction underwrites the complex cycles of life, in which death is the grand equaliser. Humans like to consider everything as linear when, in reality, everything is cyclical. We see evolution as a race along a straight racetrack, a race we think we are winning by a long margin, but are afraid to ever slow down in case life catches us. The reason the world is a mystical, enchanting place is because of the cycle of life; our bodies will decompose, but some little element may be transformed into a particle of dirt, over years and years, and then a glorious flower may be nurtured by it. This flower may then nourish a random bumblebee, who in turn will be eaten by a raven. So, in some future life, we'll be able to fly. I look forward to that; I've always admired the freedom of birds.[746] The earth will continue to exist with or without us.[247]

It is the purpose of the mind to seek. When it does not discover what it seeks, it gives birth to hopelessness and, given our undying spirit, from that hopelessness rises hope itself, taking us to the quest all over again, churning us in an endless cycle of suffering.[746] This cycle is called life; suffer you will, one way or the other. Once you understand the cycles of life, and when you realise the part you need to play, you will gain power from this knowledge of balance and how to make everything right.

I love lifecycles. From the weather, the seasons, the tides and the moon, to the physical cycles of humans, animals and plants linked to ageing, reproduction and biorhythmic processes, to cultural and civilisation cycles widely recorded in history. I must not forget the unseen cycles, too, that we have determined with the power of our minds: the astronomical cycles (orbit, wobble and tilt), geological cycles and cycles of the birth, death and oscillation of stars. We experience many different, self-inflicted economic cycles, in the form of market crashes, real estate/property booms and plateaus, and changes in elected governments. Finally, we can include the astrological cycles, the Hindu Yugas and the Mayan Baktun, that have many different significances. We are ruled by cycles within cycles, wheels within wheels, clocks within clocks. 'All human things are a circle' is an inscription at the temple at Athens, which rings as true today as it did when it was written.

We tend to distrust what we can't physically verify, measure or analyse. We don't know much about the spiritual cycles, reincarnation or the thought that the sudden, traumatic death of a young soul can speed the decision for it to come back in physical form earlier than other souls. There are thoughts that those souls that share a deep love and connection make mutual, sacred agreements (with guides and teachers in the spirit realm helping, guiding and counselling them with encouragement, wisdom and support). Deep consideration is undertaken on what is best for the soul and the form – timing and location of their physical arrival, the lessons they wish to learn and purpose they wish to experience – when they return to Earth, as well as with the impact they will have on souls that are already here. A soul returning to Earth does not repeat a previous life (just like the current season is not an exact replica of the last), and between leaving and returning, just like seasons, there must be a natural break, a period of healing and of grief, a period of rebirth of the new after the death of the old. Cycles occur in predetermined phases that can't be rushed; we must trust the process and allow it to happen in its own good time. If in doubt, people often call the eyes the windows to the soul, though we seem to have lost a lot of our natural intuition and ability to recognise Old Souls or souls we have made sacred agreements with. Many people believe that birth, death and rebirth to the earth are among the most sacred spiritual transitions any soul can make, which will forever be covered with mystery, uncertainty and lack of control.[747]

SECTION 2 - THE BODY

The adult human body is a remarkably complex machine made up of 60% water. By comparison, 71% of the planet's surface is covered by water. Humans each contain the same 3 billon DNA base pairs, packaged into 46 chromosomes in the nucleus, that make up our entire genetic material. The heart is the only muscle that never tires, and by the time you reach 70 years old it has beat around 2.5 billon times. Spread across your lifetime, you will spend, on average, 25 years asleep, a whole year going to the toilet, 13 years at your workplace over a 50-year working period, and spend many of your formative years in education. The body itself regenerates during every 7 to 10 years, replacing every single cell.

As humans, we generally survive by learning, and our educational systems teach us many things – some things are immediately useful, other things are useful later on and the remaining things are never used again. We forget things we learn very easily, and often need reminders even for simple things. Whilst our ancestors existed about 6 million years ago, modern humans only appeared in Africa around 300,000 years ago. We have no idea how much knowledge of ourselves and our world we have lost over the whole of human history, but it is probably significant, especially with regards to human health and disease. We have always been at war with ourselves and nature via our developing immune systems, with diseases, viruses or plants in our immediate environment. So, although we may inhabit a thoroughly modern world, we do so with the ingrained mentality of Stone Age hunter-gatherers and with the bodies and brains of Homo sapiens that emerged on the savannah so long ago.

The brain is a physical object that can be seen, touched and photographed, and is more active while we sleep than when we are awake. While connected, the body and the mind are not the same; when the body is relaxed, the mind can go into overdrive; the body can be busy while the mind goes into autopilot. The three parts of the brain are the cerebrum (which controls movement, thinking, emotions, problem-solving, learning, language, memory, personality, understanding, vision, hearing and sensory capacity, and interprets and processes information), the brainstem (which controls hearing, movement and basic bodily functions like heart rhythm, blood flow and breathing) and the cerebellum (which controls balance, movement and coordination of the muscles), making it by far the most complex part of the human body. The brain is composed of about 60% fat (with water, proteins, carbohydrates and salt composing the remaining 40%) and is home to 86 billion nerve cells. The 'second' or 'little' brain, officially called the enteric nervous system, has recently been discovered to be made up of 200–600 million neurons woven into the walls of the digestive system, linking digestion and moods. The brain has its characteristic folded shape (cortical convolutions) that has allowed its increase in size and complexity compared to other creatures. But it is not just the size of the overall brain that leads to superior intelligence, but the growth of particular parts, and the fact that humans have hands (enabling the development of tools) rather than flippers (whales do have far larger brains than humans). But it isn't what you have, it's what you do with it that counts.

So much has been written and passed down about humans over the years, about our emotions and psychology, a significant amount of which is still valid, still relevant and should not be forgotten. Mankind has a long legacy that we need to be reminded of from time to time, for our benefit – so we don't neglect or forget it and risk re-learning it painfully through deadly recurrence. It seems strange that the more things change (including ourselves), the more they stay the same, and that the future will flow from our current actions and trends. Although history may not exactly repeat itself, it often rhymes, just with different words and melodies; we ignore this at our own cost. We haven't yet evolved into the next-generation species, so we can't ignore what we are or where we have come from.

We are privileged to come into this world empty handed, pure and innocent; we will leave this world empty handed, with only the memories of experiences we have had whilst we have been here, none of the material possessions. These days, we do not possess things so much as things have started to possess us; this is toxic. Life is full of battles; fight for what you believe, fight to the last and stand your ground when you know you are right. The paths to self-destruction are many, and you must be vigilant for them. Aim to do your work to the best of your ability, without thinking about its results, for if we don't achieve the required yield from a task we become disheartened and disappointed. Lust and bodily desires will come into your mind and go. Anger is one of the fundamental causes of failure in people's lives; it makes reasoning fly out the window, and in that state you are doomed. Greed and selfishness obscure the truth of every situation, acting like a dirty mirror and giving a lopsided view, resulting in doubt and disappointment. And doubt achieves nothing, for it cannot create peace in this world or the next.

We are privileged to exist in a physical form, to experience the physical universe, but we must remember that we are more than just physical; we are eternal souls. God dwells within each of us, passing between the thin veil of Heaven and Earth.

CHAPTER 8

Emotions that often drive us.

"Energy in motion – when we understand our emotions and states of mind, we can start to take back control."

—Thibaut Meurisse[515] (Modified)

We may *occasionally* be the masters of our own thoughts, but we are often the slaves of our emotions. It is both a blessing and a curse to feel everything so deeply,[240] but we must control our emotions, or they will control us. Do not fall for those who perpetuate the following: negative conflict, self-promotion, secrets, lies, paranoia, conspiracy theories and thuggery. Nor for those who have a vein of meanness, who try and manipulate your emotions. For when the tide of lies goes out, it is easy to see those who have been swimming naked.

Those who can master their emotions have the ability to live in peace; those who can control themselves become free. Contrary to popular belief, the goal is not to repress or eliminate emotions, but to focus them and make ourselves stronger by knowing when to use them. Understand that emotions are not real except in our own minds, and if we decide to change our minds, we can change our emotions, we just need a process for doing this effectively.[369]

Fear

Fear is an illusion. It is a basic survival mechanism meant to keep us safe from potential danger (freeze, fight or flight modes). But then there's the fear of being rejected or failing, or of failing and being rejected for it. Children are afraid of the dark (the unknown or the unseen), whilst adults are afraid of the light (to shine or be seen), afraid to take a risk and be who they could be. We feel fear towards things that we needn't, like failure, uncertainty, emotional vulnerability and the loss of control.

Nothing holds us back like fear. Fear keeps us from taking risks, challenging ourselves and going after what we want. If you want to conquer fear, don't sit home and think about it, go out and get busy.[81] Stop worrying so much; you'll create a problem that wasn't even there in the first place. Don't be afraid of facing your fears; success has a funny way of covering your back. Remember, what doesn't kill you will only make you stronger.[334]

When fear has got the best of you, you panic and turn to false gods (someone or something that is highly revered, followed devoutly, sacrificed for and looked to for meaning).[160] Today, our false gods are entertainment, pleasure, fame, money, power, things and instant gratification. There are many influencers fighting for our attention, and the attention of our children, who have no righteousness (they seek both obedience and to tempt you to buy things you don't need), who will promise you order and peace but deliver emptiness in your soul. They demand, in return for their false promises, your silent consent for further acts that remove your freedoms and liberties, replacing them with cruelty, injustice, intolerance, division and oppression. You must never let fear rule, even when these false gods have created a myriad of problems and conspired to corrupt your reason and rob you of your common sense. Take refuge in hope because it constantly reminds the world that fairness, justice and freedom are more than words: they are perspectives.

The only time when fear is a good thing is when it increases our need, energy and actions to overcome it. Shine a light on fear by voicing your concerns, then build your courage and determination to ensure that it does not prevail or hide in the shadows until a later time. It is always worth taking some time to self-reflect; you may not like what you see, but don't forget that you have the power to change, overcome and conquer. Fear is your friend (it keeps you safe), but doing one thing that scares you each day (not putting your life at risk, of course) is actually great advice.[511]

Fear can be an indicator. Sometimes it shows you what you shouldn't do; more often than not, it expands you.[144] A little fear really wants the best for us and transforms us into better, healthier, more engaged people.[392]

The most beautiful experience we can have is 'the mysterious'. It is the fundamental emotion that stands at the cradle of true art and true science,[133] as the most human trait is to want to know why; while we can't find all the answers, we keep on asking. Some questions will make you cry, but mankind needs to stay together throughout. Why do we continue asking the same questions and how do we still have the strength to keep asking? Why are we not defeated? It is because we believe in our collective power; we kept going for those who showed us the way and showed us our purpose.

Fear is a lot more present in our lives than we may think. For example, the COVID pandemic taught us not to underestimate nature or take things for granted. Overcoming fear means discovering what winning means for you and for those around you, then taking a fresh look at the world, with respect, clarity and optimism. Even after succeeding, there can be fear of failure, not performing or falling backwards (known as imposter syndrome, an off-shoot of fear more akin to self-doubt of one's intellect, skills or accomplishments; fake people never suffer from it), which can spoil the whole period when you are at the top of your game. There are two ways to address fear: either using the combatant mode (fighting, struggling, endurance, dominance, winning at all costs) or the acceptance mode (kindness, fun, doing your best, trusting, believing in yourself, collective unity, ambition). In order to find freedom from fear, we spend a lot of our lives trying to improve and leave our old selves behind.

Think about how you would like the world to be. What would you do if you weren't afraid and fully embraced life? What contribution would you make? Look inside yourself to find out what you really want and what you are passionate about. If there is no joy when you wake up, stop doing whatever you are doing and try something else. How much of human life is lost waiting for knowledge, or fearing something that may or may not arrive, rather than looking for it?[136] Struggles are made to shape us for our purpose; the world showed us the worst, but we still found ways to triumph. And we are still searching.

I was scuba diving off the Great Barrier Reef during an open-water training exercise. My instructor told me drop my respirator to practice buddy breathing, which I did. The respirator fell down by my legs for the duration of the practice. The exercise apparently over, my buddy and the other divers followed the instructor to the surface, and I was left ten metres below with no air. Fear could have taken me over and made me swim to the surface, but there was the danger I may not make it or that my lungs might not handle the pressure change from ascending too quickly. My buddy should have waited for me to have my respirator back in my hand, but he hadn't – he had just swum off. Something in the back of my mind told me not to panic – this is very important in critical situations so you can stay objective and focused. Don't panic or give up, just remain calm. As calmly as I could, I followed my training and my respirator fell into my hand. After clearing it with the small amount of retained air in my lungs, those following breaths became the sweetest gulps of oxygen I've ever tasted.

Fear can be a mind killer[209], a body killer and a soul killer as well. A sense of serenity, which wrapped itself around me with what seemed like enhanced awareness, almost slowed down time in those moments. A similar experience occurred when I saved the life of a colleague after putting out a fire in a shared kitchen flat. Never let fear decide your fate; you are capable of so much more than fear.

When we think of love and fear, we often think of their duality. Love is expansive and conquers all, especially when you understand and practise selfless love (which often means planting seeds knowing you will not benefit from the shade of the trees). Fear, on the other hand, is restrictive, binding and holds people back from what they are capable of. The Third Way is another way of thinking about this duality beyond the individual person, and understanding the effects we have on others, that are very much underestimated. We are all connected, more than we could ever imagine, and our thoughts, words and actions reverberate through time (forward and backwards). Beware not to judge others, for we have not walked in their shoes; treat others like you seek to be treated yourself; be yourself, but don't do things that intentionally (or could unintentionally) hurt others. We are one entity where everyone is a god, made by God, delivered to Earth by God and will eventually return to God. Stop and pause, then think, is there a better way? Often there is, we just don't take time to let the Universe tells us what we should do.

There may come a time when you will face real fear, for there are entities, both physical and spiritual, that don't have our best interests at heart, who want to hurt or harm us. Remember that you have a God-seed within you, that you are all-powerful but aren't always aware of it. You are down here in physical form to perform a role God wants done, that you accepted you would do, in order to complete God's purpose (God's will and expectation of people). Come closer to God (through having fear of God, faith in and obedience to God, and selfless love to bring glory to God) and improve yourself (spiritually and by helping others). If some entity does try to harvest your soul or if you are in the presence of a demon, say, 'I rebuke you in the name of Jesus Christ.' It will save your soul.

Loving

Feeling or showing love (great care) to yourself and others is so important. When with another person, love allows us to share a bond not even death can violate.

Don't confuse love with craving, desire, lust or need. Loving transcends all these because it is given freely and expects nothing in return. Love is not easily angered, nor does it keep a record of wrongs; it does not delight in evil but rejoices with the truth; it always trusts, hopes and preserves; it is patient and kind; it does not envy, boast, nor dishonour anyone. It's not proud nor self-seeking.

Love is like a muscle; it needs to grow, so it needs feeding and exercise. It can tire quickly if overused and sometimes needs rest. Like a tank of fuel, love is finite if constantly drained without reciprocity – eventually there is nothing left.

We don't get to choose who we love and who loves us back; the right person for you to love isn't necessarily the one you think is right. We often nurture this imaginary person in our minds, and this can lead to rejecting partners who might be ideal for us.[749] The ideal person is someone who makes you happy and loves you in ways you might not notice; they are often right under your nose. Find that someone who treats you with all the love you deserve. Love, like everything else in life, should be a discovery, an adventure, and like most adventures, you don't know you're having one until you're right in the middle of it.[63]

We all want and need love and acceptance, but people often operate not out of love, but out of fear. You have the power to change anything, so change it to love. Have the courage to follow your heart and intuition, and you will never go wrong. [234 & 750] Fun is important too! If I have learned nothing else on this journey, I have learned to have fun and let loose; being playful opens you up to receiving an abundance of inspiration, opportunities and energy to accomplish your heart's desires. So, don't waste your days sitting in an office trying to make something happen, give yourself ample time to laugh, play and be curious about life.

You need to take care of the things you love, otherwise they may go away and find new love. Never ignore a person who loves you or cares for you; you never know the value of a moment until it becomes a memory. Some things are not meant to be loved forever; you will hear a song and it will remind you of romantic relationships that came to an end, but instead of feeling melancholy, rejoice that you shared a time full of good moments, feelings and passion, and that you are one of the lucky ones who has experienced love and loving. The ones we love will never leave us because they will always be there in our hearts. Don't fear the responsibility that comes with caring for other people, for caring makes your heart grow stronger.

Love isn't perfect. It is a short word, easy to spell, difficult to define and impossible to live without. It isn't a fairy tale or rom-com, nor does it always come easy. It sometimes means overcoming obstacles, facing challenges, fighting to be together, holding on and never letting go. Love is work, but most of all, love is realising that every hour, minute and second was worth it because you did it together.[751]

I consider myself a lightworker and polymath who normally works with data, evidence and analysis. However, the more I travel in this world, the more I am convinced that there are other unseen forces at work and that we are meant to connect to certain people/souls whilst we are in this Earthly Domain. These connections take many forms, from just meeting and talking, sharing knowledge with people we have never met, to becoming friends or developing temporary relationships, to loving and ultimately creating vessels for other souls to enter through. It is as if an agreement is made before we leave the soul world and we are following a prescribed path. The way I met my wife was through a series of seemingly unconnected and wildly coincidental events that played out over a number of years. When I first saw her, I knew in my heart that she was someone special and we were meant to get to know each other. This quickly turned into love. I'm over the moon that we made that agreement to meet up and share our lives in this world. It hasn't been an easy ride. Lots of hardships, challenges and upsets have been thrown our way, but life is more bearable when you are in a loving relationship, when you love and are loved back in equal measure.

There are four types of love: that which is widely linked to romantic love (Eros), which is intense, passionate, lustful; friendly or affectionate love (Philia), the kind of 'first and often temporary love' type like the first step on the ladder, which is very self-centric and self-serving; then there is the love associated with intimacy, which is deep and empathic love (Storge), shared in a mutually bonding way; and finally, there is unconditional love (Agape) that requires nothing, asks for nothing and means sacrificing yourself to save others, which is the ultimate test of Agape love. Real love is not a destination: although it can be found, it can also be lost, even after reaching it. It must be fed, watered and looked after to thrive, just like all other living things, otherwise it withers, decays and ultimately dies. Understanding the different types of love is a great start that will serve you well in your life.

Loving can be finite. I knew two people who travelled from London to South Africa by VW Transporter Van. I remember the guy buying cheap Chinese tools for the trip that broke on their first use; the care and attention you put into things is often reflected back to you. More importantly, they both went through so many intense experiences, including life and death ones, that they broke up when they arrived at their destination. Some experiences can be so intense that they are life-changing. You are not the same person you were before those experiences. You can burn each other out with intensity, and there is then nothing left to go forward with in the relationship.

Happiness

Happiness is a fleeting feeling and is only real when shared. It is simply an emotional response to an outcome, and is often fuelled by aspirations and the ego. Money doesn't inherently bring happiness, but joy does. Joy is a choice not a response to a result; it is a constant approach. In *en-joying* what we are doing, we are *in-joy* and not fretting about the outcome.

You can't achieve permanent happiness; it is just not possible. It can't be obtained or sustained because it is reliant on goal posts that move higher every time it is achieved. Chasing happiness will make you unhappy because you will frequently be let down. Satisfaction is achieved by being present in the moment, seeking the invisible, feeling the intangible, achieving the impossible and helping others – focusing on things greater than yourself. To find lasting happiness, you need to make sure your relationships get the attention and work they deserve; relationships have a huge impact on your overall wellbeing, far greater than your career or income.[241] You may want people to be constantly happy, whatever that means, but this is unachievable all the time. Giving in to people and lavishing them with everything they want is not the answer. Since when does anyone know what they truly want?

You need to take a long-term view on happiness and understand that it is always transient. Do something you're good at, as that is a route to joy; when you know that you're doing a thing well, you get into a rhythm that is really therapeutic. You can either work at a high-paying job, hating Monday and waiting for Friday, or you can work on your passion, something you enjoy that makes you feel complete and content.[752] The choice is yours. It may be tough to choose between happiness and comfort, but remember, the most important thing in life is happiness and it has to be everyone's priority. After all, it's not money but memories and experiences that define true wealth.

You should know that all happiness is inside of you. Never apologise for it. Happiness is love, especially when a mature personality does not push that love away. To be really happy you will need to be honest with yourself. You must like yourself, but that doesn't mean thinking you're fabulous and faultless; break down the blocks of the ego. Maybe you've gained all that money and fame, and fulfilled all your desires, but what if you are not happy inside despite it all?[619] Inner happiness occurs when you do something good, when you create beautiful memories to rewind, as this is something that makes you feel complete.[752] In the end, the material things in life will fade away. Happiness has to come from within; you need to search for it and cherish it when it does appear.

The kingdom of the divine is within everyone, not one person, nor a single group of people, but in all people. In you and everyone! You, the people, have the power, the power to create machines, the power to create happiness. You, the people, have the power to make this life free and beautiful, to make it a wonderful adventure. So, in the name of democracy, let us use that power. Let us all unite, fight for a new world, a decent world that will give men a chance to work, that will give youth a future, whilst giving security and dignity to those of an older age.[84]

There are three types of happiness: (1) That which allows for a 'pleasant life' filled with positive emotion. It can be considered linked to early happiness states – through material objects, ego gratification, money, addiction and that which provides temporary dopamine signals. (2) Then there is happiness that allows one to lead a 'good life' in which engagement in work makes times stand still as you cultivate a passion. It can be considered as linked to a transition to a higher state, to doing good for others and making the world a better place – elimination of resentment, not living in the past, being virtuous and staying engaged with the real world. (3) And finally, there is a deeper happiness where one leads a 'meaningful life', using their strength, wealth, energies and time in the service of a larger purpose or cause bigger than themselves. It can be considered linked to authentic happiness, accepting that this is a journey and not a destination.

There are times to be a leaf on a tree, times to break the mirror, times to not resist change and cooperate with life, times to audit happiness where you love yourself and others, times to live in the moment, times to lower your expectations of yourself and times for sacrifice. Life naturally occurs in cycles (we can't live forever at the top of the mountain of joy, excitement, optimism, contentment and love), so don't waste energy swimming against the flow of life; use your energies and actions (forgiveness, patience, forbearance, honesty, rectitude, straightforwardness, knowledge) to serve something bigger than yourself, and do it to make the future a better place for those who come after us.

Sadness

Sadness is an emotion we feel whenever we experience loss; it helps us process our grief and disappointment. Feeling sad allows us to take a step back and look at ourselves and our situation to better understand what is causing us so much pain. It teaches us to be more introspective, resilient and to learn from our mistakes.

Other people's goodwill account is not held by you. It is a separate bank funded by their sympathy and their will to assist, and they dole it out as they see fit. Your job is to keep your own goodwill account in the black.

Don't push down or suppress emotions too much, because they have a nasty habit of finding another outlet which could be far more dangerous or harmful. The next time you're tempted to feel sorry for yourself, find a distraction, because if you can change your thoughts, you'll change your mood. Life is hard and full of sorrows, so it is very important to celebrate the small joys; look around and appreciate what you have, give praise and show gratitude. It may sound crazy, but a better life comes to those who endure pain.

No one ever told me that grief felt so much like fear.[275] It is sad that we learn too late, that we regret, fear, grieve and die all too quickly. It is really sad that some people die at 25 and aren't buried until 75.[170] Don't be one of them. Don't be afraid to see what you see.[377] Even death is not to be feared by one who has lived wisely.[179] One of the greatest discoveries a man makes, one of his great surprises, is to find he can do what he was afraid he couldn't do.[167]

We often forget what it means to be human. Humans are full of emotions, desires, needs and fears, with bodies that are susceptible to disease and injury and that need food, shelter and human connection to thrive. We spend our lives chasing and satisfying these never-ending needs, like constantly pushing water uphill. We have made life hard for ourselves by creating such a complicated society: non-natural capitalism characterised by greed and inequality; technology that promised to raise our living standards and reduce pressure at work, but just increased expected output and bombarded us with advertising; social media poisoning us with unrealistic standards and facilitating humanity's dark side; and turning our backs on nature and natural things (thinking we know best) to chase the unobtainable. It is no wonder people are so sad.

In your twenties, you learn to support yourself. In your thirties, you focus on career, kids and stumbling through life.[274] In your forties, you start making roots and settling down. In your fifties, you begin to get comfortable but realise you are not as fit as you used to be. In your sixties, your health begins to deteriorate. In your seventies, you realise how short life is, what you haven't achieved and what you regret. The meaning of life is to just be alive, and part of that is to experience hardship. It is so plain and so obvious and so simple. Yet, everybody rushes around in a great panic as if it were necessary to achieve something beyond themselves.[293] We just need to be mindful and go with the flow.

Hate

Unfortunately, there are some people who do not want you to succeed or to voice your opinion.

These toxic, nasty and hateful people project their inner misery onto the outside world; those who criticise and spread negative energy do this from the overflow of negativity within themselves.[753] Calling someone 'fat' will not make you any thinner[754]; calling someone 'stupid' doesn't make you any smarter; ruining other people's lives won't make you any happier. We rise by lifting others up; dulling someone else's sparkle will never brighten our own.[445]

If people can't accept you for who you really are, that is their problem, not yours.[755] These people will not change; don't waste your time even thinking about them.[756] Don't let people slap labels on you, just be whatever makes you happy; labels don't capture who you are, what you are capable of or where you can go.

Don't hate, even when it's hard to forgive. Unscrupulous people use hate, authoritarianism, corruption, egocentrism, nativism and division to get what they want at your expense. They will take away your democracy and freedoms not in the darkness, but in plain sight. If people are propagating violence, hatred, bigotry, hostility or bias we must unite and stop them. You'll never be let into Heaven if you haven't forgiven people; you just can't take that kind of burden through the gates.

When radicalism, propaganda and lies are more accepted than free speech, debate and truth, something is very wrong with society. When there is civil unrest raging through towns and cities, and children are using guns to kill people, how can you be called a fascist for asking the authorities to restore order? Standing up for what is right is not hate, it is what is expected in every single decent society that values ethical behaviour, honesty and trust. We should never allow haters to project their twisted, cruel and poisonous values onto others to the point that they are afraid to speak. We must stand up to haters and not be pulled down to their level.

There are people who do not believe in freedom of speech when talking about certain topics. The prohibition of speech is not beneficial in a functioning democracy because to solve any issue you need to listen to the people. On real-world issues that could affect anyone, the more people speak about them, the more they are able to come up with practical and effective strategies to try and fix them. And the more ears listening the better; if more people had open minds to learning and understanding more topics, the easier it would be to solve issues.[304]

History is full of examples of people seizing power by capitalising on chaos and using political acuity, deception, cunning and restricting free speech, and it always ends badly for a lot of humanity.[757] When you think that you are wise and powerful enough to control the monsters, you invariably over-estimate your abilities and under-estimate the power of hate.[758] Do not be inhuman, lacking in sympathy, warmth, pity or compassion. Do not become cold, callous, hard, cruel, brutal, savage or violent. You are more than the inhuman that lies within every one of us. Do not let hate rule you.

Your words are more important that your thoughts, so start inspiring people. More than machinery and cleverness, we need humanity, kindness and gentleness. Without these, life will be violent and all will be lost.[84] Experiencing satisfaction and joy in who you are and in your accomplishments isn't a bad thing, except when your view of yourself outweighs the regard you have for others. The cure for pride is humility. Simple but not easy. It is all about self-respect at the end of the day, because if you don't respect or look after yourself, how can you expect others to do it for you?

Life is too short to hate. There is so much more to do, so much beauty to see and so much love that needs to be shared. I see people being absorbed and consumed by hate that they then carry through life, like a heavy load they are unable to put down. It will wear you down; it always does.

Let me say it again because it is so important. Life is too short to hate. Don't feed negative emotions your energy, time or life force; they don't deserve it. Hate consumes all it touches. There has never been a successful world leader, political party or organisation founded on hate that has lasted – never. Hate may provide some temporary empowerment, but it always turns in on itself, pulverising those who carry it with guilt, remorse and addiction in attempts to keep the pain away. As with a lot of negative things, there are three ways to deal with hate: ignoring it, burying it or clearing it. The Third Way, clearing it, is best, before it becomes burdensome to your life, the people around you and all of humanity.

Jealousy

Jealousy is our emotional response when we want what someone else has. It is connected to deep-seated insecurities and fears that people may not even realise they have, associated with oversimplification, inadequacy, abandonment and fear of being replaced or judged. It can give way to insecurity and hurt our self-esteem, making us think we aren't good enough to have everything we want.[759] It's important to pay close attention to who we feel jealous of and why,[760] because it speaks volumes about what is missing from our own lives. It's your life, live it authentically, work with and make the best of what you have. Distance yourself from distractions, energy leeches and negative people. What other people think of you isn't a 'you' problem.[750]

Lots of people are jealous of others who they perceive are happier than them. This is generally founded in the false belief that money is what makes people happy because the lack of money is one of the limiting factors in our lives. Money itself will not make you happy; it only extends the limit of things you can do, which, if you choose correctly, can make you temporarily happy, but cannot bring you full happiness. Jealously is a way of shifting the problem from yourself to another person.

Your life will change when you understand that the key to solving issues like loneliness, health and relationship problems is to stop expecting people to come to you, and to make an effort to go to them. In this social-media-focused, isolated world, lots of people are craving attention. If you give it to them, they will be your best friends thereafter. Always strive to make and keep your body healthy, have meaningful relationships and make a meaningful contribution towards anything you love in terms of your work, rest and play. Finally, try to have enough money today and for tomorrow, and a bit spare for the unexpected (inflation, unpleasant and nice surprises) to move away from the poverty line and be able to help others. Having a clear mindset about how decent your lifestyle should be (doesn't mean extravagant) will make it easier to determine how much of everything you really need.

Jealously is seeking the unnecessary and unobtainable, and comparing yourself to others, both of which you don't need to do. Jealously will disappear overnight when you remember this and become a lifelong learner. When you are curious, self-confident and aware, your overall satisfaction will grow and you will have no more room for the fake and false concept of jealousy. Ordinary men hate solitude for they are left alone with their own self and thoughts, but a real master makes use of it and embraces his aloneness, realising he is one with the whole Universe.[89]

Anger

If your anger defines you, then you have a problem. At the end of the day, anger is a loss of control; it impedes good judgement and decision-making and does not generally lead to good places. Peace it out with perspective.

Anger often makes things worse, but there are times when it is needed, such as to warn others not to cross boundaries or when great injustices have been dealt. When anger leads to violence this is not good, unless you are fighting for survival.

People are mostly wrapped, like bulbs, with layers of violence and tenderness. It is difficult to say what makes them onions or hyacinths. We have a tendency to pay more attention to the bad, shocking or ugly than to look at the good things happening around us. Anger is a manifestation of having lost control, but it can actually be useful if we take the time to understand it more. When properly focused, anger can propel us to act and fight against the problem we're facing. Don't get mad, get motivated; it is okay to have emotions, just don't let them run rampant[761]; be more forgiving of yourself, don't beat yourself up too much when handling stressful and major life changes. If people are angry with you, it is their problem, not yours. Anger is a potent spice. A pinch will wake you up, while too much dulls your senses. Calmness is a power.[762]

I remember, as a child, being angry at being blamed for something I didn't do. Enraged and sent to my bedroom, my emotions went into overdrive at the injustice being served. After what seemed an eternity, I was called down for dinner. Upon my return to my room, my bookshelves, which had been up for years, had partially collapsed. Again, I was blamed for that destruction. Looking back, I now realise that I had inadvertently called and left something, an entity or energy, in my room when I'd gone down for dinner; some negative force beyond normal science had caused the damage that day. People have reported that when severe anger takes over, it is as if another element is in the vicinity with them at the time. I can totally understand and accept this. Be mindful of your actions; there is more to this world than science and religion. Evil or mischievous spirit entities do exist.

Negativity

Don't fall into the negativity trap; it is the easy path. Negativity consumes you, leaving very little left.

Harness the power of negative thoughts and channel them into action. Channel your rage into a motivational, constructive tool, not a self-destructive one. Take comfort and confidence in knowing that you are both flawed and vulnerable, but more courageous and driven than you think. To survive and thrive you need to acknowledge what is happening around you, accept what you can and can't control, then address the parts you can change.

Everything that demands your attention takes your energy and can become all consuming. In our world of electronics, email and social media, alerts have become more pervasive and intrusive than ever. Not everything that comes across our plate needs to be eaten. Stop giving your attention and energy to the wrong things for the wrong reasons. As you get older, you realise the things you originally thought were important, may not be so, and the things you took for granted are the really important things. When you start getting your life under control, you naturally start living more in the present, becoming a more able and complete person – a kinder and happier you – which reflects on the people around you.

You have three core resources: time, energy and money. You need to ask yourself on a day-to-day basis where you are at with each to ensure that you are not selling your soul. Always ask yourself if something is going to make you stronger or weaker. If you are being oppressed in your soul by what you are being asked to swallow at work, you are an agent of you own destruction. A single task is quicker to complete than trying to multi-task. Just getting by is not being true to yourself and not getting the joy you deserve.

I try not to surround myself or my family with negative people. I call them 'energy vampires' because they are attracted to positive people. Keep your eye open for them because they can be anywhere and everywhere. It is hard to accept, but there are horrible parents out there. Parents are just people and are flawed individuals; love for your parents is not unconditional. If they are toxic they must be cut off from you, for they will not change. Life is too short to hold grudges or seek approval from these people who wish you had never been born. It may be the hardest choice you ever make, but you must put yourself first; you deserve unconditional love, compliments and mental health protection. Note: this advice is not the same as for struggling parents who are facing their own demons, have made mistakes, lack spirituality and trust or are damaged themselves, but are endeavouring to do the right thing. These people deserve a second chance. Toxic people do not deserve you; be with people who value you, care for you and share some of their positivity to make you a more positive person.

Remember, no civilisation, society or political party that has been built on negativity (hate, anger, bullying, destruction, death) has ever survived very long, because negativity is all-consuming and eventually feeds on those who practise it.

Positivity

Think positive, then be positive. What you think you become. What you feel you attract. What you imagine you create. You don't find the happy life; you make it. Life changes very quickly in a very positive way, if you let it.[476]

Be the energy you want to attract; believe you can and you're halfway there. Your life is only as good as your mindset.[763] Your mind is a powerful instrument, and when you fill it with positive thoughts, your life will start to change; if you are positive, you'll see opportunities instead of obstacles. [165] Look for something positive in each day, even if some days you have to look a little harder.[765] Grow through what you go through. You may have been criticising yourself for years and it hasn't been very constructive, so try being approving of yourself and see what happens. There is hope even when your brain tells you there isn't. Folks are as happy as they make up their minds to be.[278]

Be good to people for no reason. Life is a gift, and it offers us the privilege, opportunity and responsibility to give something back by becoming more.[384] If you see someone without a smile, give them one of yours[346] – they are free and meant to be given away.

The best job in the world is not the job you apply for but the one you create for yourself. If you don't like the road you're walking, or if there is no pathway to where you want to go, start paving another one. Believing negative thoughts is the single greatest obstruction to success. Your life isn't yours if you're always worrying what someone else thinks. The only two things you are in total control of are your attitude and your effort.[764] In order to carry out positive action, we must develop a positive vision.

The best is yet to be. The sun is a daily reminder that we too can rise again from the darkness, that we can shine our own light.[8] An arrow can only be shot by first being pulled backwards; when life is dragging you back with difficulties, it means that it's about to launch you into something great.[97]

Positivity is the key to happiness, so always turns a negative situation into a positive one. It is in knowing you have the power to choose what to accept and what to let go of.[767] When you arise in the morning, think of what a privilege it is to be alive: to breathe, to think, to enjoy, to love.[766] Whatever is worrying you, forget about it, take a deep breath, stay positive and know that things will get better.[768] Without rain, nothing grows, so learn to embrace the storms in your life. Keep your face to the sunshine and you cannot see a shadow.[266]

The rule of three applies to positivity, you can either have not enough, just enough or far too much. Too much positivity leads to an unfulfilled existence due to disappointment, despair and unhappiness. Strive for progress not perfection and don't be ashamed of slow progress; baby steps still move you forward. Work hard and don't give up. Be open to feedback and keep learning. Surround yourself with happy, warm and genuine people. When you love what you have, you have everything you need.[492] There is a light inside each of us that illuminates us when we let it shine.[463]

Positive thinking, backed up with positive action, can be a powerful enabler. I was determined to win two writing events because I felt it needed to happen. (I have never been a competitive person, but I have a connection to certain things that are meant to happen.) The first required extensive research and then replaying of the key messages in the context of my own skills and experiences, which resulted in a successful outcome. The second also required extensive research, but because of the lack of evidence, it also required a lot more of my skills, and the experience of some colleagues, to generate solutions to a specific problem area, which resulted in me becoming an award-winning author. The second submission was for another competition, but it was rejected because it was too professional and was said to have been plagiarised from another book, yet the reviewers couldn't provide that elusive source – because it was my own work.

Positivity can only get you so far. Beware of toxic positivity or suppressing your emotions too much; you need to deal with things holistically, pragmatically and with a good deal of realism. The strategies of taking a hope-focused approach, throwing more hands at a failing task or liberally sprinkling design dust to act as the silver bullet should be used sparingly, because no one can be sure of the longevity of such techniques. I've always tried to stay positive, share positivity and be a beacon of positivity, but it has been hard, for life is not an easy journey. We will fall down, but we need to pick ourselves up, not just for our own sake, but for others who depend on us.

Before you can understand anything, you need to understand yourself, your motivations, driving force, energy, limitations and daemons in your mind, body and soul. Only then will you have the power to go to the next level.

In life, you have three options. You can be 'pregnant', 'not pregnant' or 'not able to be pregnant' – nothing else. You can't be half pregnant. This applies to lots of other things in life (being positive, right, alive). In religion, you also have three options. You are either a non-believer from a place of personal purpose; a false believer who just goes through the motions and follows the rules, dogmas and regulations from a place of religious purpose; or a true believer who thinks, acts and attracts (in a way of unconditional love) from a place of following God's purpose. The mind is where everything is perceived and processed through broader lens of awareness; it is multi-dimensional in nature. Those of a physical and fleshy mind are stuck in earthly and transient things. Those of a negative and difficulty-led disposition are trapped in emotional, insecure and unconscious things. Those of a positive and spirit-led mind can transcend the previous conditions and think, act and attract that which is heavenly and lasting. This is The Third Way.

CHAPTER 9

Energy is your currency, use it well.

"You don't have to be great to start, but you will have to start to be great through energy, frequency and vibrations."

—Zig Ziglar[514] & Nikola Tesla[453] (Modified)

You give life to what you give energy to, and energy speaks louder than words.[276] Your energy is your currency, so spend it well and invest it wisely. Be aware of the energy you allow into your space and vibrate good energy into others' souls, making them never forget the beauty of yours. The energy of the mind is the essence of life[769]; match the frequency of the reality you want and you can't help but get that reality.[477] It can be no other way. This is not philosophy but basic physics.

Vibrations

If you want to find the secrets of the Universe, think in terms of energy, frequency and vibration.[453] Everything is energy in physics, and that's all there is to it. Match the frequencies of the reality you want, and you cannot help but get into that reality.[187] Everything moves and vibrates. At the most fundamental level, the Universe and everything it comprises is pure vibratory energy manifesting itself in different ways. The Universe has no 'solidity' as such. Matter is merely energy in a state of vibration.[773]

Everything is vibrational, your thoughts, your ideas, every human being.[770] The law of attraction is all about vibration; you will draw to yourself whatever vibration matches yours, wanted or unwanted, so vibrate at the highest frequency possible. What you vibrate, therefore, is what the Universe echoes back to you in every moment. It's not the words of your intentions that manifest your reality, it's the vibration of the energy of your intentions.

There is a sacred energy that guides you, and it distances itself from who and what no longer serves you, and lowers the vibrations in those areas. You are then able to attract and manifest who and what does serve, elevate, nourish and inspire you to vibrate higher.[771] This means you can change your frequency by changing your thoughts, attitudes and assumptions. When your energy vibrates at a frequency that is in direct alignment to what the Universe has been attempting to deliver to you your entire life, you begin to live in its flow and true miracles start to happen.[772]

Some of the most difficult daily challenges we face are a result of dealing with human energies. That vibe someone sent you is as real as the chair you are sitting on. Our souls are struggling, fighting, winning and losing on all the battlegrounds of human energy. The Universe is not punishing you or blessing you but merely responding to the vibrational attitude that you are emitting.[211]

Your vibration equals your point of attraction for everything coming into your reality and everything you're experiencing.[774] Your personal vibration or energy state is a blend of the contracted or expanded frequencies of your body, emotions and thoughts at any given moment. The more you allow your soul to shine through, the higher your personal vibration will be.[352] Your emotions are the indication of what vibration you are holding; always try to live in the higher vibrational frequencies of love, gratitude and possibility. We say people are full of energy when they create vibrations all around them that fill them with positivity, which we can see and detect immediately. I love that feeling.

All of life is energy and we are transmitting it every moment.[777] Be the energy you want to attract. Your thoughts begin it, your emotions amplify it and your actions increase its momentum. Treat energy the same way you treat money – as if it's a finite resource that needs to be wisely managed and invested.[776] The Universe doesn't recognise the difference between small goals and big ones, it responds to your emotions and intent.[778] Your life is influenced by the energy you bring to every moment.[379] It is the key to creativity and the key to life. Passion is energy; feel the power that comes from focusing on what excites you. If you always try to be normal you will never know how amazing you can be with energy. Throughout the infinite, the forces are in a perfect balance, hence the energy of a single thought may determine the motion of the Universe.[453]

Energy is the currency of the Universe. When you pay attention to something, you buy that experience.[299] Love is the energy of life. Without passion, you don't have energy, and without energy you have nothing. Some days, it seems like the purpose of life is to convert energy into beauty.

You can care about someone without letting them drain you of your energy.[779] Let others vibrate as they vibrate, and want the best for them. Never mind how they're flowing to you, concentrate on how you're flowing, because one who is connected to the energy stream is more powerful and more influential than a million who are not.[775] The smarter you get, the less you speak. You grow to realise that not everyone is worth confrontation. Your time is valuable; your energy is priceless.[780] Don't waste either on people who don't deserve it.

There is a lot we don't yet know about energy. We all know about its ability to drive technology, manufacture products, and heat and light our homes, but we know less about its healing powers, the life force in our cells, the connection to our bodily energy flow channels and its destructive capabilities. I feel a lot of our diseases, mental issues and unhappiness are related to incorrect energy levels. But fixing energy levels is not as profitable as prescribing drugs that treat your symptoms, not the underlying cause.

We sometimes focus on the wrong vibration level. Try to focus on the right level for the right outcome. Things that kill your vibration levels permanently are: negative self-talk, toxic friends and relationships, complaining, neglecting your body, media and music, not living authentically, never laughing and taking yourself too seriously. Oh, yes, this is very true. I stopped watching news of any kind long ago. If a given army does not stand up as one against their psychopathic, murderous, bloodthirsty leader in order to stop a war, then that is their business and no one else's. We average news consumers are absolutely powerless to change anything with regard to catastrophes or war (for instance), so there is little sense in absorbing those daily loads of information about destruction, misery and death. Some people even warn against 'war fatigue', which refers to the mental exhaustion of stuffing your mind with horror, death and doom, resulting in a disinterest in, even apathy for, the atrocities still being committed. Remember to say out loud 'go away, you mind poisoners'.[781]

Good and Evil

Everything in life involves a negotiation between doing nothing, something positive or something negative. Your life will not go as planned, you will get knocked back and encounter evil, for nobody is perfect; you must get up again and again to confront failure and evil in order to overcome it. Humanity uses many different languages, which are connected to their history, culture and environment, but they all transfer a sense of morality to our actions (right, wrong or indifferent) and refer to a separate entity (God, the devil, angels/demons) or place (Heaven, Hell, purgatory/in-between).

The greatest trick evil ever pulled was convincing the world it doesn't exist. Sometimes evil allows people to live lives free of trouble because it doesn't want them being compelled to turn to righteousness. Wickedness, depravity and immorality are like a nice and comfortable jail cell, until one day when time runs out and the cell door slams shut, and suddenly it's too late.[151] Look after your soul. Avoid the seven deadly sins: envy, gluttony, greed, lust, pride, sloth and wrath.

It is common sense to stay away from things that take our energy or don't service us well in the long term, especially those that may lead to us getting caught up in bad things. When you give negative energy to things, they grow; it is just the way things work. Give your finite energy to good things and be kind to people, because this normally leads to better outcomes and better places. Treat others as you would like others to treat you. The effect you have on others is the most valuable currency there is.

There is a lot of good, bad and ugliness in the world. Why is it so difficult to do the right thing, and so easy to be bad?[362] Inside each of us, there are the seeds of both good and evil, and it is a conscious decision which one we choose to let rule our world.[69] The good within us is not just capable of doing good things, it is capable of greatness. The bad within us can spread lies, conspiracies, fear and misinformation; it fans the flame of conflict, does terrible things to others and turns away from justice, integrity and our duty of care for everyone and everything in this world. Never forget that life always offers you a second chance; it's called tomorrow.

It is a constant struggle as to who will win at any given moment – evil or good. One cannot exist without the other. The best of us accept the 'Third Way' of uniting the goodness and evil, and redirecting their energy onto greater things. There may be times that you hate mankind, especially those who engage in unrelenting warfare, recklessly sacrificing the lives of others to satisfy themselves. Sometimes the only way to find peace is by moving away from the chaos.

We need to remain vigilant against those who would erode our liberties and stability. We are all in this together and need to keep our eyes and ears open for perils that often lie hidden in plain sight. We cannot ignore them and say nothing when we know they are wrong. Remember, the standards you walk by are the standards you accept. When things are bad and our freedoms are rolled back, it is not until they are lost that we realise how fragile they were and that we should have stood up to autocracy at the time.

Humans are not perfect and never can be. We are deeply flawed in so many ways, but there is beauty that can shine from our imperfections. As individuals, we sometimes disagree and argue; having different viewpoints and priorities is in our nature, but at the end of the day, we are here to solve problems – to bring justice, to give people a fair shot, to protect and improve peoples' lives and to fulfil our duty of care for all other living creatures and the environment. We are meant for greatness, and that doesn't mean ignoring the bad things we are capable of, it means acknowledging and accepting both the good and the bad, then choosing to do the right thing. We are temporary custodians of this world, just looking after it for future generations. Our power comes from within and doesn't need validation when we are on the right path. That is The Third Way.

A lot of life is lived in the 'fret' zone, the area between good and evil; however good this may be for individuals, it may not be so good for others, society or the environment. I like the expression 'holy person' because it represents the coming together of the two parts that exist in all of us (great good and great evil) to create a new, third entity: an imperfect human striving to do their best for everyone and everything, who is willing to share, sacrifice and seize the moment.

Why does God allow evil and suffering to exist? It is a test and the price we pay for choice. God knows us and what we can handle and has equipped each of us accordingly. God remains all-knowing, all-good and all-powerful because it is a free humanity that is the cause of evil, not Him; God cannot restrain evil without violating free will and eliminating the possibility of real relationships anchored in genuine love.[782] God does prevent and restrain some acts of evil; this world would be much worse were God not restraining it.[783] Nothing forces a person to confront their true self like suffering. It causes our focus to turn inward, to face those parts of ourselves we might otherwise ignore. God can use suffering then to develop us into better people, those who can love and enjoy Him forever.[784 & 785]

Much has been written about the human condition, and many think that humanity is in the last chance saloon because we don't fully understand the duality of our nature (our capacity to do good and evil) that is learned when we become conscious. There is a lot of dodgy science, ranting and pseudoscience out there, coupled with an army of hecklers, critics and social media poisoners that attacks anyone who dares to comment on, criticise or offer a differing opinion from the mainstream. But nobody is the final arbiter of truth, for we are all different and live in a multi-dimensional world; what works for you, may not apply to or work for me. Beware of the information you consume and aim to be like a restaurant critic: consider every dish flawed because we don't live in a perfect world, not everything is good for you. We all have choices – is something worth fighting for or not? What is worth dying for? Choose carefully.

Dishwashing

Life, and the energy we put into it, is similar to a dishwasher. Just because you can jam it all in doesn't mean it will all get cleaned. There are specific requirements to get the best results: you need some space around the moving parts to allow them to operate effectively, and people need space to allow them to grow; there is an optimal way to stack things, and doing things in an organised fashion prepares people for what lies ahead; time is needed to allow certain processes to take place, and people can't rush through life and do it well. A little preparation and attention to detail goes a long way to help improve the overall performance of things.

There are right ways and there are not-so-right ways. Life can be made much easier by following some simple rules and techniques to get things done. But there are times to follow the rules, and there are times to break them (if you need a utensil and the cycle has not yet finished, for example). You need to know which approach will yield your desired outcome. If you want a Plan B, then make sure it will work when you need it to (when the dishwasher breaks down, and it will because nothing lasts forever, at least you will have thought of what to do then). Sometimes you need a Plan B, and sometimes you don't even want to consider one. Know the risks for both scenarios and be willing to accept the consequences of your choices.

I still struggle to get my children to properly load the dishwasher. I've now come to the conclusion that if the time is not right, I just have to be patient. Sometimes you just need to go with the flow of life and wait for things to happen in their own glorious, good time. You can't really rush the dishwashing cycles; they take as long as they are programmed to take. Simple really. When you find yourself repeating the lessons your parents taught you, then you have reached the threshold of understanding. Some people never get there.

Everyone is intelligent; they may have just never had the opportunity to explore, express or enjoy it, to practice, participate or play with it, to communicate, collaborate or create with it. At the end of the day, intelligence is not remembering everything, it is knowing what you know, knowing when to seek help or ask questions, and knowing how to overcome issues and barriers. It is a mindset thing. I have a PhD in Engineering and can solve some of the most complex problems in the world, yet I often forget one of the six items my wife told me to buy at the shop, including dishwasher salt.

We often make things harder than they should be. Dodging doing the basics like loading and unloading the dishwasher is a form of avoidance, which (like self-help sometimes) can reinforce perceptions of inferiority and shame – for not hand-washing dishes, for creating unrealistic expectations that we can do it all, for thinking you are okay and don't need the help of others. The answers are out there – you just haven't found or implemented them yet.

Effectiveness

Energy is easily wasted on the wrong kinds of things. Any orienteer will tell you that the easiest and quickest route between two points is not necessarily the shortest, most direct route. You need to follow the contours of the land, understand the attack points and possess the skills to determine where you actually are on the map.

Highly effective people sharpen the saw so as not to work themselves to death. They are proactive, not reactive, and begin with the end in mind. They seek to understand before trying to be understood, using synergy. Effective people find their voice, then inspire others to do likewise. They adapt to and operate in the times and environments they find themselves in; in life and death situations, they have intense focus on what is happening around them, accept the unfolding circumstances and then do what is within their control to move to a more advantageous position. They don't panic, nor lose control, so they don't waste energy.

Life can be compared to a series of steep hills and rough terrain; you need to know how to navigate these obstacles because they can drain precious energy from you.[786] Life is a journey of finding out who you are, accepting yourself, then being the best you can be; put your family (or the tribe that loves you) first and be confident in who you are and what matters to you without letting your ego rule. You can achieve anything you want, but you will need to do so one small, manageable chunk at a time.[787] It might take a while, because all things come to those who wait and keep on trying, trying and trying. Those who can get up after they fall are practically invincible because there is no obstacle in this world that can withstand the power, might and intensity of persistent assault hour after hour, day after day, week after week, or year after year.[788]

I see lots of organisations wishing to improve their overall effectiveness, yet they stand firm on wrongly made assumptions, uncoupled dependencies driven by management egos or a lack of resources and budgets, and they don't want to put the right prerequisites in place to effect change. Effectiveness is more difficult to accomplish if you blindfold your employees, tie them down with processes and accept their incompetence or laziness. It takes brave people to admit they are wrong, but that is often the only way to turn the ship around.

You are only as effective as you choose to be. You have three options for responding to the question: Does it feel right? If 'yes', then follow it; if 'not quite', it is probably blocking you, so clear it; if 'definitely not', then it is probably not right for you, so drop it or leave it. Effectiveness (getting the desired result) is not the same as efficiency (accomplishing things with the least amount of wasted time, effort or money). Effective people have things in reserve when things go wrong; efficient people and organisations often don't.

Levels

I am going to help you take yourself to a new level of excellence. Creating the next level of results requires the next level of thinking.[471]

We are all in the same game, just at different levels.[789] As you go higher in the game, you still have to deal with difficulties, just new and different ones. You are what you think and do; every next level of your life will demand a different you.[791] Whether you think you can or think you can't, you're right.[790]

Don't think that just because you made it to the next level that the haters and naysayers disappear. Stop explaining yourself when you realise that others only understand from their level of perception.[792] Don't dumb yourself down for the comfort levels of others.[793] It helps if you remember that they are doing their best from their level of consciousness. Help someone and you earn a friend; help someone too much and you can make an enemy. It is a fine balance that will be different for every person.

There are two levels of love. There's the physical level, which is a lot of fun, and there's the emotional level, which is extremely mercurial.

There are also different levels of involvement. Everyone has finite levels of energy, love, intelligence, etc. The higher your energy level, the more efficient your body.[7] When there are blockages in energy levels is when problems arise. Dreams may be limitless in terms of energy levels, but the application of those dreams into reality certainly does put energy levels and limits back on the agenda. Your sacred space is where you find yourself and recharge your energy levels over and over again.

We should start referring to 'age' as 'level', because 'I'm at Level 50' sounds a lot more bad*ss and deserving of the sh*t you have had to shovel than just being an old person. When we are born, we start with very little energy and lower levels and awareness, then acquire and build them up. They are like muscles that must be exercised; you need to use them or lose them. However, they must not be overused otherwise they get tired.

Life is lived in three phases: the past, which is what must be accepted and learnt from; the present, which is the continual now we all occupy and must really appreciate; and the future, which is what we should plan and save for, so that when we arrive, we have reserves to still enjoy life with. Life levels all men; death reveals the eminent.

There are always more levels than you can image. People who are better off than you, people worse off than you, people more intelligent than you; faster people (no Olympian can stay at the top forever), people with more money than you. We move between levels often without knowing it, but that is just us surfing the cycles of life.

Effort

Life is much more interesting when you make a bit of effort.[794] Appreciate effort, no matter how small. Care less about the material things someone could give you and more about their time, attention, honesty, loyalty and effort. Those gifts mean more than anything money could buy.[795]

Work hard to progress, then work harder to get better; the results you achieve will be in direct proportion to the effort you apply.[478] To double your gains, you have got to triple your effort. Great work demands great sacrifice and those who are not capable of great sacrifice are not capable of a great work, but all the effort in the world won't matter if you're not inspired.

Effort is the best indicator of interest. Someone who seriously wants to talk to you, wants to see you, wants to make you a part of their day, will seriously make the appropriate effort. No reasons. No excuses. If the feelings are mutual, the effort will be equal. Know who's worth the effort and who's not. Respect people who find time for you in their busy schedule, and love those who never even look at their schedule when you need them.[796] The most attractive thing is effort. It is the most perfect thing a woman wishes to feel from her partner. Don't bother reserving a space in your heart for someone who doesn't earn the right to stay there.[20]

The greatest effort is not concerned with results.[797] Slower is faster, and if you practise every day with patience and correctness, you will get there. It's like preparing for a jump; you can't rush, you must summon the appropriate energy with split-second timing and have an understanding of purpose to get up in the air. It requires training, confidence and mental effort.

Effort gives meaning to life as it shows you care about something and are willing to work for it; success is a ladder you cannot climb with your hands in your pockets. And when you bring that to every single day, that's when change occurs. Effort is normally directed towards the five pillars of life: relationships and love, career, money and time creation, health and fitness, and personal and spiritual growth. It can be difficult to achieve balance and fulfilment when each of these categories is demanding more and more of your time, energy and resources. Don't tell people your dreams, show them. Focus on being open to the truth, open to love, open to yourself and open to others in order to move towards happiness.

It may sound harsh, but hard work doesn't equate to success; effort doesn't equate to reward. It is a trait that is admired in many cultures around the world, and it does play a key role, but success is more likely to be related to your personal circumstances — where you grew up, your family, your attitude, your current location, what is happening around you, your endurance, your ability to fail and keep going, your willingness to break the rules, your access to opportunities and the power of timing and luck. Effort also doesn't equal results if you are approaching the problem in the wrong way, barking up the wrong tree or going down a blind alley. You have to be very specific about the effort you are expending; if the goal is right for you, you'll get the results you want and, more importantly, you will gain this understanding and become defined by it.

Some of the hardest things I've done, I did just to get onto the next step of the ladder. Some of the easiest things I've done, or have just happened, were because I went with the flow; these have been the best things I've experienced. Beware of working harder not smarter. I once ran a project connecting black boxes that wasn't going well. I stopped the project and got the engineers to develop a monitoring device, much to the annoyance of the management. The project went smoothly after that, and management even sold the monitor to offset undelivered requirements in another part of the programme. I didn't get any real thanks because I was just doing my job. Be careful what you wish for because you may get it, and it may not be as you expected or anticipated. It must be soul destroying to put in so much effort to get a job or profession that you then do not enjoy and dread going to work.

Less

Less is often more. Less clutter to maintain tidiness; less money spent on things that don't matter[798]; fewer excuses for why we did what we did; less time spent on things that don't mean anything, so you can spend more time on the things that do mean something; less gossip, hate and jealousy, because they consume you and eat away at your heart; less letting life pass you by and more time appreciating all the aspects of this beautiful world inhabited by beautiful people; less 'eyes closed' and more seeing the divine in everything; less killing with negativity and more killing with kindness (difficult people don't know how to react to that); less saying 'yes' for the sake of others and more saying 'no' so you can focus on what matters to you and your loved ones[799]; less thinking about 'what if?' scenarios, and more just going for it; less crying and guilt so you can make more time for fun and laughter, as they are the best form of medicine (even laughing at yourself); less caring about what anyone else thinks, and more doing what is right for you; less living in regret; less thinking you know it all and more learning; less negative, more positive; less idling and going around in circles, and more planning to reach your dreams and goals; less comparing the start of your journey to the middle of someone else's; less wasting time and more valuing your time; less trying to control everything.

We all do lots of unnecessary things. Start dropping non-critical tasks; leave behind that which is no longer useful and de-clutter your life to make room for new, useful things. Tasks will fill your available day, but not everything you do adds value. I love changing jobs because I get a clean and empty inbox at the start. You could always 'accidentally' delete your current inbox, because any critical tasks always find a way of coming to the surface again. Let critical tasks, your own pursuits and personal priorities help define your workload, and make sure there is time left at the end to enjoy yourself and spend time alone or with your loved ones.

The KonMari method is Marie Kondo's[260] minimalist-inspired approach to tackling your stuff category-by-category, rather than room-by-room. It teaches you to ask a simple question of each item when you go about tidying up: does this spark joy? If it doesn't, get rid of it.[260]

Innovation

Innovation means looking at life with new eyes.[800] Go to places and hang out with people who inspire you. This world is made of an intricate, seemingly invisible web that connects us all to amazing possibilities. Your job is to take the first step and follow that web using inspiration as your guide.

If, at first, the idea is not absurd, then there is no hope for it.[801] If you do not express your own original ideas and listen to your inner being, you betray yourself.[802] An idea that is not dangerous is unworthy of being called an idea at all.[498] Ideas are like rabbits; you get a couple and learn how to handle them, and pretty soon you have a dozen.[802] The way to get good ideas is to have lots of ideas and throw the bad ones away.[349] There is one thing stronger than all the armies in the world, and that is an idea whose time has come.[220] You can kill a man, but you can't kill an idea. Ideas won't keep; something must be done about them.[803] A new idea is delicate and can be killed by a sneer or a yawn, stabbed to death by a quip and worried away by a frown at just the right time. All achievements, all earned riches, have their beginning in an idea.[802] The air is full of ideas, they are knocking you in the head all the time; you only have to know what you want, then forget it and go about your business, and suddenly, the idea will come through. It was there all the time.[807] I've had periods in my life when I've had a bundle of ideas come along, and then I've had long dry spells.[808] If I have a thousand ideas and only one turns out to be good, I am satisfied.[807]

You can have brilliant ideas, but if you can't get them across they won't get you anywhere.[188] The ability to express an idea is well-nigh as important as the idea itself.[810] Simple steps turn into big hits of inspiration opening doors of opportunity you never knew were possible.[800] No grand idea was ever born in a conference, but a lot of foolish ideas have died there.[161] If you want to kill any idea in the world, get a committee working on it.[254] Money never starts an idea; it is the idea that starts the money.

It is the essence of genius to make use of the simplest ideas.[351] Nothing is more dangerous than an idea when it is the only one you have.[804] Everyone is in love with their own ideas.[805] Why is it we always get our best ideas while shaving? One's mind, once stretched by a new idea, never regains its original dimensions.[806]

Curiosity, obsession and dogged endurance, combined with self-criticism, have brought me to my ideas.[807] A pile of rocks ceases to be so when somebody contemplates transforming it into a cathedral. Take up one idea and make it your life. Think of it, dream of it, live on that idea. Let the brain, muscles, nerves and every part of your body be full of it, and just leave every other idea alone.[807] This is the way to success. This is the way great spiritual giants (people who point the way to greatness and are witnesses to a life worthy of modelling) are produced.

No idea is so outlandish that it should not be considered.[809] If you are possessed by an idea, you will find it expressed everywhere. You even smell it. The man with a new idea is a grumble, until the idea succeeds.[466] To turn really interesting ideas and fledgling technologies into a company that can continue to innovate for years requires a lot of discipline. An idea is salvation by imagination. I can't understand why some people are frightened of new ideas; I'm frightened of the old ones. The new idea either finds a champion or it dies.[811] Our best ideas come from clerks and stock boys. Daring ideas are like chessmen moved forward; they may be beaten, but they may start a winning game.[812] The true sign of intelligence is not knowledge but imagination. Insanity is doing the same thing over and over again, and expecting different results.[813] Try not to become a man of success, but rather a man of value.[814]

We as a race love to categorise things. We have categories for race, nationality, sexual orientation, body size, economic income, almost everything. Once we accept our limits, we go beyond them.[242] It is the supreme art of the teacher to awaken joy in creative expression and knowledge. The difference between stupidity and genius is that genius has its limits. To raise new questions and new possibilities, and to regard old problems from a new angle, all require creative imagination and mark real advances in science.[802] It has become appallingly obvious that our technologies have exceeded our humanity. We cannot solve our problems with the same thinking we used when we created them.[178] The world is a dangerous place to live; not because of the people who are evil, but because of those who don't do anything about it.[133] Many aspiring entrepreneurs are held back, waiting for a good idea to come to them, but in reality, there is no such thing as a bad idea. Any idea can be a great if you think differently, dream big and commit to seeing it realised.

I ran an innovation team for newbies appointed by senior management, who wanted to test me to solve a particularly complex problem and develop the newbies at the same time. I'm a firefighter kind of worker: call me in when you have major problems, not routine maintenance activities. I taught the newbies, showed and guided them through a series of fun-filled activities and events that resulted in us winning an innovation award. I instructed them in Higher Order Thinking Styles (HOTS), which we are all capable of using. It was a great project, the newbies loved it because it was, at the time, the best experience the company had provided them with, and people still mention it every now and again.

Purpose

Each day is born with a sunrise and ends with a sunset, the same way we open our eyes to see the light and close them to hear the dark.[247] You weren't asked if you wanted to come into this world, nor given the choice of parents or where you landed. However, you did come about by an act of love (which comes in many forms: IVF, adoption, osmosis [grandparents assuming care when the parents are no longer able], for example) and/or passion. You are here to reignite this feeling, to find out what is important, what you are destined to do and what you are willing to sacrifice to make a real difference. You may have no control over how your story begins and ends, but by now you should know that all things have an ending. Every spark returns to darkness, every sound returns to silence, every flower returns to sleep with the earth[247], every soul returns to where it came from. The journey of the sun and moon are predictable.

The mystery of human existence lies not just in staying alive, but in finding something to live for.[815] Your purpose while you are on this earth is your ultimate art because life is not made unbearable by circumstances, but by lack of meaning and purpose. Clarifying your purpose and discovering the *why* behind everything you do is very empowering. The path becomes clear. The things that excite you are not random – they are connected to your purpose. Follow them.[818] If you can't figure out your purpose, figure out your passion. Alternatively, find your wound.[816] Follow your passion as it will lead you right to your purpose. Appreciate where you are in your journey, even if it's not exactly where you want to be; every season serves a purpose.[817] Stay patient and trust the journey.

Everything you do and create will not satisfy or make everyone happy. All you have to do is to open your eyes and look around. What you create in your mind is going to be more intriguing than anything other people try to give you. You must learn to accept feedback and love your critics; this is one of the simplest, most transformational (and free) tools that helps us realise our full potential. Feedback from the right person at the right time can motivate us, challenge us to get better, direct where we need to learn and gain more knowledge and reveal to us who we truly are and what we are capable of, thereby building stronger, more talented individuals.

It is time for you to be a creator, an inventor, an experimenter, a risk-taker, a rule-breaker, a cultivator, a mistake-led learner, a fun-seeker and a friend. Be active, healthy, happy, soul wealthy, responsible, accountable, productive, appreciative, self-reliant, prepared yet patient. Be an individual, a team-player, a contributor, a forgiver, a lover, an understander, a negotiator, a first-class communicator and listener. Be respectful, ready to commit and trust, innovative, self-aware, thankful, ready to serve with a server's heart and able to forgive, forget and move on. Be a student (a constant learner), a teacher, a protector, a little crazy, a visionary and the change you want to see.

In business, the purpose of our interactions should be to promote wealth and prosperity for all, whilst putting the interests of citizens ahead of those of the company. Unfortunately, shareholders' and bankers' interests generally override those of local communities and the environment. Big companies need to accept that they have broader social responsibility and should not exist if they are only out to use our precious resources to make money for the minority, or to influence tax, environmental, foreign and/or trade policies for their own benefit. Big companies need to be more accountable for where they source their raw materials, how funds are distributed throughout their supply chains, how they treat their subsidiaries and whether each of these elements are sustainable or not. We must not allow people or companies to engage in 'purposes' that counter the wellness of humanity or the environment.

Your purpose in life isn't your spark nor is it your reason to live. We always see films, stories and self-help books about chasing your dreams, but it is important to know that your life has merit even if you don't achieve your dream. Enjoying the journey and making small differences is just as valid as reaching for the stars; you don't have to have it all figured out. You may not have landed your ideal job, but there are so many other ways you can find fulfilment when you have something that you love or a passion for developing real mastery at. It has nothing to do with being rich and famous, or earning your way into being worthy; these goals often end up being self-defining or self-limiting. We all have value just by being alive; we are already enough and deserve to enjoy what life has to offer. We are here for such a short period of time, so don't waste it – get on and live your life.

We often internalise things and think everything is about us. Humanity first thought the geocentric model of the solar system was correct, in that the Earth was at the centre. We then developed the heliocentric model that placed the Sun at the centre of the solar system. We now understand that our solar system is located on the inner edge of a spiral arm about 24,000 light-years from the centre of just one of the 125 billion galaxies in the observable universe. Our purpose in life may not be an internal mission of enlightenment; it may require us to be externally focused. We may need to look up at the stars, to teach others, to drive the bus each day to take the next Einstein to school, to save someone else or guide others to find their spark or true purpose in life.

The meaning of life is to find your gift; the purpose of life is to give it away.[819] There's no exercise better for the human heart than reaching down and lifting someone up. It is not enough to have lived, we should be determined to live for something. Purpose is the sense that we are part of something bigger than ourselves, that we are needed and have something better to work for. It is what creates true happiness.[817] It informs all your life's decisions. Everyone's purpose is to explore and experience, to cultivate their gifts and inner knowing on their lifelong quest of soul to that point in place and time where what you do is who you are and who you serve, and to take care of yourself is to take care of the world.

There is only one thing that makes a dream impossible to achieve: the fear of failure.[821] Yet failure is a prerequisite for great success; if you want to succeed faster, double your rate of failure. Success is the result of preparation, hard work and learning from failure. It consists of going from failure to failure without loss of enthusiasm. Obstacles are those things you see when you take your eyes off the goal.

You are more powerful than you think you are. It is through adversity and being out of the comfort zone of one-dimensional living that we often achieve our best and show our true character. If you know you can do better, then do better.[819] The heart of human excellence begins to beat when you discover a pursuit that absorbs you, faces you, challenges you or gives you a sense of meaning, joy or passion.[340] Efforts and courage are not enough without purpose and direction. Singleness of purpose is one of the chief essentials for success, no matter what may be one's aim. Activity without purpose is the drain of your life.[384] Be willing to go 'all out' in pursuit of your dream. Ultimately it will pay off.[820]

Remember: don't be pushed by your problems, be led by your dreams; you choose the life you live – if you don't like it, it's on you to change it because no one else is going to do it for you; if you hang out with chickens, you're going to cluck, and if you hang out with eagles, you're going fly.[298] Love with purpose; you won't be distracted by comparison if you are captured with purpose; the real secret of life is to be completely engaged in what you are doing in the present, so instead of calling it work, realise it is play.

It doesn't interest me what you do for a living. I want to know what you ache for, and if you dream of meeting your heart's longing.[816] There is no greater agony than bearing an untold story inside you. While on Earth, we do some things that are important and things that are not. It is the important things that give our lives meaning and happiness. What will you do with your time that falls into the 'important' category?

My old company invited some people, who had travelled a long distance for a remote, international task, over for a debrief session about their experiences. I sat in a conference theatre with over 200 people, right at the back. The visitors gave their presentation. It was clear on their faces that they were tired but had been instructed to come along for the purpose of taking part in a PR exercise and so were doing as requested. The host asked if there were any questions, and nobody in the theatre responded. I felt embarrassed and sorry that these people had travelled so far for what seemed to be nothing. I decided that I would change the world that day, so I put up my hand. I asked what they really needed to help improve their experience, though I did caveat with, 'Don't ask me to give you any Star Trek or Star Wars technology.' They huddled together to discuss, and a few moments later provided me with a scenario that really frustrated them. I thanked them and said I would personally look into it. That night, I went home and, with a bit of 'outside the box' thinking, found what I thought could be a solution and ordered it. It arrived a few days later. I tested it in a representative scenario and was very impressed with the result. I then sent more of the solutions to the visitors' boss and told them what I had done. One month later, I received a fantastic letter from a representative saying it was the best solution they had ever come across. It took a little longer for it to enter service, but I'm proud I asked the right question that day and followed it up with a solution. I gained a small innovation financial award that I used to buy a music device, which I still use often. Every time I look at the device, I know that I made a difference and solved a very frustrating customer problem.

Too often we don't solve the right problems because we don't have the right perspective. We don't address the reality of the situation that actually exists and needs to be prioritised. Often, what we need is an overview, the ability to see the big picture: that we are an interconnected and interdependent structure of all reality; what affects one directly affects all indirectly. I'm reminded of part of Martin Luther King's Peace Speech: 'As nations and individuals we are interdependent'. That orbital perspective is the call to action to address the injustices we see, the sobering contradictions and unfortunate destructive realities being played out on our indescribably beautiful planet. We are not from Earth; we're of Earth. We are not in the universe; we are the Universe becoming conscious of itself.

Keep the multi-generational, multi-perspective big picture to see the depth of the problem, but stay focused on the people. People maintain their value as members of holistic human society, not numbers on a spreadsheet or workforce, nor a voting or consumer block or category. However, focusing on what we can do now, in the short term, doesn't mean quick, temporary wins, symbolic victories or impressions of progress that are, in fact, backward steps. Making lasting, effective and efficient change is the key that benefits everyone, not just someone. Moving away from a two-dimensional (us versus them) mindset into a true, multi-dimensional appreciation of the Universe we live in, puts us on the right track.

We all have significant power to effect real change in the world, but many don't realise it. I'm an optimist and have faith that humanity can become a blossoming example of unity across our planet, with awareness of and appreciation for our interdependent nature. When this reaches its critical mass, then we will have the power and resources to really start solving our problems, humanely and across all our societies/civilisations. It will give us courage during the dark times ahead (there will be some) to keep doing what we know is right, to never give up hope and keep marching forward. For a future we all want to be a part of and that is our true calling/purpose, one that follows God's purpose that has been designed for us.[822]

CHAPTER 10

Take action.

"You are never too old to set a new goal, dream a new dream or start to make a difference."

—C. S. Lewis[275 & 823] (Modified)

Change will not happen until you make it. Nothing happens without action; the best intentions in the world are nothing more than that: intentions. This chapter covers choices: fighting, doing, helping, starting, sacrificing and urgency, all of which contribute to both failing and winning. Decisions are the sparks that ignite actions. Until decisions are made, nothing happens. Then comes the hard part, putting your first foot forward on your journey, then the next.

Choosing

Life is choice. It is said that life comes down to two simple paths: get busy living or get busy dying; do or do not. There is no starting or stopping, only doing. It is not our abilities that show who we truly are, it is our choices.

Give your obstacles the credit they deserve. You need to a make a conscious choice to see challenges as something beneficial so you can deal with them in the most productive way. Obstacles are great opportunities to pause, re-think, recharge your batteries and exercise the mind by considering alternative solutions; they challenge you to learn more about yourself (and others and in some circumstances) and are life's way of telling you that you are walking down the wrong path. Failing can be especially good if you are going in the wrong direction.

There are three types of failure:

- Failing at what you don't want: so, you might as well take a chance on doing something that you really do want or love.

- Failing to learn a lesson: either from the past or an acknowledged best practice.

- Fear of losing: the danger of trying to hold on to something while strangling the life out of it.

Don't hold on to or stay in the proximity of the bad things in your life. Learn to recognise that some things and relationships just weren't meant to be, or that the time you had with them was just the allotted time you were meant to spend with them. You now have to move on to other things. You are ready; you were born ready to do the things you were destined to do. When you walk out the door today you have two options: love or fear. Choose love and start doing. Fear will turn you against your playful heart.

In this life, we are taught to believe in the duality of a heroic triumph over an evil oppressor. In reality, there are grey areas within the simple choices of good or bad, hope or fear, humanity or evil. People often start with the great intention of making things right, which can ultimately lead to a tragic downfall when glimpsing the revelations, meanings and motivations that lead to realistic outcomes. There is no reset button, no going back and making another choice. There is no redemption, reconciliation, absolution or hope; we have to accept that we have done what we have done. Life and the world are not binary; there are no easy answers for a lot of our questions. Whatever path we set ourselves on, there is no going back. On whatever path we take, there lies a set of troubling reverberations and often unforeseen, unintended consequences that will echo through time, landing differently for each active or passive participant. For uncertainty and intangible conclusions uproot the natural order we seek to maintain, terrorising and plaguing us in our inability to control them and the fact that we won't find some redeeming truth at the end of our journey. Sometimes we don't have a choice and must accept that we can't walk away from our own story.

Fighting

I look around and see these young faces and think, 'I've made every wrong choice a middle-aged man can make. I've wasted away all my money, I chased off anyone who's ever loved me, and lately, I can't even stand the face I see in the mirror.' When you get old, things get taken from you. It's just a part of life. But you only learn this when you start losing stuff. You find out that, like football, life is a game of inches. The margin for error is so small – half a step too late or too early and you don't quite make it, half a second too slow or too fast and you don't quite catch it.[824] The inches we need are all around us. They're in every break of the game, every minute, every second. Fight and claw with your fingernails for that inch, because when you add them all up, that's what is going to make the difference between winning and losing, between living and dying. In any fight, it's the guy who's willing to die who is going win that inch.[147]

Staying positive leads to success, but that positivity sometimes needs a reality check, and although others can help you, they can't do this bit for you. It will be down to you at the end of the day to get across that line and defeat what needs to be defeated. Remember, our true character is revealed when we lose, and as we will not win every time, we need to lose with dignity, with respect for others and the ability to move on. We don't need to be defined by loss, because we can get up, prepare better and then try again. When the fight turns to war, other dimensions come into play. It is no longer just winning and losing, but also surviving to fight another day. Make sure you are fighting for a just, universal cause in the best interests of humanity and the environment.

Be very selective with your battles for they drain your energy, damage you and make you vulnerable, often making the situation much worse. There is being right and being wrong, but there are times when peace is better than being right.

We are always told about fight or flight, but there is a Third Way: favour (to use love and compassion). An incident at Pristina airport in Kosovo resulted in a confrontation between Russian and NATO forces. Russian troops occupied the airport ahead of a planned NATO deployment. NATO told the local commander to take the airport by force but, instead, the British lieutenant general flew to the airport and met with the Russian general, and they shared war stories over whisky. NATO forces blocked the airfield, preventing the Russians from re-supplying and raising tensions, whilst the famous singer, then British Captain, James Blunt refused to overpower and destroy the Russians, which would have been even more provocative. What is not generally known is that the British started supplying the Russians with food, drink and entertainment; they were effectively treated as if they were on a holiday camp. Russia doesn't like their troops to get too soft and enjoy themselves, so when the British favours came to the attention of the Russian high command, they ordered their immediate withdrawal, peacefully and without any loss of life. They saved face by deploying Russian peacekeepers throughout the region. This example goes to show that there is a Third Way between doing nothing and fighting. Acting with consideration in this case resolved a very difficult situation.[825]

Doing

It is the daily doing of tasks that changes you, your situation and the world. Start each day by completing a task; the way you live your days is the way you live your life.

Respect everyone; take time to contemplate and review what needs to be done; take some risks; step up when times are toughest and face down the bullies (most of them are damaged children in adults' bodies); lift up the downtrodden and never, ever give up. If you do these things, then the next generations will live in a world far better than the one we have today.

Life is full of circuses (additional challenges designed to push you to your limits). You will likely fail often. It will be painful. At times, it will test you to your very core. But if you want to change the world, don't be afraid of the circuses. Make your bed first thing in the morning (start the day off right with a sense of achievement); find someone to help you through life, to hold a paddle; measure a person by the size of their heart not the size of their flippers; get over being a 'sugar cookie' and keep moving forward; slide down the obstacles headfirst; don't back down from the sharks; be your best in the darkest moments; start singing when you are up to your neck in mud.[826]

Risks and opportunities are just part of life. To expand yourself, you need to move into the unknown, otherwise your life boundaries get smaller each day. You need to ask yourself: what is worth risking and putting yourself forward for? What is worth losing because you don't really care about it? Let the latter opportunities pass you by. We are all different, we walk multiple routes, and there aren't any right or wrong answers. Life is fairly simple when you are looking at action; you are either moving forward or you are moving backward.

Your ambition means nothing without execution. It is time to start working on the changes you want to make happen in the world. No matter where you are in your life, you will always be able to come up with an excuse to justify your delay – when I have more money, experience, time or courage, or when I'm bigger, wiser, healthier or more mentally prepared. The truth is there is no *perfect* time to do anything. Life changes daily and as long as you procrastinate, you'll never begin.[827] Do yourself a favour and start now, start today, go out there and do it.

Today is the beginning of the best days of your life. Action doesn't have to be radical to make a difference, but a dream will remain a dream unless there is a plan of action to make it come alive.

There are those who talk the talk and others who walk the walk. Then there are those rare individuals who talk the talk and then walk the walk. Which are you?

If I had the choice between work, rest and play I would select play every time. Doing the things you love, even if you aren't getting paid for them, is bliss. I love designing and building things myself rather than destroying or dismantling, but sometimes you need to dismantle the old before you can put new things up. Many years ago, I visited my uncle who was very proud of the LEGO^{TM} model he had created for his daughters, who were not really interested in it. He had followed all the instructions (established rules), but within two minutes I had modified it to create something even better, adjusting it as I played and, for me, continually improving it. My uncle was aghast that I had deviated from the instructions and 'ideal' model set. I offered to rebuild it before I left, but I think he was so shell-shocked that I'm not sure he ever got over it. We never did see any more LEGO™ at his house after that. Life is a bit like LEGO™: you are given a lot of pieces, but it is up to you to put them together in the way that you want, that suits your needs, and you can always change them in the future if they no longer work for you or you need something else.

Helping

Help others make sense of life. Don't be afraid to ask others for help either; no individual has all the answers. They may not know the answer, but they might know someone who does or can point you in a better direction.

Our lives are not our own; we are bound to others past and present, and by each crime and every kindness, we birth our future.[322] As we remember all the people who helped make us who we are, we carry a piece of them into everything we do. Lots of people have invested in your upbringing, education and development. Never forget them, and try to pay it forward by helping others.

The world needs you. You need to get out there, whether it is your time, talent, prayers or treasure to give, everyone has a unique gift that is meant to be used to help others. What are you going to do with yours? There are myriad stories about folks who had the chance to sit back and do nothing, but they were holding on to something so precious that they needed to use, give or share with others – Mother Teresa, Bono, Jacques Brel, Buddha.[828] Helping others can often be the best medicine as it takes you away from yourself and your problems, and seeing how others live and suffer can help put things in perspective. At times, we don't reflect, acknowledge and thank the Universe for what we have.

There is always some good in this world, and it is always worth fighting for.

I was shopping early one morning when a young mother and her child were in front of me at the checkout and, for some reason, unable to buy some basic provisions that were clearly meant to feed them both that day. I could see what was happening and stepped in to pay. She was ever so grateful and offered to pay me back, but I just asked her that if she ever had the opportunity to help someone out in the same way, that she would. Why not share out help?

On a separate occasion, my friend Andy came to my college room asking for help. He wanted to be the Law Chairperson that year, but everyone knew he was the department joker and so nobody took him seriously. I asked him if he really wanted it and he said yes, so I told him I would help him make it so. I didn't do law, public relations or anything like that; I loved drawing cartoons and designing things at that stage of my life. I put my skills to the test and created a one-page cartoon manifesto for my friend that was so out-of-the-box and engaging it swung the popular vote, and he got his wish that year. He 'helped' me later that year when I was Hall of Residence Chairperson by getting me a policewoman stripper at the end of year ball. Help comes in many forms, sometimes requested, but often unexpected and out of the blue.

On another occasion, I was walking to work in the Netherlands when a woman stopped me in the street and asked if I could help her. The locks on the car she had borrowed to get to work had all frozen up and she couldn't get into the car. I asked for the car key and started blowing on it furiously – she must have thought I was crazy. After about three minutes, I had sufficiently warmed the key to melt the ice and she was able to get in the car. She thanked me and I walked on to work. It didn't cost me anything, but I helped someone in need and that felt good. Sometimes you are just meant to be in certain places to help people out.

On a further occasion, I felt an immerse desire to donate money to some charities for my birthday. All the charities thanked me, but one in particular called me up and asked if I would mind putting my money to a specific appeal because another donor was matching all contributions. I agreed. It didn't cost me any more, but it meant so much. Small things do count.

Starting

Life-changing advice is only worthwhile if you do something with it. We all have problems, burdens and challenges to overcome, but many of us delay sorting them until the last moment. If you are brave enough to start, you are strong enough to finish.

Discarding, decluttering and organising allow you to focus your limited time, energy and resources on what matters most. Start with clearing your mind, taking care of yourself first and prioritise so that you don't overload yourself.

Say 'no' to things that don't bring you joy with honesty and politeness; you are not put on this earth to complete everyone else's to-do list. Stop saying 'yes' straight away; think about what is being asked of you and whether it fits with what matters most to you, with what you need and deserve. Saying no can be very liberating as it allows you to spend more time on the things that matter most to you and give you more energy. Don't be afraid to do things differently from the crowd, and don't overly care about what other people think of you. Put your own oxygen mask on first because you can't help anyone if you've passed out as well.

The key is to treat others as you would like to be treated yourself; do unto others as you would have them do to you, considering their feelings, happiness and harmony.[829] Start by using the disciplined values you possess so the other person feels nice after meeting you. Life is not a competition with others; it is about coming to terms with yourself and accepting who you are (your strengths and weaknesses) in times of success and failure. If you don't know or acknowledge your weaknesses, how on earth can you address and resolve them?

Make decisions rationally, not when you are emotionally charged; deal with the things you can control or prevent happening, not the things you can't; chase joy not happiness, because if you have joy, happiness will follow; worrying doesn't change anything, you need to take action to fix things; don't worry about the future, it may not happen.

The secret to time management is creating a strategy and associated set of actions to focus you on achieving your goals in small, manageable steps that you can commit to. Expect degrees of difficulty along your journey and keep something in reserve to deal with them. It is our attitude at the beginning of a difficult task that informs its successful outcome. Success doesn't come from what you do occasionally, but from what you do consistently[168]; people of mediocre ability sometimes achieve outstanding success because they don't know when to quit.[830] Most people succeed simply because they are determined to. Most people can do awe-inspiring things, they just need a little nudge.

I love starting something, it can be very satisfying. My dad was a great starter, but not-so-great a finisher, especially on jobs he started around the house. I love that quote from Douglas Adams[516] when he said that he 'loved deadlines. The whooshing noise they make as they go by'.

Everyone starts with a white belt, seeing more competent teammates, finding themselves in over their heads and trying things they've never done before and failing. You just need to start properly, listen, learn and practise. One of the hardest things to start doing is loving yourself; self-care and self-love are the answers to all your questions, for there you will find self-appreciation, kindness and compassion. Until you can practise fully loving and honouring yourself, how can you choose things, people and situations that are right for you and can move you forward? You need to make sure you have got all the basics right and chosen a watertight boat before you start sailing into the middle of the ocean to rescue or even find others. Everyone has choices; stop pleasing people and seeking happiness in broken relationships, set boundaries and start making more courageous and conscious decisions. That is how to sail safely into the ocean and get back in one piece; you may even start enjoying being with yourself.

Sacrificing

Whatever you are working towards will need an element of sacrifice. Although anything of real value in this world is freely provided, your goal will need paying either with your time or your resources to care and nurture it. Never forget that the harder something is to find, the more precious and beautiful it has the potential to be.

The process of elimination is the first step towards determining your identity by defining who you are not. Who you are not is just as important as who you are. Let's jettison the computer screen that stops us getting out in the world so we can spend more time with our families and having human interaction. Jettison those unhealthy foods we eat; stop giving bad things and people our energy and time. Stop going to places where bad things live so you can spend more time in the good places that bring you joy.

There are things worth making sacrifices for, and there are others that are not. Be very, very specific about what you want to sacrifice things for. There are often too many options; get rid of the excess and reduce your choices. Focus on what is important to you; it will help you find out where you should be and what you should be doing. Your hands can't hold everything; to pick something up you will have to put something else down. Not everything is worth keeping or dying for.

You must go through the pain to get to the gain of being changed by it. Let everything happen to you, both beauty and terror, and just keep going, for no feeling is final. We need, in love, to practise the art of letting each other go. Holding on comes easily; we do not need to learn it.[831] Perhaps all the dragons in our lives are princesses who are only waiting to see us act, just once, with beauty, courage and sacrifice.[381] There is no better way to die than facing fearful odds, for the ashes of your fathers, the temples of your gods, to sacrifice yourself so others can survive.[286]

We have to sacrifice to achieve what we want. Sacrifices teach us how to prioritise our values and goals, they challenge us to be creative and resourceful.[832] The value of sacrifice is in teaching us that making sacrifices is never easy, because all things, situations and events have their own importance.[833] Sacrifice is to withhold from or forfeit something for a greater cause. You're not just giving something up; you are exchanging it for greater good.[834]

There are three types of pain: pain that hurts (including grief, loss and attachment issues), pain that alters and thus teaches, and pain that endures, never goes away and is a constant. Understanding the different types of pain means you can deal with, mitigate or accept it in the right way for you.

I sincerely pray that whatever is causing you pain, anguish or stress will pass or subside. May your negative thoughts, excessive worries and doubts disappear and be replaced with self-care, clarity and understanding. May your cup of life be filled with inner peace, tranquillity and love for others. Remember, you are never alone.

I've sacrificed many hours to study to get to where I am now. Preparation for each test, each exam, each qualification. Each one building strength, character and knowledge. One exam I initially failed, but all my colleagues gave me the determination to pass the next time. All I was told by my employer at the time was that I had passed. Years later, someone told me that, eventually, someone had got a higher grade than me, and that my employer had been holding me up as an example for years, without my knowledge. I sacrificed a lot for that employer, but it was never acknowledged to my face. But that's life. Make sure your sacrifices are worthy of your time, effort and resources, for not all are.

Urgency

You need to have a sense of urgency to get things done, and each step you take should be one closer to the place you want to be. Start counting down not up, this creates a sense of urgency as it has a clear end, as opposed to counting up, which can go on forever.

What you focus on is what you get. The path from *can* to *want* requires that you ask yourself, 'Do I really want this?' Be discerning. Do it because you want it. Actions speak louder than words, so hold yourself accountable.[835] Noble intentions should be checked periodically against results.[66] Reflection is valuable but, unlike Hamlet, you need to *act* on it. Life is simple; everything happens for you, not to you. It all happens at exactly the right moment, neither too soon nor too late.[284]

Bliss comes in waves, so look for it all the time otherwise you will miss it. Set and maintain an intention as strong and sure as a guiding beam of light sent from a lighthouse, because that is the way to get things done. Our need to consume things and our tendency to overthink can get in the way; get out of your own way, live in the present, forgive yourself, be at one with your god and move on. Focus on what is in front of your eyes and give things the justice they deserve.

Put yourself in a place for the truth to find you. Remove yourself from the noise – prayer, meditation, a road trip, being with friends. Personalise the truth in terms of how it works for you, how it applies to you and how you need it in your life. Have the patience to germinate ideas; they will soon emerge from the mind and evolve into bones and soul. Then comes the time for courage, the time to act, to take it into your daily life and practise it so that it becomes part of who you are. That is when good things happen, when what we want becomes what we need.

There are times when you should tell yourself to 'go for it' in the sternest voice, but just because you are doing more, doesn't mean you are getting more done. Don't confuse movement with progress; busy does not equal productive. Rushing into things without prior planning or commitment is just as dangerous as procrastination.

When I was a student, I was woken one night by the fire alarm going off. Thinking it was another false alarm, I opened my bedroom door and was immediately engulfed in smoke. Some automated process took over as I started shouting 'fire, fire, fire', to wake my peers and get them to leave the flat. Through the smoke, I made my way to the kitchen to check that everyone had left, only to see my neighbour drunk and asleep on a chair in front of the flaming cooker. He had attempted to cook some sausages in a drunken state and had fallen into a deep sleep. I shook him and shouted at him to wake him and get him out of the flat, threw a fire blanket over the cooker, left the building last and called the fire service while everyone around me was in a state of transfixed shock. I made my way to the road outside our flat to direct the fire service to the entrance and opened the automatically-locking doors to allow them in. I breathed in a lot of smoke that evening and felt unwell later, but recovered the next day. Fear hadn't come into it. I knew what needed to be done, and just did it. Did I save a life? I don't know, but I did help people and save a bad situation from getting worse, without any expectation of thanks, gratitude or reward. It is the deeds that make the man. There is no need to fear at the end of the day, for everything will unfold in divine order. Everyone and everything has a purpose in life; sometimes it means just doing little things.

Failing

Success feels great but it can be temporary. There is always someone who will be faster, more successful and achieve more than you. Success dulls the edge, whilst failure can sharpen it.

Don't focus totally and negatively on failure, or talk only of your flaws and limitations – this is how to become disillusioned. We try our best, but don't always do our best. Learn from each failure what you are good at and what you can succeed at and seek constructive feedback. Don't use negative words like 'can't', replace them with 'can't *yet*'. This attitude has a positive impact on the unconscious mind, which plays a large part in who we are and what we do; it can't tell the difference between what is real or imagined.

Life has a very strange way of pointing you in a certain direction; failure is an opportunity to stand back and reconsider whether you are heading along the right path. Life doesn't give up its secrets easily; things worth fighting for are worth more than things given to us or achieved with ease. Failure helps make us the people we are. It changes us, making us better versions of ourselves. As architects of our own lives, our actions feed our successes, but we're not perfect, so don't expect to get things right first time. All great successes come from multiple fails and repeats.

Failures often result in things being modified, iterated and improved until they achieve the required state of quality or performance. Perhaps individual personalities can't be changed, but one's outlook on life can be. The secret lies in learning to take advantage of bad times.[238] Learning to fail faster so you can recover faster, and get to where you want to be faster than the competition, is a great skill to learn; once you've learnt how to fail, you understand a key change accelerator, because you can avoid repeating it. Picking yourself up, taking ownership and moving on is how you become empowered and stop falling into self-pity, self-loathing and guilt. The way you respond to failure says more about who you are as a person than the way you respond to success. The victors of the last war fight their new enemy with their old tactics. Having previously prevailed, they are content with the approach to battle that worked for them, whereas the vanquished want to know why they lost. Don't be defined by your successes, they are only road signs on your journey; dissect your successes with gratitude, find out what they mean, where they are taking you.

Unsuccessful people daydream a lot, avoid being in the driver's seat and don't want to listen to other people's opinions nor learn from their own mistakes. Unsuccessful people often don't take care of themselves, both physically and mentally, and doubt their abilities because they are unaware of how much potential they have to achieve.

Sometimes it takes a good failure to really know where you stand – I can laugh because I have known sadness. I want you to promise me something: if you love someone, you will tell them – even if you're scared or it will cause problems, even if you think it will burn your life to the ground – say it and say it loud, then go from there.[431]

Never apologise for being sensitive or emotional – it is a sign that you have a big heart and aren't afraid to let others see it. Showing your emotions is a sign of strength.[333] The best and most beautiful things in the world cannot be seen or even touched; they must be felt with the heart. The emotion that can break your heart is sometimes the very one that heals it. Pity those who don't feel anything at all.[837] The world is a tragedy to those who feel, but a comedy to those who think.[482] A feeling is no longer the same when it comes the second time. It dies through the awareness of its return. We become tired and weary of our feelings when they come too often and last too long.[836] Our emotions make us human; even the unpleasant ones have a purpose. Don't lock them away. If you ignore them, they just get louder and angrier. In order to move on, you must understand why you felt what you did and why you no longer need to feel it.[836] Holding on to anger is like drinking poison and expecting the other person to die with you.[840]

The secret of being happy is accepting where you are in life and making the most out of every day.[838] The struggle you are in today is developing the strength you will need tomorrow. Life is not lost by dying; life is lost minute by minute, day by dragging day, in all the thousand small, uncaring ways.[839]

Love is the most powerful emotion, and that makes it the most dangerous. No one cares how much you know until they know how much you care. Most relationships don't die from natural causes but are killed by selfishness, neglect, lack of consideration, lies and secrets. Life is not about being rich, popular or the best looking; it's about being real, humble and kind. One thing you can't hide is when you're crippled inside.[836]

Some things that attempt to come into being are before their time, and so you will struggle to bring them forth. I've run projects where I've tried to create items in advance of when they are ready to be accepted, and failed. But there is nothing wrong with failing; I used the opportunity to make the items better, improve communications and better articulate their value and benefits. Very few things are made on the first attempt, and the effort you put into things is a reward of its own. Failing is a proven fast-track method of getting to a better solution.

Winning

Let me tell you something you already know: the world isn't all sunshine and rainbows, it's a mean and nasty place. I don't care how tough you are, it will beat you to your knees and keep you there permanently, if you let it.[437] Nobody can hit you as hard as life, but like Rocky Balboa said, it isn't about how hard you hit, it's about how much you can take and keep moving forward.

The difference between winning and losing can be very small. Being perfect is not about achieving a perfect score. Life is not about winning – it's about you and your relationship with yourself, your family and your friends. Nobody can be perfect when it's defined according to unrealistic standards or by comparing yourself to others; this only creates suffering. Being perfect is not about the scoreboard. Being perfect is being able to look your friends in the eye and know that you didn't let them down, because you told them the truth, that you did everything you could, that there was not one more thing that you could have done.[176]

Once you have achieved, you need to decide where to go next, and that can be very difficult. Do you press on to a higher peak? Or, satisfied that you have done your part, do you walk back down the mountain and pass the baton to others to continue the race while you look for the next challenge? If you only think about the peaks and valleys in life, you will forget to live where we spend most of our time – between the high and low points. Look out the window and see the beauty of the present wherever you are and whatever you are doing.

If you are driven by fear, anger or pride, nature will force you to compete. If you are guided by courage, awareness, tranquillity and peace, nature will serve you.[374] Real winning is about living a fulfilling life, helping others, sharing and realising your true purpose. We need to redefine winning so that it means more than individual accomplishments, but team, community and universal accomplishments as well; too often, winning is achieved at all costs and irrespective of the means. People look for greatness only in the extraordinary and completely overlook the wonder of the ordinary.[841] Sometimes, a miracle can be just getting through each day, because it requires almost superhuman strength. Progress and winning are the natural results of staying focused on the process of doing anything.

To be alive is power and winning at the same time. Where there is life there is hope; taking personal accountability is a beautiful thing because it gives us complete control of our destinies.[411] You can't wait around for something to become good, it either is or isn't.[13] There is no tomorrow and no yesterday; if you truly want to accomplish your goals you must engulf yourself in today.

There is more than enough winning to go around. The real things of value are those that money can't buy. Unlike material things, which are finite, there is no limit to the amount of love, compassion, trust, support, forgiveness, care, happiness, beauty, humour, joy, respect and peace that can exist in this world. Believe in the wonderment of life, the magic of love and the reality of death.[62] The magic of each day lives in the unknown, the most beautiful experience we can have is to exist within that mystery.[376]

There are four types of play that teach the rules of what play is: unoccupied play (a baby learning body movements), solitary play, spectator/onlooker play, parallel play. Associated and cooperative play (socially induced concepts to prepare the individual for a life of work, play and societal introduction, acceptance and contribution) are where we learn the concepts of winning, succeeding, planning, preparing and practice. We are expected to move up from novice, through beginner, to proficient and aim towards expert, which comprises purpose and autonomy. Only some people become true masters through mindfulness, though there are a lot of false masters who followed a path of corruption, complacency and criminality.

Society expects and rewards winners, and undervalues the benefits of losing, of failure and the power of regret, learning, reflection and retrying. It is physically and virtually impossible to be right first time, especially when you are trying something new (yet we continue to set unrealistic expectations). Failing helps you learn what doesn't work for you; prototyping helps de-risk future endeavours based on this and teaches you to move off the wrong path towards a better one, or improve the current path for the time being. You will need to take many different paths, routes and methods to get to where you want to go. Some never get there; they get stuck on the same path that leads only to a dead end. We are all different, so what works for one may not necessarily work for you. Choosing to fail, to allow others to experience winning, is one of the most beautiful things to witness.

Finally, there is the draw, the playing for fun, exercise and mutual benefit, to experience the joy of joint celebration, the win-win of every action and transaction. This is linked to big-picture thinking, understanding its effects on society, the environment and the world, and considering and addressing the law of unintended consequences.

Understanding the different types of play allows you understand the effect your thoughts and actions have on others, in all aspects of your life. Take a moment to think how they affect others, and what it must feel like from their perspective. At the end of the day, we are all connected, we just don't realise how deep this connection goes; all we see is the surf on top of the unimaginably deep ocean.

Planning

The true definition of waste is spending the majority of your time in the past or future, and rarely living in the reality of now.[10]

Everything has a past, be it a person, an object or a word. *Everything.* If you don't know the past, you can't understand the present and plan properly for the future. Acquiring wisdom is great, but the goal is to apply it. The intelligent have plans; the wise have principles. When you establish a destination by defining what you want, then take physical action by making choices that move you towards it, the possibility for success is limitless and arrival at the destination is inevitable.[298]

A goal without a plan is just a wish.[192] All successful people are big dreamers. They imagine, in every aspect, what their future could be, then they work every day toward that distant vision, goal or purpose. A clear vision backed by definite plans gives you a tremendous feeling of confidence and personal power.

Is it dangerous to plan too much? Yes. We all need to have a plan, but life goes on regardless, and we know all too well what happens to so many of the best laid plans of mice and men.[72] Plans are of little importance, but planning is essential.[134] If you don't know exactly where you're going, how will you know when you get there? All human plans are subject to ruthless revision by Nature, Fate or whatever one prefers to call the powers behind the Universe.[95]

Sometimes you just need to dive into the water and swim. Breathe, trust, let go and see what happens.[845] Elegance under pressure is the result of fearlessness.[846] In the planning stage of a book, don't plan the ending; it has to be earned by all that will go before it.[460] You will never be fully ready, it's just a leap of faith at the end of the day, that's all it is. You don't always need a plan. Without leaps of imagination or dreaming, we lose the excitement of possibilities. Dreaming, after all, is a form of planning.[439]

Life is not fair and sometimes things don't go to plan. You can talk all you want about having a clear purpose and strategy for your life, but ultimately this means nothing if you are not investing the resources you have in a way that is consistent with your strategy. In the end, a strategy is nothing but good intentions unless it is effectively implemented.[92]

The majority of people don't want the responsibility of planning. They want to be free of it. What they ask for is merely some assurance that they will be decently provided for.[430] However, with adequate planning, passion and perseverance, you can achieve the loftiest of goals. Each day, wake up with a plan. Don't just approach your days in an unfocused void, as that state of mind leaves too much room for discontent, opposition, unhappiness and hopelessness.[847] Discover a purpose that gives you passion; develop a plan that makes you persistent. Design and prepare to motivate you to optimise your potential. Spontaneity is one of the joys of existence, especially if you prepare for it in advance.[169]

Two things seem to have been crucial in tipping the outcomes of some of history's greatest achievers: long-term planning and the flexibility to reconsider their next move with a Plan B if it all goes south. If you put your faith in slow, deliberative planning in the hopes it will spare you failure down the line, you're deluding yourself. The time to repair the roof is when the sun is shining.[253]

It does not do to dwell on dreams and forget to live.[396] You will never reach your true potential living solely in comfort and routine – you've got to take some calculated risks. Take the risk or lose the chance. If you are not willing to risk the usual, you will have to settle for the ordinary.[390] Only those who will risk going too far can possibly find out how far they can go.[135] If it's still in your mind after planning, then it is worth taking the risk for. The biggest risk a person can take is to do nothing.[428] Be brave, but take educated not mindless or careless risks, because that is how great achievements are made. You cannot swim for new horizons until you have courage to lose sight of the shore.[141] If you don't go out on the branch, you're never going to get the best fruit.[344] Living with fear stops us taking risks; move out of your comfort zone. You can grow if you are willing to feel awkward and uncomfortable when you try something new.

When you do the things in the present that you can see, you are shaping the future that you are yet to see. A man may plant a tree for a number of reasons: perhaps he likes trees, wants shelter, or he knows that someday he may need the firewood. Someone's sitting in the shade today because someone planted a tree a long time ago.[66]

Remember: life is what happens to us while we are making other plans.[842] By failing to prepare, you are preparing to fail[843]; if you don't know where you are going, you'll end up someplace else.[474] Plans are useless, but planning is indispensable.[134] You can't plough a field simply by turning it over in your mind; unless commitment is made, there are only promises and hopes, no plans.[844]

Don't expect any strategy, plan or schedule to survive contact with reality, the enemy or the universal forces. For life is not meant to come easy to us; we are destined to work for what we need because then we appreciate and care for what we have that much more. The Universe is far more complex than our simple minds, so to expect that we can map out our future in nice, easy steps is naïve. There are inherent errors and assumptions in our thinking, incoming issues just over the horizon and significant internal and external forces beyond our control. Plans must be robust enough to adapt to change and the unforeseen.

Expect plans to change. Plans are full of wild assumptions, predictions, constraints, leadership expectations, unknowns, risks and vagaries. I've never delivered an initial plan to cost, schedule or scope, because plans never survive contact with reality, required improvements, other opportunities or the human spirit to succeed in the face of adversity.

Organising

Organising isn't about perfection, it's about efficiency, getting things in the right order, reducing stress and clutter, saving time and money and improving your overall quality of life.[407] It is being in control, and with it comes empowerment. It isn't about getting rid of everything you own or trying to become a different person, but living better by being the best version of yourself.

Decluttering can be overwhelming, so start by getting rid of one small thing. Clean out your junk drawers and you'll soon find yourself clearing the rest of the house. The first step to getting what you want is having the courage to get rid of what you don't. If you have something you haven't used in six months, then it's probably clutter. This isn't just limited to what you can see on the outside, it's about how it makes you feel on the inside. Clutter is chaos. It's a suffocating presence that robs us of peace and joy. To truly cherish the things that are important to you, you must first discard those things that have outlived their purpose. The space in which we live should be for the person we are now and are becoming, not for the person we were.[260]

The difference between who you are and who you want to be is *what* you do.[356] Don't be busy, be organised. Organising always seems impossible until it's done. It's not about changing your personality, just your habits – a place for everything and everything in its place.[170] Getting organised is easy, staying that way requires discipline. Cleaning and organising are practices not projects. A minute spent organising is an hour earnt. Good order is the foundation of all things.[70] Nobody ever regrets organising their house. If you want to improve your life immediately, clean out a closet. Often what we hold on to holds us back.[379] Getting organised is a sign of self-respect.

Imagine yourself living in a space that only contains things that spark joy. Have nothing in your house which is neither useful nor beautiful. Tidying allows you to tend to your psychological and spiritual spaces. Strive not to get more done, but to have less to do.[233]

Any fool can get wet. A little organising, reviewing of previous lessons and critical thinking about what lies ahead can go a long way.

Controlling

When you try to control everything, you enjoy nothing and control nothing.

People who feel the need to control others don't have control over themselves. It's not what you say to everyone else that determines your life, it's what you whisper to yourself that has the greatest power.[85] You have the real control. Controlling people often demean or criticise others as a way of building themselves up and appearing superior. In fact, a controlling person is easy to spot from the constant monologue about how rotten, stupid, evil, ridiculous and annoying everyone else is, on the presumption that they are never any of these things themselves.

Start every day with an attitude of gratitude. You always have the choice to be happy. You alone get to choose what matters and what doesn't; the meaning of everything in your life has precisely the meaning you give it. If you can stay positive in a negative situation, you win. Learn to understand the purpose of bumps in the road, grow from them and stay positive.

Control your own destiny or someone else will.[493] Challenge yourself to control the way you respond to what's happening – that's where your power is.[849] You can't control other people's reactions, you can only control your own. Nor can you control what goes on externally, just what goes on inside of you. No man is fit to command another who cannot command himself. Self-control is strength, calmness is mastery.[395] Don't allow others to control the direction of your life or permit your emotions to overpower your intelligence.[850] True power is restraint. Breathe, and allow things to pass. Self-control is taking the emotion out, sitting back and observing things with logic.

Know the difference between guiding and controlling. Guiding is done with *their* best intentions, while controlling is done with *your* best intentions. Abusive relationships are characterised by control, games, violence, jealousy or emotional blackmail. When it comes to relationships, less control equals more freedom and engenders trust. If there's no trust, there's no connection. Controllers, abusers and manipulative people don't question themselves or consider the problem is them – it's always someone else who is at fault. An emotionally abusive man is skilled in making you think you aren't good enough or that everything is your fault. It is just as difficult to recover from emotional abuse as it is from physical abuse.[851]

Be aware that your mind is controlling you most of the time, and don't let it. To be happy or not is a matter of your mind, your choices and actions. The thoughts coming to your mind are just thoughts: don't let them control you, make you sad or accept what shouldn't be accepted. Simply let them go.

There is a lot of mistrust of global monopolies and industries, especially to do with the perceived control they have. Most of the time, Big Business, Big Government and Big Banking operate as they are designed to do. However, we must maintain the free press using Big Media and Big Journalism to shine lights into their dark corners. Hollywood entertains but should never be allowed to rewrite history or blur the lines between fact and fiction for secret agendas. Big Pharma manipulates regulations to keep natural, cost-effective remedies out of the marketplace, putting profits before patients. Big Oil keeps the world moving, but its fossil fuels damage the planet. The creation and disposal of plastics has still to be addressed, together with how slowly we are transitioning to more sustainable materials; these issues are not helped by them buying up competing patents that threaten their sector, and causing environmental scandals, all to maintain control and profit. Big Tobacco is shifting from their traditional products to smokable hemp. Big Agriculture controls the strains of seeds, and virtually all aspects of the food chain, blocking other more sustainable competitors from entry into markets.

Every industry, and their effect on the environment, really needs looking at. From Big Paper (Forestry and Logging) and Big Coal/Big Hole (Mining) to Big Car (Automakers), they are all trashing the environment and are major carbon-dioxide emitters. Big Pot (Drugs and Criminal) is the other often-neglected monopoly that ruins lives and fills prisons with worker bees whilst the kingpins walk free. Big Tobacco, Big Chemical and Big Food (everything we ingest) are slowly poisoning us with disinformation, unnecessary fillers, salts, sugars, fats, preservatives, artificial flavours, packaging and microplastics, their lack of quality control and accountability, overuse of pesticides, antibiotics and growth hormones. This is all before we talk about monopolisation, the lack of competition, environmental degradation, animal welfare, government lobbying and manipulation, supply chain control and the prioritisation of obscene profits and maximum efficiency over quality and associated public health issues.[852] If we are ever to get back to a sustainable way of life, these 'Bigs' need to operate not only for financial benefits, but also for the social and spiritual wellbeing of humanity.

Silence may be a source of great strength, but we should never remain silent about the things that really matter. Each person dies a little every time they refuse to stand up for what is right. We need to take control of ourselves, our minds, bodies and our souls, so we can take the right path to creating better societies and governments, and a better world for the future.

Technology is a powerful, multifaceted tool that can manipulate and influence people as well as affect the arrangement of power in our cultures and societies. But while it is not intrinsically good or bad, technology can't act independently of human action. The impacts and effects it has on people depends on how it is wielded. It can assist kids in working together, help teachers motivate students and be used to inform, inspire, empower and initiate change. However, it often uses partial or flawed data, and makes assumptions and predictions using algorithms that humans are losing control of due to their complexity and the sheer number of computational instructions being run every second.

Everything around us is beginning to look like it isn't part of the natural world. We create our tailored worlds within the world, for we have gone beyond just neglecting nature to a relationship that is now totally dysfunctional. Every decision is driven by greed, ignorance or apathy, and the biggest lie we've been sold is that we can't afford to care about the natural world until we're all rich. That is never going to happen. Our modern lives have become so disconnected from nature; we are destroying our ecosystems upon which everything depends for survival.

I have serious doubts that economics and technology will ever save us; we need to start thinking of a Third Way to save us all. A way in which we rebuild our connection to nature, care about it thriving, and protect and restore the resources we have used for future generations that don't currently have a voice. When nature turns on humanity, don't expect any mercy.

CHAPTER 11

It is how we react that matters.

"When you need to handle yourself you must use your head, to handle others you must use your heart."

—Eleanor Roosevelt[392] (Modified)

Action and reaction, ebb and flow, this is the rhythm of living. You can't change how people treat you or what they say about you, but you do have the power to decide how you're going to react to it.[386] It is not necessary to react to everything, sometimes it's better not to react at all. This chapter looks at aspects of reactions, kindness, confrontation, confidence, smiles, reflections, influence, regrets and loyalty.

Reacting

The three responses to threats are freezing, running away and hiding, or confrontation. This last response is associated with the growth mindset (suppressing the amygdala and encouraging the neurochemical dopamine reward pathway), where the decision to take some physical action, even just a lateral eye movement, pushes you across that fear threshold and instantly rewards you. These responses are ancient, hardwired mechanisms in the brain, installed by Mother Nature for our survival and wellbeing.

Life is 10% what happens to you and 90% how you react to it.[853] When you can't control what's happening, challenge yourself to control the *way* you respond,[854] for that is where your power lies! Don't get upset with people or situations; both are powerless without your reaction.[230] Sometimes the best thing to do is nothing.

You are in charge of how you react to the people and events. You can either give negativity power over your life or you can choose happiness instead. Take control and choose to focus on what is important. Those who cannot live fully often become destroyers of life.[335]

Maturity doesn't refer to age: it is your sensitivity, manners and how you react. Resilience is how you react, respond to and recover from what has just happened to you. There may be a 'normal' or a common way to react to different things, but that's mostly all it is; people are often dazed and confused when you react differently from how they were expecting you to. This gives you the power and time to respond in a far more appropriate manner. You're only responsible for being honest, not for someone else's reaction to your honesty.

Ethics are the principles or rules for how we act in the world, but they are only a guide; you can choose what you believe to be the right response. The thing is, it doesn't matter whether or not the person 'had it coming'; what matters is your behaviour, not theirs, your ethics, not theirs. It's the way *you* conduct yourself, not the way they conduct themselves. How people treat you is their karma, while how you react is yours. Your environment shapes who you are, but how you handle emergencies, or how you react when someone is rude to you, that's up to you. We must all learn to act, not react.

Most distraction doesn't start outside us, but from within. The root causes are internal triggers and uncomfortable emotional states from which we seek to escape, and so we do things against our better judgement. We need to go back to the first principles of why we do anything and start to understand the nature of human motivation. The common understanding is that we respond to avoid pain, and perhaps in the pursuit of pleasing others. However, at a neurological level we only do something to avoid discomfort or regain physiological homeostasis. The same applies to uncomfortable psychological sensations we seek solutions to. We must remember that we are always trying to escape discomfort when we become distracted, and so must learn new methods to deal with it. A person who never made a mistake never tried anything new.[848] We are not built to be bored or to do nothing, but to discover, experience fresh feelings and improve our lot in life. If we harness our restlessness, it can help us be inventive and desire to do more good. We should not want, crave or desire; channel these internal triggers into traction rather than distraction.

We have more information and power at our fingertips than ever before, so there should be no excuse for not doing something. However, we lack the ability to follow through and the training to avoid being distracted, especially when our technology has been designed to be pervasive and persuasive. It is easier than ever to get distracted, for we have become slaves to artificially constructed, perceived 'urgent' activities at the cost of critical activities linked to the health of our own hearts and souls. If we accept distractions, we develop learned helplessness, where we think there is nothing we can do and so stop even trying to focus. The key to being happy is knowing you have the power to choose what to accept and what to let go of.[855]

Strict abstinence is to stop something completely. But we always need to feel something, so it often leads to a behaviour backfire response, especially of the very behaviours we are trying to avoid. The sensation of giving in relieves the discomfort of telling yourself not to do something; we inadvertently re-wire our brains to anticipate that giving in feels so pleasurable, not because the behaviour itself is pleasurable but because it relieves us of the discomfort of privation.

So, strict abstinence often backfires. Rather than saying 'no', try employing the ten-minute rule – tell yourself you can have whatever you're craving, but you just have to wait ten minutes to reflect on the sensation first – talking to yourself with compassion and not blaming or shaming, as you would with a good friend – effectively 'surfing the urge', which is often enough to override temporary impulses. Remember, emotions don't last forever; they are like incoming waves that eventually subside. Surfing your urges and emotions, like a surfer riding a wave, won't make you contemptuous, but curious. This is a simple yet effective technique, but is not a solution for everything. If you are in serious trouble, consider talking to a professional. You are never alone nor too far from someone who can help you.

The id, ego and super-ego are three interacting agents in your mental life. Understanding of intercultural human behaviour and reactions is thought to be founded on the notion of cultural differences, not cultural deficiency. Rudeness, or any behaviour that violates social or organisational norms, is not a universal concept and varies by culture and geographical location; thus, the same action may well prompt different reactions in different places. For instance, patting a child on the head, as one might in Dingle, Ireland, is downright unforgivable in Phnom Penh, Cambodia, where the head is considered to be the seat of the soul.

The concept of duality is a misnomer; there are other ways beyond 'yes' and 'no': 'let me think about it', 'I haven't decided', 'both options don't look good so let me look at alternatives', 'this is the view from your perspective, I have a wider viewpoint and a larger number of variables to consider', 'I must consider the unintended and long-term consequences of these options', 'I prefer to keep my own council and opinions to myself' 'are you feeling alright?', 'this seems a very quick decision to make when we haven't looked at other options', 'I have other commitments that mean I can't participate in this, it's not my problem', 'I wish you all the best, but my path is in a different direction', 'I don't want to be tied down at this moment', 'I'll wait until God shows me what to decide', 'this isn't even on my radar as a priority, I have other issues to deal with first', 'I'll meditate on it and come back to you', 'that is a decision for another day', 'I'm going to sit on the fence until it develops', 'it is too early for me to decide at this stage', 'you are on your own on this one, best of luck', 'that is your question, not mine'.

The key to any situation is how you react, because that is what you are in control of, if you choose to be. Or you could just let your emotions, ego and primeval nature take the wheel.

Kindness

Kindness is one of the greatest gifts you can bestow upon another person. If someone is in need, lend them a helping hand and do not wait for a thank you; true kindness lies in the act of giving without the expectation of something in return.[208] It is a passport that open doors and fashions friends, it softens hearts and moulds relationships that can last lifetimes.[129] Happiness is the new rich, inner peace the new success, health the new wealth, and kindness the new cool.

Ah, kindness… what a simple way to tell another struggling soul that there's love to be found in the world.[293] Wherever there is need, there is an opportunity for kindness to make a difference.[203] It costs almost nothing but can mean everything. Kindness begins with the understanding that we all struggle. We rise by lifting others. Be kinder to yourself and then let your kindness flood the world.[90] Unexpected kindness is the most powerful, least costly and most underrated agent of human change.[856] Love and kindness are never wasted; they always make a difference. They bless the one who receives them just as they bless the giver.[203]

Kindness is spreading sunshine into other people's lives regardless of the weather.[371] Try and be a rainbow in someone else's cloud.[16] A single act of kindness throws out roots in all directions, and the roots spring up and make new trees.[856]

In a world where you can be anything, be kind. Kindness is the best nourishment for humanity. When you are kind, it not only changes you, it changes the world.[265] It may be the most vital key to the riddle of how human beings can live with each other in peace, and care properly for this planet we all share.[283] Be kind to everything that lives; no act of kindness, no matter how small, is ever wasted.[856]

Cleverness is a gift and natural talent only takes you so far, but kindness is a choice and can take you everywhere. Constant kindness can accomplish much.[856] As the sun melts ice, kindness evaporates misunderstanding, mistrust and hostility. If you have been searching for ways to heal yourself, then kindness is the best way; you cannot do it too soon, for you never know how soon it will be too late.[856] Sometimes, miracles are just good people with kind hearts.

The effect you have on others is the most valuable currency there is.[82] Be the reason someone smiles. Be the reason they feel loved and believe in the goodness of people.[38] Kindness is a gift that everyone can afford to give, and it always matters. The smallest acts of kindness can make the biggest impact.

The kind heart loves deeply and forgives quickly, for there is no room in it for grudges to grow. There is so much goodness in the Universe that there is enough for everyone. Like love, kindness is an infinite resource.

If you want something you've never had, you have to take a risk, follow your intuition, do something you've never done, go somewhere different and put yourself out there. Take one small step forward, don't stay still and definitely don't take any steps back. This will teach you more about yourself, new skills and even new life lessons involving compassion, kindness and sharing. It's called getting out of your comfort zone.

Confrontation

If you don't fight for what you want, how will you ever get it? [45] Knowing is not enough; we must apply and fight for what we believe in. Willing is not enough; we must do what needs to be done.[272]

No one puts it quite like Winston Churchill[93]: 'There are times when we need to stand up and fight to be free, so the life of the world may move forward into broad, sunlit uplands; knowing that, if we fail, then the whole world that we have known and cared for will sink into the abyss of a new dark age made more sinister, and perhaps more prolonged, by the lights of a perverted science. We need to brace ourselves to do our duty and if we survive and last another thousand years, men of the future will say as we have said of others before us, that this was their finest hour. We all have a "finest hour" within us, when linked together in a righteous cause we will be willing to defend to the death our native soils, our previously fought-for freedoms and for those we love. We shall go on to the end, and fight on land, seas, oceans and in the air, on the beaches, in the fields, on the hills and in the streets for what is right; we shall never surrender, even if large parts of the world are subjugated and starving, we shall carry on the struggle, until in God's good time, the new world, with all its powers and might, steps forth to the rescue and the liberation of the old.' [93]

You will never know how strong you are until being strong is the only choice you have. There will be times when you have nothing else to offer but blood, toil, tears and sweat. If you fight hard, know who you are, and are proud of who you are, you've got a good chance of winning.

The biggest fights are with the people you care about the most, because those are the relationships that you're willing to fight for. Be the one to give endless chances and accept people for who they are, even if the rest of the world doesn't.

Don't back a man into a corner without giving him a route to escape; don't underestimate the cornered man nor ever think that the reason people are peaceful is because they don't know how to fight or be violent.

The supreme art of war is to subdue the enemy without fighting, but if you have to fight, victorious warriors win first then fight. The best fighters of old put themselves beyond the possibility of defeat; when they went to war, their plans were as dark and impenetrable as the night, they moved like a thunderbolt and never interrupted the enemy when they were making mistakes. The art of war is of vital importance to everyone as it is a matter of life and death, a road either to safety or to ruin. Hence, it is a subject of inquiry which can on no account be neglected.[468]

Never take your eyes off your opponent or wild beasts, even when you're bowing. Engage people with what they expect, as it is what they are able to discern, and it confirms their projections. This will settle them into predictable patterns of response, occupying their minds while you wait for the extraordinary moment, that which they cannot anticipate, to strike and fight. [895]

He who respects himself is safe from others, he wears a coat of mail that none can pierce. He who will win knows when to fight and when not to fight; the expert in battle moves the enemy and is not moved by him.[468] The successful warrior is the average man, with laser-like focus.

Do not wish for an easy life; pray for the strength to endure a difficult one. Battle against the unjust, work past the pain, overcome the disappointment, forget your doubts, face your fears and educate yourself enough to realise how little you actually know. Good fighters sometimes need to lose the small battles in order to win the war, so pick your battles, don't let others do it for you.

Sometimes you need to go through darkness to get to the light.[302] We don't live in darkness, darkness lives within each one of us. Every person has their secret sorrows, which the world knows not, and oftentimes we call that person cold when they are only sad, because we have not walked in their shoes. Live in each season as it passes, breathe the air, drink the drink, taste the fruit and steel yourself to fight and influence the future earth upon which we rely for the air we breathe, the water we drink and the food we eat.

There are times when we should not advocate for confrontation, when we have to let old feuds die and let personal quarrels be forgotten, to keep our eye and anger directed towards the common enemy. Let personal interests be ignored, let all our energies, the full ability and force of the team, organisation or even nation be harnessed, then we will be unbeatable.

When life has a balance, everything will be better. Your spirit is the true shield; listen to it more often. It never gets easier; you just get better. As you think, so shall you become, so don't say something or think something that you don't mean or are not prepared to do. Know that victory is right around the corner, so never ever give up. If people do give up, understand that it took everything they had out of them and don't judge them for that.

I have found that a soft answer can turn away wrath, but never go so far as to shy away or respond with harsh words and actions because they tend to have the opposite effect and stir up anger. Acknowledge the feelings, share wisdom and respond with control. Be a master at confrontation, always with efficacity, never acting out of any motive but love, and if possible, endeavour to live peaceably with all. Start by attempting a personal one-on-one to tell them their fault. Only escalate if this doesn't work.

Confidence

Confidence doesn't come in a bottle; it is part of your make-up and character, but it can be learned. It is the most beautiful thing you can possess.

A person cannot be comfortable without their own approval. Confidence isn't walking into a room with your nose in the air thinking you are better than everyone else, it's walking into a room and not feeling the need to compare yourself to anyone else in the first place.[469] If someone is judging you, that's their problem, so don't make it yours. Confidence is silent, insecurities are loud. It is not 'will they like me?' but 'I'll be fine if they don't.' The only person you need to compare yourself to is your yesterday self. When you accept your flaws, no one can use them against you.[858]

Whoever is trying to bring you down is already below you. When you start seeing your worth, you'll find it harder to stay around people who don't value themselves. Never apologise for having high standards; the people who really want to be in your life will rise up to meet you.

You can gain strength, courage and confidence by every experience in which you really stop to look fear in the face, when you are able to say to yourself, I can take the next thing that comes along.[392] The quickest way to acquire self-confidence is to do exactly what you are afraid to do.[18] Confidence is like a muscle: the more you use it, the stronger it gets. It is not the mountain we conquer, but ourselves.[213]

Self-confidence is a superpower; once you start believing in yourself, magic starts to happen.[423] So, stop comparing and stay focused on yourself. Relax, go with the flow and don't stress over the little things. Love yourself, you are a gift, and nothing would be the same if you didn't exist. Be positive and look for the good in every situation. Do what you love; life is too short to waste time doing anything otherwise. With the realisation of one's own potential, and self-confidence in one's abilities, one can build a better world. Don't wait – the time will never be *just* right.[212]

It is confidence in our bodies, minds and spirits that allows us to keep looking for new adventures.[503] Your success will be determined by your own confidence and fortitude.[337] If you don't ask, the answer is always no. If you have no confidence in yourself, you are twice defeated in the race of life. Confidence isn't optimism or pessimism, and is not a character attribute, it's the expectation of a positive outcome. Experience tells you what to do, while confidence allows you to do it. As long as you keep going, you'll get better. And as you get better, you gain more confidence. That alone is success.[451]

Don't become over-confident, arrogant or careless. Over-confidence sinks unsinkable ships. Astronauts try very hard not to be over-confident, because it is when you get over-confident that something snaps and bites you; you'll end up having a very bad day, or having to rely on your backup equipment that was built by a contractor who was appointed because they were the lowest-cost bidder.[185]

A flower does not think of competing with the flower next to it, it just blooms.[423] You were born to be real, not perfect. Beauty begins the moment you decide to be yourself[857]; let people see the real, imperfect, flawed, quirky, weird, beautiful and magical person that you are. The most beautiful thing you can wear is confidence.[142] Self-respect, self-worth and self-love all start with looking inside of yourself for your value; nothing can dim the light that shines from within.[16] Too many people overvalue what they are not and undervalue what they are.[164] You may never be good enough for everybody, but you will always be the best for *somebody*.

By creating so many illusory images of physical perfection – whether in shops, magazines, TV or social media – big brands are thinking more of their profit margins than the self-esteem of today's young people, who they don't care about. Confidence is the ability to feel beautiful without needing excessive 'beauty' products or someone to tell you that you are. To all the young people out there: don't worry so much about your weight or other perceived flaws; what matters is what makes you different or weird – it is your strength. Understand that when you buy something genuine it is often expensive because a lot of time and effort has gone into making it; there will be slight imperfections that make it beautifully real and truly unique. When you buy something mass-produced, it is cheap, but quickly manufactured and not built to stand the test of time. Confidence is the genuine, and realness is the best fashion accessory.

Smile and let everyone know that today you're stronger than you were yesterday.[124] Be a girl or boy with adventure, a lady or gentleman with confidence and a woman or man with bravery.

Never apologise for being sensitive or emotional. Showing your emotions is a sign of strength.[420] Let others see that you've got a big heart and aren't afraid to show it.

Confidence comes from being able to admit who you are and what you've done, and loving yourself for who you've become. For the person you are today, you need to thank the person you were five years ago for not giving up. Be faithful to that which exists within you[311]; embrace the glorious mess you are. You are unique.

We can all achieve something great and influential in life. Of course, hard work and persistence are parts of the puzzle, but above all, we need to have confidence to remind us that everything is possible. Remember, every great thing in the world starts with just one belief, and there is always the person who perceives the dream for the first time, who thinks beyond the possibilities. Confidence has no competition and is the key to success and a sound future. Confident feelings drive a person to life fulfilment and create a belief in their actions. The confidence to do something big starts with a hint of self-worth; it is the key to success and a sound future and is probably the most important thing in your life, as without faith in yourself nothing can happen. Keep reminding yourself, 'I can and I will do it.'[469]

Having the confidence to focus on the important things in life, such as education, is a necessity. Having goals, a strong work ethic, the power of determination, real friendships, family and health is everything. Helping others (if you are reading this, it is no coincidence) is the key. What is not often spoken about is the power of being sure and keeping up your strength, even through the difficult times in your life; everything will work out. Rest assured that God is always on your side.

Remember: time is money; take time to present a token of gratitude every day; life is not all work, so entertain loved ones periodically; take timely and quality rest; work on your self-confidence; smile more; seek inner happiness; have a life purpose and develop a passion for it; you are the most important thing in life; make good memories to live by and recall with joy; seek great things from challenges and rough times (you might learn something about yourself or get redirected onto your right path); maintain a positive approach to life; seek to achieve self-awareness, so you know yourself every day; and we each have our own 'most important thing', perception and approach to life.[469]

I wasn't great at school, I just worked very hard to get through each challenge without thinking too far ahead. To be honest, I wasn't really great at anything, though I was a good swimmer. I wasn't lazy, I was an under-confident, late developer. I did work hard and try my best, and managed to get the minimum number of required achievements to allow me to proceed to the next level. I just kept going and going and have never stopped, all the time growing in confidence, skills and experience. I'd like to keep on going for as long as I can, putting my mind, body and soul into things I enjoy doing that also help others. I know people who are so confident that they know exactly how many hours of study are needed to pass a test, and then do that absolute minimum, knowing they will pass. They thrive on that kind of experience. I'm not like that; I now like to have a little safety margin built in.

We all have different confidence levels and they can vary depending on our circumstances. That is one of the great things I love about life, the fact we are all different. How boring the world would be if we were all the same.

Smile

If you're reading this: congratulations, you're alive! If that's not something to smile about, then I don't know what is.[447]

Smiling is the best way to face every problem, to crush every fear, to hide every pain.[432] I love those who can smile in trouble.[104] A smile doesn't always stand for a perfect life.[432] When things are difficult, smile with faith. Don't wait until you feel better, smiling is one of the best remedies. Sometimes your joy is the source of your smile, but sometimes your smile can be the source of your joy.[502] The real man smiles in trouble, gathers strength from distress, and grows brave by reflection.[343] The robbed person who smiles steals something from the thief.[419]

Peace begins with a smile.[326] Smile at strangers and you just might change a life.[298] A simple smile, that's the start of opening your heart and being compassionate to others.[105] A gentle word, a kind look, a good-natured smile, can work wonders and accomplish miracles.[419] Use your smile to change the world; don't let the world change your smile.[88]

If you have only one smile in you, give it to the people you love.[16] Your smile makes life more beautiful.[199] A smile is happiness you'll find right under your nose.[309] Lighten up, enjoy life, smile and laugh more, and don't get so worked up about things. Smile, smile, smile – it will considerably reduce your mind's tension.

Don't cry because it's over, smile because it happened.[123] Never regret something that made you smile.[466] You'll find that life is still worthwhile, if you smile.[391] Look back, and smile on perils past.[415] Keep smiling, even if things are going badly.

I eat every two hours. I sleep for eight hours. I have lots of water. I pray to keep calm. But most importantly, I have a smile on my face.[28] The greatest self-care is a peaceful smile that always sees the world smiling back.[309]

A mother told her child that every time you smile, a very tiny bit of the smile stays stuck to your face, so as you get older your face starts to show all the tiny bits of all your smiles and you look like you are smiling all the time, even when you are just thinking about what to have for breakfast. She also said that if you frown a lot, the frown sticks to your face and you look cross all the time and people are scared of you. Wrinkles should merely indicate where smiles have been.[466]

A smile can move mountains; it can also break hearts.[414] Always find opportunities to make someone smile, and to offer random acts of kindness.[38] Smile more; smiling can make you and others happy.[441] Strong people are those who can smile for others' happiness.[368]

Be the living expression of God's kindness: kindness in your face, kindness in your eyes, kindness in your smile.[326] Everyone smiles in the same language[484]; it is the universal welcome.[131] Children, with their playful smiles, show the divine in everyone. Share your smile with the world; it's a symbol of friendship and peace.[53]

Let us always meet each other with a smile, for a smile is the beginning of love.[326] Every time you smile at someone it is an act of love, a gift to that person, and a beautiful thing.[326] A smiling face is a beautiful face; a smiling heart is a happy heart.[87] The people who make you smile from just seeing them, those are my favourite people.[172] If you see someone without a smile, give them one of yours.[469] Nothing shakes the smiling heart.[244] A smile is the key that fits the lock of everybody's heart.[103] A smile is a friend maker.[195]

Keep a smile on your face and let your personality be your autograph.[469] When life gives you a hundred reasons to cry, show life that you have a thousand reasons to smile.[469] It only takes a split second to smile and forget, yet to someone who needs it, it can last a lifetime.[298] Today, give a stranger one of your smiles – it might be the only sunshine they see all day.[56] It's hard not to feel happy when you make someone smile.[38]

Nothing you wear is more important than your smile.[443] Smile, it increases your face value.[200] If you can't sing and dance, then smile a lot.[98] Before you put on a frown, make absolutely sure there are no smiles available.[35]

If you're not using your smile, you're like a man with a million dollars in the bank and no cheque book.[181] Beauty is power; a smile is its sword.[375] A smile remains the most inexpensive gift I can bestow on anyone and yet its powers can vanquish kingdoms.[296] Let my soul smile through my heart and my heart smile through my eyes, that I may scatter rich smiles in sad hearts.[512]

Smile in the mirror every morning and you'll start to see a big difference in your life.[339] A smile cures the wounding of a frown.[419] If you smile when you are alone then you really mean it.[391] You haven't lost your smile at all, it's right under your nose; you just forgot it was there.[502] Learn to smile at every situation; see it as an opportunity to prove your strength and ability.[60]

Too often we underestimate the power of a touch, a smile, a kind word, a listening ear, an honest compliment or the smallest act of caring, all of which have the potential to turn a life around.[75] All the statistics in the world can't measure the warmth of a smile.[201] A smile is a curve that sets everything straight.[118] We shall never know all the good that a simple smile can do. An enigmatic smile is worth ten pages of dialogue.[55] It seems to me that what we call beauty in a face lies in the smile.[458] Everywhere you go, take a smile with you[24]; the world always looks brighter from behind a smile.

The source of a true smile is an awakened mind.[199] Consider yourself a lucky person if you have at least one person in life with whom you can laugh and cry honestly, someone who understands you well and encourages you. And if you don't have that person, then be one for someone else. Keep your natural smile bright and let it bring a smile to others' faces too.

We don't smile enough. Too many of us are far too serious and don't know how to smile or laugh at ourselves.

Influencing

To get what we want from another person, we must forget our own perspective and begin to see things from their point of view.[81]

Human nature does not like to admit fault. When people are criticised or humiliated they rarely respond well, often becoming defensive and resenting their critic. To handle people well, we must never criticise, condemn or complain, because it never results in the behaviour we desire.[81]

People rarely work at their maximum potential under criticism, but honest appreciation brings out their best. Sincere appreciation is one of the most powerful tools in the world; it must not be simple flattery, it must be meaningful and with love.

Arouse in the other person an eager want. When we can combine our desires with their wants, they then become eager to work with us and you can mutually achieve your objective.

Become genuinely interested in other people. You can make more friends in two months by being interested in them than in two years by making them interested in you. If you can make people feel important in a sincere and appreciative way, then you will win all the friends you could ever dream of.[81] The only way to make quality, lasting friendships is to learn to be genuinely interested in them and their interests.

Happiness does not depend on outside circumstances, but rather on inward attitudes.[81]

A person's name, to that person, is the sweetest and most important sound in any language. People love their names so much that they will often donate large amounts of money just to have a building named after themselves. We can make people feel extremely valued and important by remembering their name.

Be a good listener and encourage others to talk about themselves. The easiest way to become a good conversationalist is to become a good listener. To be a good listener, you must actually care about what people have to say. Much of the time, people don't want an entertaining conversation partner, they just want someone who will listen to them. People will talk to us for hours if we allow them to talk about themselves. When you do talk, talk in terms of the other person's interests.[81]

If you talk to people about what they are interested in, they will feel valued and value you in return. We love to feel important and so does everyone else. Make the other person feel important, and do it sincerely. The golden rule is to treat other people how we would like to be treated.

The only way to get the best out of an argument is to avoid it. Whenever we argue with someone, no matter if we win or lose, we still lose. The other person will either feel humiliated or strengthened and will only seek to bolster their own position.[81] If you must argue, show respect for the other person and their opinions. Never say, 'You're wrong'; it will only offend them and wound their pride. When compassion awakens in your heart, you're able to be more honest with yourself.[81] If you're wrong, admit it quickly and emphatically.[481] When we fight, we never get enough, but by yielding we often get more than we expect. When we admit we are wrong, people trust us and begin to sympathise with our way of thinking.[81]

A drop of honey can catch more flies than a gallon of gall (bitterness, resentment, harshness). If we begin our interactions with others in a friendly way, they will be more receptive. Even if we are upset, we must remain friendly in order to influence people to our way of thinking. Start with questions to which the other person will answer 'yes'. Do not begin by emphasising the aspects on which you and the other person differ, but by emphasising the things on which you agree. Let them rationalise and talk about the idea, because it will taste much sweeter to them in their own mouths, as if the idea is theirs. Ideas can best be transferred by allowing others to think they arrived at it themselves.[81]

Try to see things from the other person's point of view[859]; we must seek to understand them. Success in dealing with people requires a sympathetic grasp of their viewpoint, then they will be more able to appreciate your side and are more likely to come around to your way of thinking. If you can appeal to others' noble motives, you can successfully convince them to follow your ideas.[81]

Dramatise your ideas; the truth must be made vivid, interesting and dramatic. The thing that most motivates people is the game, so if you want someone to do something then give them a challenge and they will often rise to meet it. Everyone desires to excel and prove their worth.[81]

I'm known to be a kind and considerate person, but people are well known to take advantage of 'nice' people; from experience, this is a very common trait. People attempt to influence, direct and control others, but get very annoyed when we say, 'Enough is enough, now please go away and don't come back.'

Regrets

The common regret people have on their deathbed is that they wish they had spent more time with the people they love, on relationships and a pursued purpose, rather than trying to please others.[860] It's easy to let time slip away, but once it's gone you can never get it back.

Kids love their parents, but they love doing stuff *with* their parents even more. It doesn't have to be a holiday at the Four Seasons: it could be raking leaves, learning how to throw a football or cleaning up the playroom together. We learn all the little habits that we take for granted in our own behaviour from mimicking our parents; if we're not making the time to do stuff with our kids, we're robbing them of the chance to mimic us.[861] And remember to turn you phone off when you are in your kids' company; there is nothing worse than being there in body but not in mind.

A common regret is not having done the right thing when someone dies – should I have said something different, done something different, not said something or forgiven them? Many people also regret not being able to say goodbye – we don't know when we are going to die, so for those left behind, this can be a really big issue. Thus, prioritise spending time with the people you love and regularly tell them how much they mean to you. After we die, it is the little things that make great memories for those left behind, those special little moments where you emotionally connect. A thousand small, special, delicate moments are worth a lot more than one big thank you at the end.

Those soon to die wish they'd worried less and felt less anxious during their lives. Worry is just using your imagination to create the things you don't want. Most of us place way too much importance on what other people think about us and how will they judge us. Ultimately, these are just opinions from people who don't fully share your reality; be who you are and say what you feel because those who mind don't matter and those who matter don't mind.

Many wish they had been better able to forgive. It takes a strong person to say 'I'm sorry' and an even stronger person to forgive. Forgive. Let go. Free yourself from grudges and enjoy happiness instead of wasting it. Burying the hatchet with a family member or old friend can be difficult, but in the act of forgiving them we take the issue off our plate and are able to move forward. This doesn't mean you necessarily go back to 'old ways' and resume the relationship; you don't have to have that person in your life going forward.

Some wish they had stood up for themselves, had more confidence and been more assertive. *Never* allow yourself to be bullied or silenced; no one is more important in this world than you.[862] Why do we allow the concerns of others to weigh so heavily on us instead of trusting our own beliefs? Maybe we don't think we are worth having what we want; maybe we just think poorly of ourselves.[861]

Another common regret is not having lived *your own life*. Spend your time working on the things you want to accomplish – build a business, cultivate your dream career, build a family, run a marathon. The greatest success is living your life in your own way. We can fall into the trap of living the life that our parents want us to because we think it's what will make them happy, but working constantly for something you don't care about adds nothing but stress to your life. Even if the passion is there, keep your workload in balance with the rest of your life.

A very difficult wish is to have been more honest. If you don't own up to your own elemental truth, falsehood will ultimately end up owning you. Honesty is the clearest path.

Don't end up regretting that you didn't live up to your full potential. Always live up to your own aspirations, not down to others' expectations. There is no passion to be found in settling for a life that is less than the one you are capable of living.[862] Trust that voice in the back of your head more because, most of the time, we learn later that it was dead right. It is more important that you internally succeed, because that is what matters, rather than externally achieving.

Life is found in the distance between your deepest desire and your greatest fear. Another common wish is to have faced fears. Remember, fear is only temporary, but regret lasts forever. This includes not being braver and risking vulnerability by declaring love for someone. Some people have declared their love and ended up having their hearts broken, but, while there's always a possibility of rejection, it is always better to try than to live with the regret of not knowing. Nothing in life is to be feared, it is only to be understood; now is the time to understand more so that we may fear less.

With the benefit of hindsight, we can see that we often spend a lot of our time on inconsequential things. When you let go of the meaningless, you have more time and give the right things a chance to catch you. Remember to live in the moment and make a difference today. Make it a day worth remembering and be sure to smell the flowers along the way.

Make sure you have the courage to speak up against the damage, trauma and pain that can come from so many areas. It is your right to let it out, and is the only way the abused can take back control; so many people taking their last breaths regret not having exercised their control.

Many people regret having taken their lives too seriously. Strange as it seems, most of us don't know how to have fun and look for the humour in situations. We don't joke around because we're too task-focused, or perhaps we don't think we're funny. Humour brings us smiles, which tell the brain we are content, so it gifts us a shot of serotonin, the happy chemical.

It is difficult to travel when you are very young, very old or very ill. Visit the places and people you want to see before it is too late.

Few study a second language, and this is a big regret down the road for many people, even though it might seem like a small thing next to family, career and romance.[861] When we take the time to learn a new language, whole new cultures open up to us.

It is too easy to let your marriage break down; today, statistically, more people will divorce than stay together. If you ask, many will tell you they couldn't take it anymore and that it was for the best. (And, of course, there are some marriages that shouldn't go on and where divorce is the best for all parties involved.[861]) However, many people privately will tell you they regret their marriage breaking up. It's never just one thing that ends it – even if that one thing is infidelity, there are usually lots of problems leading up to it. The regret most of us have is that we didn't correct these 'little things' before they became a big thing; we can't control our spouses, but we can control our actions, and we know (deep down) that we could have done more.

Everyone wants to fit in when they are kids, so don't regret getting involved with the wrong crowd when you were young. Everyone does dumb stuff when they're young and impressionable and think these friends are the only ones who will ever understand them. The wrong people can have a profoundly negative effect on our progress through life.

Similarly, there are major issues affecting everyone, so don't end up regretting not taking care of your health when you had the chance – nobody really thinks of their health until there's a problem. It's at this point that we promise ourselves, 'If I get better, I'll do a better job with my health.' It shouldn't take a major calamity to get us to prioritise our health and diet. Small habits every day make a big difference over time. Take care of yourself so you can take care of others.

Finally, don't regret not being a better parent. There's no bigger legacy than our children; most of the time, they turn out great, but there is nothing that makes us feel guiltier than seeing our kids struggle. When they start showing signs of problems – at school, with friends, etc. – there has often been many years in which we could have (and should have) spent more time with them. But no situation is ever lost; there is always time to improve our relationships with our kids, but it can't wait another day, especially if it's a relationship that's been neglected for years.[861]

Ask yourself if there is anything you might regret not doing. If there is, take action now.[862] Later will be now before you know it; time doesn't stop for you, and you're only here for a short visit.[862] Don't hurry, don't worry, but *do act*.

Other Regrets

- Not responding appropriately and proportionally, and reacting instead.

- Staying with addicts and becoming their caregivers rather than their lovers, losing yourself and your friends in the process.

- Moving miles away from family to be with boy/girlfriends, only to be dumped.

- Loaning people money that is never paid back.

- Becoming involved with a married person, loving them and wanting to be in their life, but always being a side-person because they will never leave their marriage.

- Standing by people who've committed many crimes and getting caught up in it.

- Staying with people who don't care for you, make you unhappy or make fun of you.

- Taking people back who dumped you and being fooled twice.

- Not learning from nasty experiences.

- Not listening to your inner voice and protecting yourself and your finances.

- Inviting another person into bed with you and your partner.

- Drunk-dialling an ex (who still loves you) for a booty call; it never ends well.

Remember: don't worry about those who talk behind your back, they're behind you for a reason; it is better to be a lonely lion than a popular sheep; the best way to deal with the past is to face it, stand strong. Start peacefully accepting your past; weak people take revenge, strong people forgive, intelligent people ignore; people underestimate people, if someone mistakes kindness for weakness that is their fault not yours; don't ever mistake silence for ignorance, calmness for acceptance, or kindness for weakness.[308] Listen before acting; compassion and tolerance are the real signs of strength. Be kind to everyone, trust everyone and support people, because that is the way decent people like to be treated and how decent people treat others, but when others are unkind to you, deceive or hurt you, weakness is not what they are going to remember about you. *Nemo me impune lacessit* (No one provokes me with impunity).

I am reminded of these wise words: if life were a circle and we were the point in the middle, our perception of reality would be a line from the edge to the centre. We have mastered that line, and it is called misery. We invariably live in the past, with pain and regret; we wish we had done things or said things; we wish we hadn't done or said other things, or that we had taken opportunities, different routes, or made different decisions. We find we are often conditioned by our past, our culture and our fears, perhaps thinking of others and not ourselves when it comes to our future. Stay alive, stay in the now (present time) and stay with loved ones.

Loyalty

The faithless are those who say farewell when the road darkens. Hold faithfulness and sincerity as first principles.

When you belong to the people you love and they love you back in good times and bad, it forms part of your identity far more than any word or group ever could. The strength of a family, like the strength of an army, is in their loyalty to each other.[863] When loyalty runs through your bloodstream, you can't get away from it because you have committed to it thoroughly. When you have honesty, respect and loyalty, you can conquer anything. If put to the test, an ounce of loyalty is worth a pound of cleverness.[864]

Where the battle rages, the loyalty of soldiers is proved. Don't give up on people when they need you; friends may come and go but enemies accumulate.[864] If you can't value a commitment made by someone else, your own commitments lose their value, too. The first step in the evolution of ethics is a sense of solidarity with other human beings.[865] When loyalty is a one-way street and demands complete support from those around you, expect the lies to flow and people to defend their personal interests.

A child is born without feelings of envy and hate, a blank canvas upon which anything is possible. If, between the ages of one and seven, they start down a negative path, it can lead them to violence and crime, and the abandoning of loyalty and good faith.[774] Children will learn this as they grow up and most will redeem themselves, but weak people will perpetuate fear, sow discord, trade lies and misinformation, undermine others and the integrity of systems in an attempt to hide the fact that they have no loyalty except to themselves.

Humanity is at a crossroads. Western countries are teetering on the brink of losing democracy, and globally, there are increasing levels of ignorance, poisoned political atmospheres, the rise of pseudoscience and anti-science sentiments. Daily overstimulation, homogenised media, addictive social media and excessive comfort is ruining many of our lives. We must fight for what we believe in and for critical thinking, otherwise we will lose them.

Stop telling yourself you're not qualified, not worthy or not experienced enough; growth happens when you start doing the things you're not qualified to do.[458] *The more you understand people, the more you will realise that ability and experience are less important than finding those who are genuinely kind, empathetic, positive, motivated and want to make a difference. It's far easier to teach new skills than it is to unlearn old toxic behaviours.*[469]

Watch for signs that you're getting burnt out, like procrastinating a lot, isolating yourself, becoming very impatient or unable to sleep. If you quickly lose joy doing hobbies or activities that previously excited you, if your performance is deteriorating or you start turning to addictive habits for comfort, then it's time for a rest, re-evaluation or change of course in your life. When you think that you are lost, you are in fact redirecting; when you feel that you have failed, you are learning to try another time or another route; when you think that you are behind, you are preparing to move forward with calculated determination, energy and vision. Life happens for you, not to you. Just be yourself – that is all you need to be.

We always have time to recognise the humanity in other people and respect their dignity. I wish people could see themselves the way I see them. Whoever is bringing out the best in you, always stay connected to them.

Always live in the present moment, stay connected, be grateful and don't take for granted your health or all the little things. Don't work away your life if you don't have to; make it so you don't have to. Spend time with those you love, those who love you back and those who make you feel loved. Nobody needs to die of broken heart syndrome. We are all soldiers of life without an army sometimes – betrayed, forgotten, abandoned – but in this moment, we are all brothers and sisters together.

If loyalty isn't a two-way street, then it isn't loyalty, it is blind obedience. The three ways of loyalty are: awareness, consideration and hard-core commitment (jumping in both feet first). I have noticed that people either have the loyalty of a dog (thorns may hurt you, men desert you, sunlight turn to fog; but you're never friendless ever, if you have a dog), a cat (unlike dogs who come when called, cats take a message and get back to you later, if you are worthy) or a tortoise (no concept of loyalty at all), and that people generally stick to their patronus like glue, which can be a limitation. Be therianthropic and shape-shift depending upon your specific needs and requirements. Never forget that loyalty should be continually earned and respected, not taken for granted, expected or exploited.

There are those who want to know and then there are those who want to believe, especially unsubstantiated beliefs; which are you? When you see someone ahead of you stop suddenly or swerve for no apparent reason, you do the same, for they often see something you don't and that can save your life. Memories are like waves: no matter what, distant or close, they always come back, but we do all have the choice to stop absorbing other people's negative emotions.

Reflections

You don't come out of the womb with all your abilities. Self-reflection, self-examination and insight are skills (just like any other, whether mental or physical), which means that every individual has to develop them. Some become good at it, some don't. It takes practice to be good at anything, so those who lack the ability have just not practised enough. When you meet individuals who claim to be opinionated or are highly argumentative ('no one changes my mind', 'I'm right, you're wrong'), lump them into the 'not very good at self-reflection' category.[920 & 348]

Humans are a reflection of the different aspects of the Universe. The human mind is a microcosm of the mental Universe, expressed as conscious, subconscious and unconscious levels of mental reality. The human soul is a microcosm of the spiritual Universe, the connection point between the human being and the Divine. We are connected to the Universe in a way that makes us something greater than ourselves.

Self-knowledge[30] is the way we can change the world, but we need to start by changing ourselves; we must know ourselves deeply, understand our emotions, thoughts and behaviours before we can begin to understand how our actions affect the world around us. Everything that happens to us reflects our choices and actions, for which we must take personal responsibility. We cannot blame others for our problems; we need to look inward to see what we can do to change the situation.

Compassion and respect relate to everything in the Universe being interconnected; we must treat others as we would like to be treated ourselves. When we are helping others, we are in fact helping ourselves; when we are harming others, we are harming ourselves. At all times, we must remember that we are all reflections of each other.

We have free will.[426 & 930] When you go against your life plan, you slow your soul's progress. If you take the scenic life route, have relationships with the wrong people and let your ego or materialism take control, things will not go as you planned, and you may need a reset of one of your landmarks to get back on track. We also have soul contracts with others in our soul cluster that either provide a positive or negative experience – the more intense or painful experiences are normally reserved for Old Souls, while the easy lives are left to the young souls. Miss elements of your soul contract, and you will have to repeat it, just like a school test to be retaken. If in doubt, ask your Soul Guide[9]. Connect to Source.

In life, we are all different. We all have different purposes, drives and approaches. As an example, there are people that don't have or need dishwashers. Then there are people who stack the dishwasher like a Scandinavian architect. Finally, there are other people who stack it like a raccoon on crystal meth. People who are raccoons often drive the Scandinavian architects crazy. Accept that we are all different, and one size doesn't and will never fit all. Take time to stop for a moment, pause and reflect, and then respond. You will probably feel better later on and may have even responded slightly differently from your initial automatic reaction.

CHAPTER 12

We will not always have it.

"Always look after your body so it can look after you in old age, as old age never comes alone."

—Alan Phillips (family saying)

When you realise that the Divine is sitting in the temple of every human body, it is a moment of reverence. The human body was not designed for a sedentary lifestyle; we were designed to act and to do great things. Remember that without the body and sex, humanity would have gone extinct a long time ago. This chapter explores the topics of ageing, respect, yourself, movement, medicines, food, our limitations, DNA and health in general.

Ageing

The human body is the most complex system ever created and the best work of art we have. The more we learn about it the more we come to appreciate just how richly complex it is; just imagine the rhythm of the body, the melody of the mind and the harmony of the soul combining to create the symphony of life itself. Everyone gets old at different rates. You *are* as old as you feel, but there are cycles that will inevitably occur.

In your teens, you think you know everything. Teenagers take little advice from others and do exactly what they want to do. They think and feel invincible, which can be very frustrating and upsetting for others, especially those close to them. This attitude is due to a significant part of the prefrontal cortex of the brain being undeveloped at this stage, which is the part of the brain responsible for planning ahead, managing emotions and delaying reactions, empathy, self-awareness, morality, consciousness, taking in the big picture and understanding cause and effect.[301] One's virginity tends to be lost between seventeen and twenty-three.

In your twenties, you are in your physical prime and your prefrontal cortex becomes fully formed. Twenty-six is the average age of Olympic medal winners, and as you head towards thirty, you reach the average age of great cyclists, tennis and basketball players.

By thirty, ballerinas have normally retired. It is the decade in which most professional athletes retire, except for golfers and rugby players, who seem to retire a little later or go into media. The average age to get a PhD is thirty-three.

By forty, you should have realised that everything will be okay, and if it doesn't turn out to be, it is probably not the end of the world. Things you thought of as 'big!' earlier in your life have now been put into perspective. Hopefully, you have found out what you love and are really owning it and making it work for you. Forty-seven is the age most people start their own business. The average age of men giving a Ted Talk is forty-five, and slightly lower for women. Women generally go through the menopause between forty-five and fifty-five.

The fifties are a very interesting stage. It is the average age of world leaders, professors and Nobel Prize winners.

The average age people die in the UK is around 78 for men and 82 for women. Life on Earth is short (though the soul is eternal), and life seems to go faster the older you get. It can be snuffed out in an instant, so live it to the full; you owe that to yourself and the people you care about.

'Everything in excess! To enjoy the flavour of life, take big bites. Moderation is for monks.' (From *Time Enough for Love*, my favourite book as a teenager.[205])

Don't sweat the small stuff and you will realise that money is not the measure of success. It's not about what you have, it's about what you *do* with what you have; you really do reap what you sow. Happiness doesn't just come to you automatically; you make it with your thoughts and actions.[867] All those songs you listened to as a youngster now have new meaning as you realise what they were actually singing about. The past has passed for a reason, so you must let it go, otherwise it will hold you back.

It is never too late to live a life that makes you proud. Take life's lessons, learn from them and live every moment so that you have no unfinished apologies of business.[867] When you hear the phrase 'overnight success', you know it means between two and ten years of preparing, consistency, patience and perseverance. It takes some people forty years of wandering in the desert, searching and testing the waters, before they have the confidence to use that experience and knowledge to make the rest of their lives amazing. The sooner you can stop 'wandering in the desert', the more amazing your journey will be.

It has been said that there are seven ages of man that focus on physical appearance: the helpless infant, the whining schoolboy, the emotional lover, the devoted soldier, the wise judge, the old man still in control of his faculties and the extremely aged who returns to the start in a second state of helplessness.[419] What is not well understood is the associated stages of mental knowing, listening ability, spiritual awareness and being awake. When you are young you crave to be older, yet you don't want to listen to the older generation because you think you know best; when you are old you crave to be younger, yet won't listen to the youngsters because you have seen it and done it and think you know best. There is power in all generations coming together and sharing their thoughts, ideas and understanding.

Old age does not come alone, it can come with myriad ailments and the feeling that life is passing by. For those lucky enough to have looked after themselves and are not suffering any major ailments or feeling too tired and worn out, old age can come with advantages: having a happier outlook on life, spending more time with loved ones, sharing wisdom and having an opportunity to pursue your remaining dreams. The aim is to keep going (stay alive) as long as you can, embracing a healthy, productive and empathetic life, keeping an open mind to new ideas and a willingness to keep learning and bringing joy to yourself and others.

Never lose the 'inner child' within you who has the ability to play, have fun and rebel slightly. I had a rather strict upbringing compared to my sibling, one that emphasised compliance, obedience and not stepping out of the shadows. Who would have guessed that I would become the editor of the humorously subversive postgraduate underground monthly magazine at university? I wasn't identified until my graduation and, even then, I didn't confirm or deny. Never lose your sense of humour or take yourself too seriously – life is a game and soul experience.

Respect

Always listen to the people who value you and consider doing what they say, but remember, they will not always be right.

There are bad, oppressive men who seek power and domination over others, but we must avoid suppressing human nature, ideas and love. As a parent, it is your duty to raise responsible, kind and awake children, recognising that the world is filled with injustice, corruption and lies. Treat every girl like a princess because that is what she is.

It takes great strength to love, be gentle, kind and respectful; these traits are the most valuable currency we shall ever have. Life is all about seeking meaning through sacrifice, not happiness through pleasure. When you say you are going to do something, do it; your word is your bond.

Before you judge the world, you need to take responsibility for your own life, so take care of yourself like you would a loved one. Progress is not made by comparing yourself to your past achievements, or others. It is what is yet to come and is only defined by your soul contracts, dreams and imagination.

Lies are a common tool of self-deception, but we should strive towards a truthful and respectful life. Do not delude yourself by believing your own lies, falsehoods and frauds; it makes other people lose all respect for you. You become an unethical, corrupt excuse for a person, who is not being true to themself or others.

Respect, like loyalty, is earned and should be given freely, not due to power, money or influence.

Yourself

Treat yourself with kindness; don't give yourself too much of a hard time when nothing great is materialising. Self-worth should come from within; you are meant to thrive, and that means doing great things and enjoying life, believing in yourself and following your own path.[868]

Small steps are the route to great advances; you can't reach far-off places in one great leap. You've got to ask the right questions; many don't, because they think they already know the answers. You need to let the Universe know what you want and work towards it, letting go of *how* it comes to pass. Be forensically specific with your goals and be careful what you wish for, for you may just get it.[228] We live the lives we create for ourselves, so perhaps the greatest lesson anyone can learn is to take responsibility for their own life. However, never feel negative, never let life grind you down. You're here once, you've got one shot at this life… so enjoy it.

Investing in yourself isn't selfish, it is the most worthwhile thing you can do. Just because you are breathing doesn't mean you are alive. If you have an active addiction, compulsive behaviour or significant untreated health condition, be sure to start there – as hard as it might be. Without addressing such underlying issues, it is impossible to succeed in deepening intimacy in your life; you can't look after others if you can't look after yourself.[869]

There comes a time when you have to let go of all the pointless drama and the people who create it, and surround yourself with those who make you laugh so hard that you forget the bad and focus solely on the good. After all, life is too short to be anything but happy.[303]

There are some things in this life that are important and a whole lot of things that aren't. Dedicate your life to something, starting with a simple, internal mission statement. That will do. Keep it under your hat[882], don't preach, propagate or try to convert.[452] Be flexible in your thinking, try to see life not as the enemy but as a friendly sparring partner. We get torn between what we want and what is good for others; be on the side of the angels, not the beasts. Some days it's okay to give up, because a good player knows when they're beat and when to try a different approach.

Take an interest in the outside world because that will develop you. Dedicate yourself personally to things you can change and areas where you can make a difference. Then aim to be the very best at everything you do; failing is fine but aiming low isn't.[452] Only dead fish swim *with* the stream, and that is what life is, a series of struggles and lulls.

Be the last to raise your voice, as shouting is a sign that you have lost control. Be your own adviser.[452] Maintain your composure by counting to ten before you react, as it allows you to collect your thoughts, calm down and find an appropriate response. Calm people are trusted and live longer. Calm people are relied on. Calm people are looked up to and given responsibility.[870]

The world is divided into those who look at others enviously and those who see others as a motivational tool.[452] We all have regrets for the things we haven't done, but you still have time to do some of them. Don't be afraid to dream. Plans must be realistic, but dreams don't have to be. Don't expect to be perfect, celebrate your flaws and imperfections as an important and necessary part of yourself.

Don't try to be understood before you understand yourself. People may never understand your intentions, but *you* know them. They may never appreciate why you do what you do or say what you say, but they have never walked in your shoes, lived your life or been in the environments you have been in. *You* know why. They may never understand the strength it takes to be the way that you are. You know your weaknesses and your struggles, and you are the one who works to overcome them, so your strength means more to you than it could ever mean to anyone else. You don't need to be accepted by others.[199] You just need to accept yourself.

You'll get older but not necessarily wiser, because wisdom is not just about making mistakes but learning to escape afterwards with your dignity and sanity intact. Accept that what is done is done and you need to just get on with things.[452]

Everyone deserves one opportunity to be given respect. However, if they blow that opportunity and show themselves to be unworthy of it, then they can't expect to receive it again. After that, respect will need to be earned the hard way through kindness, acting respectably, listening well, acting fairly, not making excuses, owning issues, taking responsibility for things, letting go of anger and the ego and being willing to change when they are wrong or when things are not working out as planned. We must all demonstrate our values through the words we use and our actions. Communicate well, address issues promptly (with no bias) and build relationships based on trust, safety and the wellbeing of others.

Movement

Dancing can promote wellness by strengthening the immune system through muscular action, physiological processes and maintaining balance. Dance can condition an individual to moderate, eliminate or avoid tension, chronic fatigue and other disabling conditions that result from stress. It builds up core muscular strength, endurance, coordination and harmony. It is one of the most powerful artistic mediums to engage in or witness and has been called 'body language'. The technical skills required to dance using correct body placement, alignment and timing whilst creating beautiful, aesthetic lines is truly breath-taking, especially when synchronised with other dancers. It is a combination of the physical and mental that can provide an almost spiritual experience. Once you have learned to dance, it is important to keep practising to continue benefiting from the results; use it or lose it.

A key element that makes dance so impactful is the conscious intention it has when coupled with the emotional power of music. Numerous scientific and psychological studies have shown that music can lift our mood, combat depression, improve blood flow in ways similar to medicines, lower stress-related hormones and ease pain. As such, music can be very therapeutic; it can bring people together and be a source of fun, entertainment and joy.

Yoga is the bringing together of mind and body and incorporates breathing exercises, meditation, mindfulness and poses designed to encourage relaxation, reduce stress and relieve anxiety. Our bodies accumulate stress and toxins, and we need to remove them to keep our energy levels flowing correctly, thus reducing inflammation, improving heart health, promoting quality sleep and improving our general quality of life. It is also a good way to maintain flexibility and balance, otherwise our range of movements gets smaller and smaller, just like our lives, as we get older.

Keep moving every day, as much as you can. You are meant to move, meant to keep everything working to rid yourself of toxins and keep those energy centres working and flowing.

Food

Life is too short for fake butter and fake people.[871] One cannot think well, love well, sleep well if one has not dined well.[509] Food is the foundation of genuine happiness; it is our common ground, a universal experience that binds us all together.

First, we eat, then we do everything else.[872] A recipe has no soul; the cook must bring soul to the recipe. Cooking is all about people; no matter what culture, everywhere around the world people eat together.[145] Food brings people together on many different levels; it's the nourishment of the soul and body; it is culture, habit, craving and identity. Eating and food also has symbolic meanings associated with love, sensuality, comfort, stress reduction, security, reward and power. Hard work should be rewarded by good food.[109] It is symbolic of love when words are inadequate.[873] The best cooks always leave one or two ingredients out when they give people their recipes, ensuring that people always come back to them.

We are what we eat and drink, so don't be fast, cheap, easy or fake. We need to pay more attention to the taste, smell and texture of food we eat, and any thoughts, feelings and sensations we may experience at the same time. We should understand what our food and drink does to our bodies in terms of weight gain, blood sugar levels – be it eating disorders or allergies – and how it affects our behaviour. We should know which foods are good for us and which are not so good. We are only beginning to realise that the health of our gut and dietary restrictions are more important than we ever imagined.

Every cell in the body depends on a continuous supply of calories and nutrients, whether obtained through food, IV fluids or tube feedings. Nutrients are substances that provide energy for activity, growth and repair and all bodily functions such as breathing, digesting food, keeping warm and having an active immune system. A healthy, balanced diet can help improve a person's quality of life.[874] The good news is that adding any amount of healthy foods may help lower the risk of an early death. Improving diet by just twenty percent was linked to an eight to seventeen percent lower risk of premature death. Eating less food also increases life expectancy. You don't need a silver fork to eat good food. Many foods such as nuts, turmeric and other plant-based foods contain antioxidants and have anti-inflammatory properties that seem to protect against cancers and age-related diseases.

However, the good stuff is outweighed by the bad stuff we create through our industrial processes and by not properly dealing with our waste materials. Saturated and trans fats in humans and animals tend to contain small amounts of toxic chemicals and selected heavy metals (arsenic, cadmium, lead and mercury) which are not good for our bodies or brains and lead to illness, impairment and, in high doses, death.

Tap water, too, can reasonably be expected to contain small amounts of contaminants. More and more households are adding water quality interventions such as carbon and UV filters, but these do not remove the chlorine. Chlorine is a very reactive compound and, when mixed with certain naturally occurring organic compounds, produces harmful by-products. Synthetic hormones and microplastics are also getting into our drinking water, reducing male fertility rates. The introduction of microplastics into the environment and our food supply from synthetic fabrics, car tyres, non-stick pan coatings, paints and microbeads from cosmetics is a recent concern. The health implications are still unclear, but there is growing evidence that inside digestive systems they could be facilitating the release of more toxins. The detection of microplastics in our blood shows they are now inside our bodies and accumulating in our organs, where they shouldn't really be.

Unfortunately, we have intentionally and unintentionally contaminated many of our natural environments and, ultimately, ourselves. Environmental defences are being torn apart as big corporations are now able to navigate safe drinking water and clean air legislation.[9] Good health is not something we can buy. However, it can be an extremely valuable savings account.[408]

There is still a lot we don't know about the world, our bodies and how we interact with each other. Research is beginning to uncover that the foods we eat and how they are grown, treated and transported is far more important than initially thought. This is before we even consider when we eat, the negative impacts of certain foods in our diet related to cancer, certain diseases and even hair thinning, and the general ignorance around the benefits of other foods and techniques. More to follow in Book 2.

Limitations

We may be living longer today due to improved diet and medicines, but we are still as fragile as ever. As we get older, we have an increased susceptibility to infections, greater risk of heat stroke and hypothermia, a slight decrease in height as the bones of our spines get thinner, our bones break more easily and our joints change, exhibiting symptoms from minor stiffness to severe arthritis. The most common outward signs of ageing are wrinkles, dullness of skin, blotchiness, age spots, hair loss, and gaunt hands and neck. The inward signs are associated with a decrease in performance of our organs, gradual breakdown of our systems and faculties and reduced mental capacity and response times.

Age most certainly does not come alone. Even though you may take preventative steps as you get older – keeping fit, watching what you eat or even taking anti-ageing medicines – you will eventually lose muscle mass, your skin will sag, you'll get more injuries and recovery will take longer. In some instances, you may not get the injury to heal at all, even after trying multiple techniques such as acupuncture or physiotherapy. Your sex drive will diminish, you will have a greater tendency towards anxiety and depression, you will have a higher likelihood of losing your balance and are at a greater risk of falling, which could result in hip fractures or other complications.

The most common age-related diseases are cardiovascular and chronic lower respiratory. Humans are very susceptible to heart issues and, over time, the heart muscle can weaken. High blood pressure doesn't help, nor does the narrowing of the arteries by built-up fatty plaque. As you age, your heart loses efficiency as blood vessels get clogged and much stiffer and less flexible. This all means the heart is one of the major single points of failure in humans as they get older. Other common issues include: strokes, hypertension, cancer, osteoarthritis, diabetes, osteoporosis, Alzheimer's and Parkinson's, not to mention complications due to having multiple chronic conditions.

We all have limitations. We just need to acknowledge them and work alongside them.

I, like a lot of people, have at least three major limitations: (1) Thinking that people will operate rationally, pragmatically and sensibly for the good of everyone, not just for themselves. (2) Trusting that people will do the right thing, are not just out for themselves and will not step on you and others to get ahead, whatever the cost. (3) Giving people the benefit of the doubt multiple times after they've made the same old mistakes again and again and have proved themselves to be totally inept, causing huge amounts of collateral damage everywhere they go, and believing them when they have no intention of delivering what they say they will.

Health

Health is everything, more precious than fame, wealth and everything else, except love.

We are fragile beings; how easily and quickly we lose our health, from catching a disease or having an accident to ageing. It is something we take for granted until it is not there. Your health is your wealth, so take care of your body; it's the only place you have to live in. It's never too early or too late to work towards being the healthiest you. A healthy outside starts from the inside. There is no magic wand or shortcut to wellbeing; you have to eat healthy and live healthy to be healthy and look healthy.

Middle-age spread is a fact, not folklore, but our metabolism does not increase or diminish with age. Muscle loss and a general slowing down are just natural processes of ageing. There is a whole industry created around health and dieting, which is wrapped around commercialism and shifting products or services. Most focus on only one part of the problem space that they can sell. Statistics show that only twenty percent of people are successful at maintaining any weight loss in the long term (at least one year), so when dieting is synonymous with suffering and ninety-five percent of diets fail people, it is no wonder so many flock to any new fad, exercise trend or quackery.

To understand the whole issue, you need to look at the whole problem. Our bodies are very complex machines that have been designed to deal with food shortages, to protect us as we age and to be exercised daily. Yes, you should watch what you feed your internal machine and choose fresh produce over processed and salt-rich foods, sugars and alcohol,[395] but what is not so widely known is the importance of getting enough sleep, understanding your hormones and other substances in your body and recognising the impacts of stress and inconsistent, irregular eating patterns. Exercise can be a great weight balancer, but when augmented with weight and hormone monitoring, as well as controls and mitigations (drinking more water), then tackling weight gain can start to move into an area within our control.

The body constantly surprises us as we learn more and more about how it really works. If we want to live happy, healthy, fulfilled and extended lives, we need to start sharing this knowledge, living it and making sure our younger generations fully accept and appreciate its subtleties so they can benefit from what we didn't know at the time. There are so many threats to our health (trauma, injury, alcohol and drug misuse, cancer, medications, obesity, diabetes, sleep apnoea, etc.) that we need to look beyond mental health, occupational health and rehabilitation and put more effort into preventative health, hormone health and overall wellbeing.

Don't start a diet that has an expiration date, you need to develop a healthy lifestyle that will last forever.[875] Success happens when we're not in the mood to make a healthy choice but do so anyway. Instead of focusing on all the reasons you can't do something, focus on all the reasons you *can*. Eat wholesome foods, drink water and stay active. It costs money to stay healthy, but it's even more expensive to get sick.[52] When diet and lifestyle are wrong, medicine is of no use; when diet and lifestyle are correct, medicine is of no need. The preservation of health is easier than the cure for the disease. No matter who you are, what your goal is or how you define success, a healthy body and mind are vital if you want to lead a truly productive life.[877] Happiness is healthiness, so create healthy habits.

Health is a state of complete physical, mental and social wellbeing and is not merely the absence of disease or infirmity.[876] Stories of when one partner dies then the other loses their will to live and dies within three weeks show there are life forces that can affect our health state. The doctors of the future will not treat the human body with drugs, but will cure and prevent diseases with nutrition, sound and energy flows.

Our vital energy flows through twelve meridian channels and they follow a special rhythm. The pairing of body parts with the points of the body through which *qi* flows can now be achieved with 'electro-dermal' measurements. Chakras are the circular vortexes of energy that are placed in seven different points on the spinal column, and the seven chakras are connected to the various organs and glands within the body. They are responsible for distributing life energy, also known as *qi* or *prana*.[878]

Make your mental health a priority. Mental health is not a destination but a process; it's about how you drive, not where you're going.[879] You don't have to struggle in silence anymore; you can live well with a mental health condition so long as you open up to somebody about it. Give yourself the same care and attention that you give to others and watch yourself bloom.[32] The way you speak to yourself matters; you are more than any illness or condition; not everything you think is true. A beautiful day begins with a beautiful mindset.[462] Today is your opportunity to build the tomorrow you want.[880] If you get tired, learn to rest but not quit, just like Olympians do. Don't feel guilty for doing what's best for you. A little progress each day adds up to big results.[881] Learn to love the sound of your own feet walking away from things not meant for you. It's okay to worry, or to not know how not to, but not all storms come to disrupt your life – some come to clear your path.[18] We're not meant to stay the same. Change is good.

Diet plays a critical part in all our lives, influencing our overall health, the diseases we are likely to be more susceptible to and our longevity. We are aware that many things can hamper or interfere with our health (sugar, smoking, alcohol), but we often forget that even healthy things contain elements of bad things, so we must consider our portion sizes. Bigger fish tend to contain more mercury, bigger vegetables can contain more insecticides, and too many vitamins can be unhealthy, even dangerous.

When food is less important to you because you have learned to control your appetite, simply by occupying your mind elsewhere, you will find that when you meditate on other aspects of your life, you can go without eating and don't miss it. There are great health benefits to periodic fasting, which include boosting cognitive performance, supporting weight loss, improving overall fitness, decreasing the risk of metabolic diseases, lowing the risk of obesity and associated chronic diseases and reducing inflammation. Our foods and environment are very fulfilling, calorific and full on, so we need to give our bodies a rest every now and then.

Nutrition also plays a dramatic role in mental health that we are only beginning to understand. More on all these topics in Book 2, including a case study that I'm currently involved in.

CHAPTER 13

Pain either hurts us, heals us, or changes us.

"You can't expect to experience real feelings or gain wise knowledge if you were never young and crazy."

—Chris Brown[58] (Modified)

Be true to your feelings, because the more you deny what you feel, the stronger they will become.[506] We may try and hide our feelings but forget that our eyes can speak. Pay attention to your gut feelings; no matter how good something looks, if it doesn't feel right, walk away. This chapter looks at aspects of touch, joy, intuition, willpower and focus.

Touch

Everyone has the ability to touch other people's lives. We do so mostly without physically touching them: with our words, smile, eyes, and courage, with our madness and in millions of different other ways! We are contacting beings without contacting!327 Some people come into our lives and touch our hearts so deeply that we will never be the same again.

We are here to inspire and touch each other's hearts. In life, we leave a legacy to our children[347], we leave our footprints wherever we travel, and we leave our fingerprints on every heart we touch.[38] Money will not last, nor fame, but how you touched others will always stay behind. When you touch minds, people are willing to walk a dozen miles for you, when you touch hearts people are willing to walk a thousand miles for you;

but when you touch souls, people are willing to walk a million miles for you.[116] A fulfilled life isn't counted in the years, awards, wealth or followers someone amassed for themselves, but in the number of faces that smiled because of them. Prove to the world that you are alive; let your words breathe life into the nostrils of the Universe.[237]

Our ability to touch other people's hearts is infinite. To touch someone's heart, please don't think it is about more detail, spending more money and more superficial things; that is not how memory works. We recall with our feelings, emotions and interactive experiences, which are invariably clouded in mist and fog and feel ephemeral to really grab hold of. That is why the best experiences are so exquisite.

Joyful

As you become more conscious of yourself and the world around you, you will begin to notice the beauty, joy and happiness hidden in the simplest of things; it is easy so to miss the little things when your life and mind are busy, and you are not living in the present. Dwell on the beauty of life, watch the stars and see yourself running with them; if people sat outside and looked at the stars each night, I bet they'd live better.[488]

There is joy in the seemingly mundane things that people often take for granted, whether this is sitting in the garden, drinking coffee, watching the sunrise or reading a book; all of these activities can fill your senses with extreme joy. A nice warm shower, a cup of tea and a caring ear may be all you need to warm your heart. A quiet and modest life gives joy through the universal elements, all of which are free: a morning walk or an evening saunter, spotting a bird's nest or noticing a wildflower in spring; these are some of the rewards of the simple life.[73] Sometimes, if you stand on the bottom rail of a bridge and lean over to watch the river slipping slowly away beneath you, you will suddenly know everything there is to be known.[319] Witness the world through the eyes of your inner child, eyes that sparkle in awe and amazement as they see love, magic and mystery in the most ordinary things. The world is full of magical things, patiently waiting for our senses to grow sharper.[357]

E. A. Bucchianeri says, 'I have never been drawn to luxury but I like things that are built well and last (I suppose that is the engineer within me). Sometimes, the simple things are more fun and meaningful than all the banquets in the world.' [63]

It's strange how the simple things in life go on while we become difficult.[51] Love the simple things: coffee shops, books and people who try to understand. If the sight of the blue sky fills you with joy, if a blade of grass springing up in the fields has the power to move you, if the simple things of nature have a message that you understand, rejoice, for your soul is alive.[127]

Whoever loves and understands a garden will find contentment within.[88] We have grown dull toward this fantastic world in which we live; it is a fairy tale through and through. There's a sunrise and a sunset every single day, and they're absolutely free. Don't miss so many of them.[483] If more of us valued food and cheer and song above hoarded gold, it would be a merrier world.[456] I am beginning to believe we're so busy watching out for what's just ahead of us that we don't take time to enjoy where we are.[488] Learn that it is the sweet, simple things of life that are the real ones.[499]

Real joy in life comes from finding your true purpose[866] and aligning it with what you do every single day.[384]

Oh, what joy it is to be alive, to wake up every morning to start a new day. Too often, we take this for granted, that is, until some misfortune arises and we realise what we had.

Intuition

It's knowing without knowing. Follow your intuition as it is the whisper of the soul where true wisdom manifests itself: the sense of knowing how to act spontaneously without needing to know why, where you don't need to explain or justify your feelings to anyone, just trust your own because they never lie to you.

There is a universal, intelligent life force that exists within everyone and everything. It resides within each of us as a deep wisdom, as inner knowing, and we can access this wonderful source of knowledge and wisdom through our intuition.[180] Your eyes can deceive you, your brain can play tricks, your heart can be blind, but your gut instinct is always right. Part of evolving and growing up is listening to your intuition then acting on it. It is the beacon that guides us to peace and navigates us through the treacherous karmic waters, an inner sense that tells us what feels right and true at any given moment.[86] A good artist lets their intuition lead them wherever it wants.[268] Have the courage to follow your heart and intuition[234]; they know what you truly want to become. Intuition can be your superpower, as the more you trust it, the more empowered you become. And the stronger you become, the happier you are.

Intuition is really a sudden immersion of the soul into the universal current of life, where the histories of all people are connected and we are able to know everything, because it's all written there.[883] It is an essential part of the whole experience of living, and although it does not predict the future or how people will behave, using intuition as a guide makes life more rewarding. It helps you follow your true path and soul contract, preventing things from being tougher than you expected and causing you to relive this life to get to where you were supposed to be.

Energy doesn't lie, so tune in to it. You may hate it when it is telling you something you don't want to hear, but no matter how good something looks, if it doesn't feel right, walk away. The intuitive mind is a sacred gift, and a rational mind is a faithful servant. We have created a society that honours the servant and has forgotten the gift.[133] Intuition is more powerful than intellect and logic and is the truest energy, for it reflects what your spirit is feeling and what your soul is saying.

If you want something you've never had, you have to take a risk, follow your intuition, do something you've never done, go somewhere different and put yourself out there; get out of your comfort zone! It will teach you about yourself.

Willpower

While many of us feel we are not lacking in strength, we know that we lack will.

Willpower is a muscle, so the more you train it, the stronger it gets.[884] It is not something that people just find, they create it. Nor is it genetic, something that gets handed out to some and not to others; it is a skill that can be developed through understanding and practice. Some people are willing to change and others are not.

Willpower is a stronger force than you may think, as the difference between a successful person and an unsuccessful person is not a lack of strength or knowledge, but a lack of will. It requires the strength to resist, and the power of a resolved mind. Everything is generated through your own willpower; it is the key to success.[318] Successful people strive, no matter what they feel, by applying their will to overcome apathy, doubt and fear.

Willpower and desire, when properly combined, make an irresistible pair. There is no great talent without great willpower; it knows no obstacles and allows you to find your greatness. Most of life's actions are within our reach, but decisions take willpower.[318] Strength does not come from physical capacity, but from an indomitable will; it is the basis of perseverance. Technique and ability alone will not get you to the top. Willpower can't be bought with money or given by others – it rises from your heart. Concentrated visualisation and willpower enable us to materialise thoughts, dreams and visions in the material realm.

A big part of willpower is having something to aspire to, something to live for.[318] It needs clear and achievable long-term goals and an established motivation for change when attempting to do something differently. People who succeed have the ambition and willpower to develop themselves. They rightly assume that with a little more self-control and delayed gratification, they would eat better, exercise regularly, avoid temptations, save more, stop procrastinating and achieve all sorts of noble goals and feats.

Research indicates that willpower can be strengthened by practice, by conserving it, avoiding the multitude of temptations, implementing good intentions and planning ahead. This is great for those who have the time to do all this, but in our busy, internet-dominated lives we are perpetually surrounded by so many temptations that our willpower reserves are running low. Don't overload your future self; be realistic about your expectations and don't overextend yourself. Bring your mind to the present and just start; once you immerse yourself in the task, you will be less likely to procrastinate. Create a habit of exercise, improve your productivity, wake up early and force yourself to practise a skill.

Persistence is the key factor in strengthening your willpower. Great things take time, often longer than you would like them to, and you are bound to endure hardship on the way. Anything of real value needs to be fought for with grit and determination. The best strategy is taking a large task/goal/dream and breaking it down into manageable chunks. *The Art of the Start* states that there is often great initial excitement but that people get paralysed because they don't know where to begin.[249] 'Chunking' shifts focus from the larger goal to smaller goals that are easier for the brain to comprehend; don't think twelve weeks ahead, think today. When your goal is achieved and you can see the end result, you will forget about all the hard work.

Willpower is like a muscle: it is not infinite, gets tired, easily wanes and needs a rest now and again. Use it carefully, cautiously and calculatedly.

Focus

Maintain your focus. Focus is directly connected to self-discipline. Use your experience, wisdom and instincts to focus on what is truly important in life.[885]

Energy is everywhere and you can use yours either to work for you or against you. It flows where attention goes, to what you are focusing on. The only thing standing between you and your goal is the rubbish story you keep telling yourself as to why you can't achieve it.[36] Anything is possible. Your dreams, your ideas, your inventions and your vision. Never let anyone tell you 'you can't', because once you start saying it, it will become true. Everything we hear is an opinion, not a fact or relevant to us until proven otherwise. Everything we see is a perspective, not the truth.[27]

Disliking, not forgiving and trying to change others takes more energy than just letting things go and focusing your efforts on your own business.[885]

You cannot be all things to all people. Don't be afraid to make people mad by saying 'no'; that's their problem, not yours. Your honesty will inspire your true friends. Focus on the important people and things in life, and everything else will fall into place; everything else probably isn't worth focusing on anyway.

You decide every day who you will and will not be. Be bold in your decision, but choose wisely.[60] Hard choices will always be hard choices, but they always have to be made. Focus.

I tried to learn the piano, but I struggled because I had short fingers. I have noticed that great musicians tend to have big hands and very long, spiderlike fingers, which give them a distinct advantage when reaching parts of instruments that others find hard to reach. Everyone has natural abilities, things they tend to be very good at picking up and learning, and other things they find it more difficult. Successful swimmers have large feet and hands; successful runners have long legs; successful horse riders tend to be of a smaller stature. Try lots of things when you are young to discover what you are naturally good at and which bring you joy; then focus your effort on these things first, for you will find them a lot easier to do.

Focus on what you can achieve (even if only in small steps), not what you can't or are unlikely to. In public life, there are a lot of people who don't focus, don't put the effort in and don't achieve, called 'backdrop people' (more about them, later in the book). If the public environment were to be compared to an orchestra, there seems to generally be six conductors and one person playing all the instruments.

I love it when the team says that they will 'lean in' when in fact they take one step back, making it seem as though you have stepped forward. It is amazing what a person of focus can achieve.

There are three pieces of a person. The first, biggest piece generally ignores things, takes the easy path, turns a blind eye to evil and walks away so they don't get involved – we can do anything, just not everything. The second, more reasonable piece (that which may be left after severe trauma) may want to forgive yet not forget – certain things can never be made even, but this part recognises that people can end animosity, go their separate ways and accept that what is done is done. The final piece (that you don't really want to awaken) really wants to play things out to the end, whatever the price and whatever the cost.[154] Choose your fights wisely and never underestimate an opponent of focus, commitment and sheer will.[153] *These are the most dangerous people, for they prioritise succeeding over everything.*

CHAPTER 14

The Art of Living.

'We bring nothing into the world, yet we all have the extraordinary capacity to leave a real mark.'

—1 Timothy 6:7[2] (Modified)

Life is a gift, and it offers us the privilege, opportunity and responsibility to give something back by becoming more.[384] If you're looking to live and grow, choose the challenge every single time. Comfortable and easy are short-term friends but long-term enemies. Give your focus to one day at a time along your beautiful journey, for it shall not last forever. The world is full of wonders, but they become more wonderful, not less so when science and objective observation look at them.[26] Most people on this planet believe in some type of life after death, and we live in a multi-dimensional Universe, where our consciousness has the capacity to pass from this dimension of reality into the next.[495]

Home

Home is where we start out, where our lives begin. The minute you start travelling, you discover new words, opinions, concepts and other languages that didn't previously exist in your life. Be a traveller and take time to absorb the full aperture of these experiences, rather than just being a tourist taking a snapshot (or selfie) out the window. Home and lost causes are the only things worth fighting for.

Your voyage away from your safe and secure home will be full of ecstasy and pain, discovery and revelation. Accept and delight in knowing that you know nothing; it will make you the smartest of all, as you will have experiences that most people can only dream of. Remember Roy Batty, the android antagonist of the film *Blade Runner*, who desperately seeks his creator for an extension to his three-year lifespan. His valediction is a rhapsody to life's great adventure: 'I've seen things you people wouldn't believe... Attack ships on fire off the shoulder of Orion... I watched C-beams glitter in the dark near the Tannhäuser Gate. All those moments will be lost in time, like tears in rain... time to die.'[148] Actual knowledge exists in knowing that you know nothing, but you must find the courage to leave home and go on a journey to discover this. Be the one, the first one who has the spine, the resolve and the determination to do what needs to be done.

Always seek out things no one has seen before, find the glitter in the dark, and always follow the path less travelled. In his book *Pathways to Bliss*, the anthropologist Joseph Campbell writes that the hero's journey begins in the 'darkest part of the forest where there are no paths laid down by others for us to follow'.[80] Life isn't about finding yourself but creating yourself. Expand your horizons by analysing your personal projects – prioritise some and drop others because you can do anything, but not everything. Next, challenge yourself by learning a new skill, changing your attitude, developing a curious mind and changing your habits. If you don't like yourself, reboot an area of your life or actively change your personality by creating an alter-ego. It worked for Bowie. Learn to embrace new roles and spend time with different types of people.

You have to go without something to find out what it's really worth to you; things that were previously taken for granted then find their true value in absence. After the loss of the 'old you' or somebody close to you, let the sorrow rinse through you. Mourn well by cherishing your new time alone, reflecting on and setting new goals and discovering who you are now meant to be and be with. What matters most is how well we loved, how fully we lived and how deeply we let go. Gaining and losing things is just part of normal life. During grief, remember that time doesn't heal anything; we only learn to live with the pain over a period of time. Grief is not a sign of weakness, nor is it a lack of faith; it is the real price of love.[886]

Healing can't be rushed. We need time to move through the five phases of grief: denial, anger, bargaining, depression and acceptance. Don't fall into the trap of longing for what can't be; accept that victory requires sacrifice.

There once was a person who'd become unstuck in the world, so they left their home and loved ones and travelled around, blind as a leaf in the wind, until they had circled the Earth and arrived back where they had started out from. Their car, job, phone, shoes, everything was right where they had left them, the people they loved welcomed them back; nothing had visibly changed. Despite this, the traveller felt excited to have arrived home, to the place they had been aiming to get to all their life. They were the one who needed to change. This epiphany only came about by developing a new mindset while travelling, to see what was in front of them with new eyes, appreciate home more than ever and care for it with even greater love. They had to endure the hardship of the journey and experience all the new things on the way to learn, understand and accept that they had always been home.

Change

If you want to change the world, you must be your very best in the darkest moments.[454] It starts with one act of random kindness: it can happen anywhere, and anyone with a pure heart and the right ethical and moral intentions can do it.

Change and uncertainty are the only guaranteed elements of life; we may as well accept that we cannot control our lives 100% all the time, but that we can control our responses.[887] Focus on what you can control. We can control our efforts but not the outcomes. Stop trying to calm the storm; instead, calm yourself and the storm will pass. However, sometimes you need to sit in the eye of the storm and experience the unpleasantness to appreciate the light.

A person often meets their destiny on the road they took to avoid it.[888] You can spend your whole life running away from an outcome only to realise you have been running toward it all along. Start small; great things can be changed with small steps. Making your bed will provide your first accomplishment of the day, you can then go on to complete others… exercise, a healthy breakfast.

What is unpleasant about developing a renewed passion for the beauty of life? Never underestimate the power of denial. Stop running away from the reality of your life, and change. Positive action begets a positive life; avoidance means never solving your problems. Start doing as much good as possible and quit worrying about other people's judgments; obsession leads to new obsessions. As visionary poet and artist William Blake wrote: 'The eagle never lost so much time as when it stopped to learn of the crow.' [46]

Luck is less 'leprechaun-guarded pots of gold at rainbow's end', and more 'preparation and good timing'. It's about being ready to act when an opportunity presents itself, like an actor with a prepared audition. This may involve some waiting, but you can change yourself and acquire new skills anytime you want. We hold the real power for change. It lies dormant in a lot of us and only awakes in those who have a dream and the will to act and make it a reality. It's not in the stars that we will find the constellation of our destiny but in ourselves. No matter who you were in the past, your future will always make room for you to change. *It* is the law of life, and those who look only to the past or future are certain to miss the present. [253]

You've got to accept that some things are not your fault and that a lot of life is far from perfect. But you can be the change that you wish to see in the world (we but mirror the world [178]). Everyone thinks of changing the world, but no one thinks of changing himself. [458] Enthusiasm is common; endurance is rare. Never doubt that a small group of thoughtful, committed citizens can change the world, [310] but beware, there is nothing more dangerous than a big idea in a small mind. [889]

Education is the most powerful weapon you can use to change the world. [295] The world, as we have created it, is a process of our thinking; it cannot be changed without changing our thinking. [133] But nothing is so painful to the human mind as a great and sudden change; those who cannot change their minds cannot change anything. [422] We are taught you must blame your father, your sisters, your brothers, the school, the teachers – but never blame yourself, it's never your fault. But it is always your fault – if you want to change, you're the one who has got to do it.[208] Taking a new step, uttering a new word, is what people fear most.[122]

Only you can change the world, and you do this by casting a stone across the water to create many ripples. Some changes look negative on the surface, but you will soon realise that space is being created in your life for something new to emerge.[457] It's never too late to change your life for the better. Change the way you look at things and the things you look at change.[890] It's only after you've stepped outside your comfort zone that you begin to change, grow and transform. You don't have to take huge steps; making even the smallest changes to your daily routine can make a big difference to your life.[38]

Maturity is when you stop complaining and making excuses and start making changes.[38] We are products of our past, but we don't have to be prisoners of it.[485] The present changes the past; by looking back, you do not find what you left behind.[114]

Believe something, and the Universe is on its way to being changed, because you've changed, by believing. Once you've changed, other things start to follow. Isn't that the way it works?[125] You never change things by fighting the existing reality. To change something, build a new model that makes the existing model obsolete.[175]

Destiny is not a matter of chance, it is a matter of choice; it is not a thing to be waited for, it is a thing to be achieved.[61] You cannot change what you are, only what you do. Fashion changes, but style endures. No matter who you are, no matter what you did, no matter where you've come from, you can always change, become a better version of yourself.[290] All that you touch, you change; all that you change, changes you. Anything that seems to be set in stone or unaltered can indeed change.[892] The only lasting truth is change. Every person who has finally figured out their worth has picked up their suitcase of pride and boarded a flight to freedom, which landed in the valley of change. The best way to love someone is not to change them, but to help them reveal the greatest version of themselves.[298] Life is a series of natural and spontaneous changes; don't resist them, that only creates sorrow. Let things flow naturally forward in whatever way they like.[467] Even if you cannot change all the people around you, you can change the people you choose to be around. Things change, and friends join and leave your life constantly. Life doesn't stop for anybody.

Life is too short to waste your time on people who don't respect, appreciate and value you. Spend your life with people who make you smile, laugh and feel loved.[891]

The only way that we can live is if we grow; the only way we can grow is if we change; the only way we can change is if we learn; the only way we can learn is if we are exposed; and the only way we can become exposed is if we throw ourselves out into the open.[78] Do it now. Change will not come if we wait for some other person or if we wait for some other time; we are the ones we've been waiting for.[892] We are the change that we seek.[366]

If you're always trying to be normal you will never know how amazing you can be. You may feel very secure in the pond that you are in, but if you never venture out of it, you will never know that there is such a thing as an ocean, a sea.[78] Holding on to something that is good for you at the moment may be the very reason you don't have something better. Incredible change happens in your life when you decide to take control of what you do have power over instead of craving control over what you don't.[298] Don't just learn, experience; don't just read, absorb; don't just change, transform; don't just relate, advocate; don't just promise, prove; don't just criticise, encourage; don't just think, ponder; don't just take, give; don't just see, feel; don't just dream, do; don't just hear, listen; don't just talk, act; don't just tell, show; don't just exist, live.[38]

When making a change, remember that there are three burdens of proof. (1) The burden of scientific (related to the mind) proof lies with researchers, not the critics/naysayers, and especially not with the establishment, who have set ways and hate change. (2) The burden of body (related to the physical) proof lies with each unique individual. They take what they want, what is useful and leave the rest. They are the judge, jury and executioner, for only then will they come to know, trust and live the life they need to. (3) The burden of spiritual (related to the soul) proof lies outside current science, its tools and techniques. Some things are unknowable, but we are given glimpses into this realm (associated with connectedness, oneness and love) through people with special abilities.

Cycles

Life is not easy, so don't try and make it so. It is a constant cycle of ebbs and flows.

If it never was and it isn't now, then you need to accept that it may not ever be. Life is full of ups and downs – it is not fair. Don't be a victim and fall into the entitlement trap. Get over it and get on with it.[307] Life is like a dark tunnel; you won't always be able to see the light at the end, but if you keep moving, you will come to a better place.[157]

You have the power to make your life free and beautiful, to make it a wonderful adventure. You don't have to prove anything to anyone, except yourself. If you haven't done what you promised yourself to do by now, then the chances are it will never happen (unless you act today). Everything is more rewarding if you break a sweat to get it because it means so much more. Changing can be strange, ugly, uncomfortable and horrible, but it is the door to the new, to opportunities and to where you were destined to travel. We all come into this world with something to do, and although it can take us some time to figure out what it is, if you relax it will appear before you.

Life moves pretty fast. It actually speeds up as you get older, so if you don't stop and look around once in a while, you could miss it all.[65] You are the author of the book of your life, so turn the page if you get stuck with a bad habit.[307] We all make mistakes; you have to own them, make amendments and move on. Guilt and regret kill many a man before their time. What we do in life, echoes in eternity.[893]

It's easy to run out of hope. No matter how bad it gets or how lost you feel, remember that where there's life, there's hope; hold on to it and keep it alive.[156] We have to be greater than what we suffer.[894] When there is so much uncertainty in the world, we must come together and remember how special life is and how fragile but powerful we are. You can't stay on life's peaks indefinitely; everyone needs to come down sometimes. You need to be prepared for the physical, mental and personal peaks, valleys and plateaus that naturally occur in cycles. The errors you make in the good times can create bad times in the future; the wise things you do in the bad times can create good times in the future. The time you take planning, observing and contemplating when on a plateau helps you see things differently and allows you to make different choices. Humans have an enduring power to inspire faith and excite hope, but it requires someone special to be fully effective and transform the lives of many.

Life on Earth is not meant to be an easy or comfortable ride. It is a series of some good and some bad. We have been sent here to learn new things, to experience the ups and downs, joys and pains, and have been granted the choice to do good things and not so good things. It is our choice.

Some of us will experience the 'dark night of the soul', which is a challenging period (not a single night) that ultimately leads to personal transformation and awakening. Afterwards, you might experience all sorts of new things, but most importantly, you will emerge refreshed, renewed and ready to walk your true-life path – a path of meaning, purpose and fulfilment with the will to love, believe and have new faith, holding the vibration level of love. It is not a place, but a state of being where you are able to hold energy and no longer perceive the outside world as taking something away from you.

You are never alone in the journey through these cycles. Stay strong by loving yourself, but every now and again, you may just need to surrender and not be afraid to reach out for help. When you awaken, you will realise we are all beings of light that are interconnected in this beautiful tapestry of physical, psychological and spiritual existence. Our respective connected futures hold boundless possibilities because we are truly remarkable, made in the image of God, and have the God-seed inside of us, allowing us to share the love of our Mother Universe and make our world a better place.

Time

Time is divided into three: that which was, that which is, and that which will be. Let us learn from the past to profit in the present, and from the present to live better in the future.[510]

Life is short, now is all we have, nothing lasts forever. Take strength from the past to create the new, but remember that now is the only time that matters; stop wasting it by ruminating on the past or planning too much for the future.[241] Things in the past can hurt a lot, but you can either run from them or you can learn from them.

Seeds grow, but not overnight. Sometimes miracles take a little time to happen. Don't judge each day by the harvest that you reap, but by the seeds that you plant. Time to reflect, time to mend, time to move on; there are different actions for different times.

Books are lighthouses erected in the great sea of time, but the ocean is wide – there are things you will never know. [496] Get over it, either apply more focus or move on to something different. It may not be the time and place for the answer to appear, or it may require more effort on your part to discover the answer.

An obsession with finding future happiness prevents many from attaining the joy that is always present; it is the matter of connecting to it and allowing it to flow through you that people find so difficult. You can worry about the pathway to the future, but there is only the now, the present, what is happening in the here and now, the decisions we make in this moment based on love or fear.[444] Don't make decisions based on fear wrapped under the blanket of practicality. It takes only one decision to change who you are. It is not what happens, it is how you react that matters.[137] Train yourself to respond in ways that lead to better outcomes now and in the future.[2415]

Time isn't on your side. It runs away from you and gets faster as you get older. So, take what you need when you need it, park the rest and come back after a while to review, because what served you well in the past may no longer serve you. You may have to drop or unlearn things or pick new things up. Think of life lessons as a backpack: what you needed (or thought you needed) when you were young is not always the same as you get older, wiser and more selective. Too many people hang on to baggage, additional things that don't bring them joy, for far longer than they need to. Minimise your burden; pack efficiently and travel fast; enjoy the preparation, planning and dreaming; enjoy the journey filled with excitement and anticipation as much as the destination of love, joy and bliss.

Waiting is a part of life that we all experience, and it's often considered challenging. It's being told to stay still and do nothing, and people can find that really hard. We're used to being active, doing things, moving forward. So, when we're asked to wait, it can feel like everything has come to a standstill, and that can be uncomfortable. Over the years, I've learned that a thought is put into motion the moment it's released to the Universe and the wheels begin to turn. It's a matter of letting go, and allowing God to make all the arrangements on your behalf. People, places and things will fall into place with little to no effort on your part. Remember, we are all beings of interconnected light. There's no need to fear; everything will unfold in Divine order. Your future holds boundless possibilities because you are truly remarkable.[894]

Art

Art is the only trace we leave of our passage on Earth.

We spend too much time on the mundane things – making money, making products, delivering services – and not enough doing the important things in life like creating truly beautiful art or spending time with the ones we love. People forget the money they've earned and saved after they have spent it, they disregard and throw away products when new ones appear, they consume the services we provide and forget about them. But humanity will always remember the artists, the people who give life meaning and help us make sense of the world.

I see art everywhere. In everything humanity creates, in everything nature creates, in everything the Universe created – in all God's work. Even in the autumn when the leaves fall on the grass. Everywhere.

Adversity

The flower that blooms in adversity is the rarest and most beautiful of all.[896]

Sadly, disappointment is an intrinsic part of life.[897] Stress is another inevitable part and a common universal truth. The key is how you respond to them. Nobody cares how difficult your life is; we are all up against something, so stop looking for sympathy and start creating the life you want to read about, one you are proud to have lived. There is a time to wait and see what happens, but there is also a moment to get active.[898]

In the middle of every adversity lies an opportunity.[897] When times are tough, just keep breathing. Tomorrow the sun will rise, and who knows what the tide will bring. Don't succumb – you are the master of your own fate. When we face impossible odds and life-threatening situations, it is not the smartest or most intelligent who prevail but those who embrace the joy of life. Joy gives them a reason, above everything else, to survive. People who survive know this and react accordingly; the hardest times often lead to the greatest moments of your life.

Don't be seduced by your own ego and think you are better than anyone else.[90] The ego seeks to divide and separate, whilst the spirit seeks to unify and heal.[90 & 43] Every day, try and do something positive, because you aren't fighting against other people, you are fighting for life. And at the end of the day, when you go to sleep, ask yourself if you are a good person or not.[44] The next day, try to do better. That is all you can do.

Challenges are what make life interesting. Run towards them, not away, because the only way to escape fear is to trample it beneath your foot. Keep going; tough situations build strong people.[261]

To every person upon this Earth, death comes sooner or later. How can a man die better than by facing fearful odds, for the ashes of his father and the temples of his gods?[286] Adversity shakes the foundation of our character to test if what we believe in and value is really worth standing for.[389]

Hard times don't create heroes, rather, it is during hard times that the 'hero' within us is revealed. Strength doesn't come from what you can do but from the things you once thought you couldn't.[389] It is only in the depths of winter that you finally learn that within you there lies an invincible summer. Life may have pounded you down time and time again, but you must still love life, just as the earth loves the rain. If you are struggling right now, please remember this: you have survived everything you've gone through up to this point. You can do this.

There are many types of adversity (physical, mental, emotional, workplace, social, spiritual, financial, household) that are multi-dimensional (control, ownership, reach, risk, threat, trauma, endurance) and affect individuals, work/family/friends and society as a whole. Just like in relationships, you can only quit, camp or climb. Adversity can make you stronger, more resilient and better prepared for the future if you plan, have help and support and deal with it instead of ignoring it.

Wealth

We are all born with nothing and leave with nothing. There's nothing like that concept to help keep perspective on money and material goods. Wealth makes the world go around and buys the freedom to do work with meaning, but it does not equal success.

All the best things in life are free because the most valuable things – love, family and friends – don't cost anything and can last an eternity. The second-best things are very expensive possessions that we are just guardians of whilst here on Earth; they are only temporary. You don't need to be poor to be spiritual; you have a right to be rich. Make money when you can, because money does make things easier, but beware of greed; you should only look to have what you need. The third best thing is the balance of money. You must keep enough money for yourself in order to live your life, promote independence and keep harmony with the world, yet also enough to give to others to help them on their way. This is to foster others' independence, not to make them reliant upon you or give you undue influence over their lives. The creative life force encourages the movement of giving and receiving because it recognises that all energy flows in circular and spiral fashions.[900] However, never lend money to family or friends unless you are prepared to write it off[899]; if you are precious about money then don't lend it in the first place.

Material wealth will not make you a better or happier person. There will be times when wealth is given to us freely or we obtain it easily, and it is then that we must give to others less fortunate and to the environment, for all living things and for future generations. But remember, giving money does less than giving time. Giving your time changes you in a way that giving money can't; it allows you to alter your perception and create a memory for yourself and others that will last forever.[241] All we have to decide is what to do with the time and resources that are given to us.[456]

Although money is not everything, you must gain control of your financial situation or the lack of control will hold you back and make your life more difficult. It takes a lot of mental fortitude to correct an imbalanced financial situation; it is a marathon not a sprint. Your emotions can really mess up your finances.[901] Unlearning bad habits can be hard, especially when we tell ourselves that making money is hard.

There is nothing worse than doing a job you hate, even if you earn lots of money. Loving what you do for a living is the definition of true wealth. Don't forget that time is far more precious than money. Time only cares for those who care for it; don't waste it, utilise every single minute to build a better tomorrow.

You don't have to buy anything new to work on yourself – this is optional.[902]

The world is made up of Old Money, New Money and Little-to-No Money. Money is generally finite, and those with it like to keep it that way. Real wealth is infinite.

There are three types of wealth: (1) That which comes with money, possessions and power but is always temporary, transient and linked to envy and greed. (2) That which comes with being poor and having to focus on survival. It is often linked to short-term thinking, getting through the next minute, next hour, next meal or next day. Some of the wealthiest people I have come across are the poorest in terms of monetary wealth, but are overflowing in love, care and compassion. (3) That which means you know you have enough for your basic needs, health and happiness, but not future desires. It often comes with a focus on comparing yourself to others and measuring your worth against them.

Understanding these different types of wealth and moving to a state of 'enoughness' brings with it more physical, mental and spiritual alignment than you could ever imagine, and often comes with awakening.

Just look at sports cars. When you are young, you can't afford them; in middle age, if you have kids and extra passengers/gear they are impractical; and when you are old and can afford one, they are almost impossible to get in and out of. Similarly, sofas are often designed for aesthetics and not for comfort or ease of getting onto and off from. Excessive wealth is unnecessary and superficial, and products are often specifically designed to tempt, to exemplify the best, when in reality they are over-engineered, overpowered or over-the-top. This is a classic situation of form over function; form should come from function to be practical and beneficial, otherwise it is just art dressed up in a shiny suit. There is one car manufacturer that produces cars that, while looking good, probably spend more time in the garage being repaired than on the road. Yet people still buy these unreliable vehicles to impress, show off or prove something that doesn't need to be proven. If, after spending lots of money, I had to recharge my battery every night just to keep it from going flat because of a design flaw, I wouldn't be impressed.

"The greatest wealth is to live content with little, for there is never a lack of those who desire more." —Marcus Aurelius.

Death

We have two lives. The second life begins when we realise we only have one life.[99]

Live life to the fullest. Every man dies, but not every man really lives. We don't want to just survive, but truly live with the courage to jump in, push envelopes and take risks. We are all seeking a noble and truly blessed life, looking for answers from someone else on top of one of those mountains. If you die before you reach the summit, at least you can say that you did your best. That is all anyone can expect of anyone. No more and no less. You're going to the top of this mountain, broken legs and all.[903]

Cherish moments with loved ones because they will not last forever. Everyone you love is going to die, some before you and some after you. Tears born from loss form profound lessons for the griever. They show us the connection of everything to everything else and remind us of the value of human life. We all die alone, yet souls want to experience new, constantly changing, dynamic, vibrant lives in all their colours, glories, joys and pains. Remember, there are heroes and legends; heroes are remembered but legends never die.[400]

Everyone has one chance to do something great, though most people never take the chance; they are either too scared or they don't recognise the opportunity when it crosses their path. This is your big chance, and you shouldn't let it go by.[159] Never stop believing there can be better.

There is no absolute truth, and nobody owns truth. In God we trust; all others must bring data.[113] Truth is not like data, information or products – truth is just out there. It is a stubborn thing, and whatever may be our wishes, our inclinations or the dictates of our passion, it is not possible to alter the state of facts and evidence.[235] The three most important truths are that you were born, you will die, and the *time* between these two events (not money) is your most valuable asset.

Your achievements and successes won't matter on your deathbed; you will be thinking about the relationships you made, and your regret for things you wish you had done during your time.[241] As you get old, things you took for granted get taken from you – the ability to walk, run, hear – and that's just a part of life.

Great things always begin from inside. We are mere reflections of our true nature, and we are here to express the spirit that dwells inside of us. All life comes and goes in cycles, but what we are is with us forever.

When I was a child and I thought of dying and going to an afterlife, I felt as if I was going home and that my time on Earth had been just a brief dream. A part of me was sad to leave it all behind as I passed through the darkness and utter despair, but I could feel this growing sense of relief, happiness and amazement that really was out of this world as I approached the light. The more I learn, the less sure I am of anything in this life. Still, there is that small flicker and feeling of home in the depths of my soul, somewhere really deep inside, that knows that no matter how bad things seem, there is always that light at the end of the tunnel,[904] that our bodies are just soul carriers until we return to the afterlife, to come back to Earth again at a later date and in a different form.

Death gives life meaning, to know your days are numbered, your time is short.[905] That it will never come again is what makes life so sweet.[117] Death is not the opposite of life but a part of it, and as natural as birth. We don't really understand it, but perhaps we are not meant to. Death is not the greatest loss in life, rather it is what dies inside us while we live.[100] The goal is not to live forever, but to create something that will. The only real purpose in life is to be our true self, live our truth and be the love that we are.

When a person is close to death and their body starts to close down, you will notice a decrease in appetite, that they will start sleeping more and become less social. Their body is becoming less active, needing less energy than it used to, and their metabolism is getting weaker as their muscles atrophy. In terms of vital signs, their blood pressure will drop, their breathing will change, their heartbeat will become irregular and harder to detect, and their urine may become darker or rust-coloured. The person may experience confusion, increased pain and hallucinations. Keep talking to them right up until they pass away, as they can often still hear what is going on. People will often look like they are sleeping after they die.

It is not long before the stress chemicals kick in and the body starts to go rigid. Beware, the seemingly asleep relative will soon look quite different, so be prepared for this. Alternatively, you can leave after a person dies so you always retain all the good memories of them and are not shocked by their final appearance.

It is said that souls will look down upon their body, often in disbelief, but that there is someone from the other side who comes to meet them and help them through the surprise and confusion of leaving their physical body and returning to spirit. We should not be afraid; we are returning to where we have come from and who we really are.

Love is the emblem of eternity; it confounds all notion of time, effaces all memory of a beginning... all fear of an end.[111] Happiness is the settling of the soul into the most appropriate spot.[22] Coming home is one of the most beautiful things.[380]

Nothing can dim the light that shines from within.[250] Give every day the chance to become the most beautiful day of your life, because one day you will enter the big sleep. Isn't it scary, knowing that any time could be the last time you talk to someone you love? Always keep that in mind, because you may not have an opportunity to tell people how much they meant to you, how much you cared for and loved them, or even to say a last goodbye.

In the precious time that we have in mortality, there are many things to be done. Some of these things are more important than others; some will be right, some will be wrong and some will be vital to meet our expectations of ourselves, to meet our purpose in life and to help move humanity in the right direction. We are capable of far more than just making a living or indulging ourselves in the beauties and pleasures of this world. We have been given tools to be used with judgement, not to excess, to help others and do things before we go back into eternal life. Eat, drink and be merry, for tomorrow we die, and it shall be well with us.[1]

Life is measured not by the breaths we've taken but by the moments that take our breath away. It is all so simple when you open your mind; that is what it takes to be human. Most of us end up going out the way we came in the world: kicking and screaming.[23] We can't escape our mental prisons; we think too much and feel too little. The fear of death follows from the fear of life; a man who lives fully is prepared to die at any time.[466]

You are not invincible or eternal, so although you don't know exactly when you will die, you can either speed the process up by not looking after yourself or you can start to structure your life in a more meaningful way. You have that unique and beautiful choice. Life is very simple. Just keep moving forward and keep getting up when you fall down, until your very last breath. Take care of the things you love. Don't wait too long to discover love or truth, don't be a person who learns life's lessons too late in life. Life is a process of continuous learning: if we stop, we start believing that nothing else can amaze us and we abandon the desire to learn new things. It is here that we begin to slowly die.

Our life is now, and it's the journey that counts. Everything is temporary; nothing lasts forever. Today's sacrifice will pay off tomorrow, but when we are young and impatient we want everything immediately. It is often not the destination that counts but the person we *become* whilst undertaking the journey. To work on what matters is to live without dying.

Accept that life is unfair and that nothing is owed to you. Don't make mountains out of molehills; you can tell the greatness of a person by what makes them angry. We have a huge capacity for tragedy, and every time we entertain our negative thoughts, we only manage to hurt ourselves and fear the worst, which never happens. When immersed in the problem, it can seem bigger than it really is, so step back to help gain perspective. Face your fears, be yourself and follow your dreams before it is too late. The people who self-fail in life are called losers because they never try, they live in mediocrity and don't embrace the power of now; they live in either the past or the future, and have lost the beauty of the present.

Persistence often pays off. If you want to do something important before you die, be ready to fail, and fail hundreds of times at that, whilst absorbing criticisms even if they are undeserved. You only live once, so don't care about the judgements of others (with the exception of constructive criticism as this helps you grow). Fear can stop you from growing. You need to overcome fear so that, having done so, you will know how to defeat it again. There is a spark of life within each of us that is fed and nurtured by our body, mind and soul. Use that spark well, for you die only once, whereas every new day is a fresh piece of paper to be written on. Yesterday is history; tomorrow is a mystery; today is a gift, that's why it is called 'the present'.[392]

Death is not the end of our existence or soul. When I visited my dad in hospital just before he died, I was talking about when he could come home; I now know that he knew he was dying, and it had been written on his face. You don't want to accept that your dad is about to die, and I probably hadn't wanted to read the signs. I just loved being there with him, chatting about small nothings, being right next to him and being totally present.

In the next bed, there was a younger man who had been listening to us, and with whom we started up a conversation. He said he had medically died a few days earlier but that the doctors had managed to bring him back. He told us the story of what he had experienced during this period of being dead, that he'd had an outer-body experience of wandering around the hospital in the form of a floating apparition, which he'd found very strange. He told me that he hadn't seen people as humans, but as the pain, hurt and suffering they were experiencing. (This brings new meaning to descriptions, from people who have had near death experiences (NDEs), of Earth as a place only brave souls come to, for it is the place of pain and suffering.)

Many people who have experienced a near death experience report that, as they stand next to their body, they are relieved the suffering is over, and are aware of a 'Being of Light' standing beside them, or being drawn to the light through a tunnel. No more pain, suffering, torment, oppression, sickness or fear, for the Universe is a friendly place. A timeless place of unconditional love, caring and sharing, with a sense of overwhelming peace and wellbeing, and a sense of oneness with everything.

Those who do come back become better versions of themselves, are more open, more welcoming, more at peace with themselves, more understanding and more loving than before, and often have a mission to start or complete, and are able to deal with newfound energy. They are no longer afraid of death for they know what awaits us all on the other side of life.

Beware. There are those that seek to harvest and feed upon your soul at the end of your life, to take you away to be tortured. They want this because we are built in the image of God (which they hate), we are weak and sinful (God values humility and wants us to consider ourselves lower, to love unconditionally and sacrificially serve others, to 'become like our Father in Heaven', whilst demons want power over us), we can be saved (demons can't, for they are trapped, restrained and evil) and we are considered territory to be conquered (they are attempting to restrain the growth of the Kingdom of God because they are depraved, have long-term malice and gain pleasure from pain and suffering).

The man I talked to in the next bed said he was at peace with himself in that ephemeral form, but that when he came across a living person, he didn't see them as we see ourselves, he saw what I can only interpret as their souls: all their heartbreak, fear and anguish. Is that what living an earthly existence means, collecting and carrying around all those painful memories and only achieving peace after death? I like to think that hospitals are not the best places to be in (for they have very difficult functions to perform). If the younger man had managed to go beyond the hospital, he would have seen some form of love, care and compassion.

We all carry around some element of pain. It hurts to live with dark thoughts and unresolved emotions from traumatic experiences, but there is always help. I have created a set of UK-centric helplines and contact details called 'LiteHows', to shine a light on safe harbours, at the end of this book. These contact details were created with the best intentions and were based on available knowledge at the time of publication. They may now be out of date, but I plan to create a website in the near future that will be kept up to date. Sail safe.

SECTION 3 - THE SOUL

The soul is not a physical object. Like the mind, it can't be seen, touched or photographed. It is the internal entity that lives, for a short period of time, within the physical constraints of the body in order to experience the world, others and the self in a truly unique form. Many people in this turbulent and traumatic world may be experiencing 'soul loss', in which part of our living essence shuts itself away, where it becomes fragmented and hinders us from moving forward.

Our over-reliance on science – with its dependence on data credibility, experimentation and repeatability – is left in a vacuum as more and more studies have shown that staggeringly few of them are actually repeatable. Scientific studies are not able to be operate across the multiple dimensions that are beginning to be recognised. Science cannot prove everything, especially ideas about the Divine and supernatural beings, or make value judgements. The scientific method is one of the most valuable tools that humanity has ever created, but it does have boundaries and limits that must be recognised.

Our over-reliance on religion – with its dependence on unquestioning faith, misinterpretation of divine messages and overzealous application – can be outdated, harmful to the individual, destructive to an integrated society and an impediment to progress. It is not helped by attitudes of religious discrimination, persecution and general non-acceptance of other faiths in the name of avoiding becoming extinct themselves. As religion often offers an easy method of dividing the world into 'good, believing people' and 'bad, non-believing people', it is no wonder that it has been implicated in all sorts of conflict and violence throughout human history. Patriots and zealots talk of dying for their country or cause but conveniently ignore the act of killing for their country or cause.

It is ironic that these institutions that purport to promote peace and harmony actually practise tribalism and thrive on existential anxiety. It seems that the least religious societies tend to be the most peaceful, prosperous and equitable.

Bertrand Russell's message to future generations, recorded in 1959, stated: 'If we are to live together and not to die together, we must learn a kind of charity and a kind of tolerance, which is absolutely vital to the continuation of human life on this planet. In this world, which is getting more and more closely interconnected, we have to learn to tolerate each other, we have to learn to put up with the fact that some people say things that we don't like. Love is wise and hatred is foolish. Look for the facts, not just the ones you wish to see, because facts don't care about your feelings.' [399]

Meet me in the middle of your story when the soul is worn but still wise, for a deep soul is aware of eternity, not just the present moment, [906] as the living soul of man, once conscious of its power, cannot be quelled.[294] The soul always knows what to do to heal itself; the challenge is to silence the mind.[329]

The world is perishable and whoever comes surely has to go one day. Whilst the body is temporary, the soul is permanent; the soul does not die, it just moves to another dimension. Fear is a disability, a deterrent to your wellbeing, for fearing death and worrying will kill your ambitions and diminish any chances of progress and real growth. You must always strive to eradicate fear from your mind. It is time to be fearless, for although it may be time for the body to die, the soul never will. After death, our soul continues to exist and will eventually be reborn into another body. We should, therefore, not pay attention to our outer body, but work for the inner soul and its satisfaction instead. For that is what we truly are and shall always be.

The meaning of life is just to be alive; it is so plain and so obvious and so simple. Yet everybody rushes around in a great panic as if it were necessary to achieve something beyond themselves.[489]

The Divine is supreme and the original cause of all causes. Everything starts from and ends with the Divine. The Divine is everywhere, omnipresent and omnipotent. The greatest thing any of us can do is to devote ourselves to the Divine and a life of service to others, because only then will every action and deed be dedicated to the Divine. Have faith, for faith brings in positive energy and momentum to make good things happen; that is how whatever happened was good, what is happening is good and what will happen in the future will be good.

As much as we would wish it so, the soul world is not governed by the laws of man, the will of kings or the models of science. It is beyond all these earthly things. It is the least understood part of being alive, human and connected.

CHAPTER 15

There are many paths to the divine.

"If you want to go fast, go alone; if you want to go far, go together; if they go low, you go high."

—African Proverb[6] (Modified)

Sometimes, the bad things that happen in our lives put us directly on the path to the best things that will ever happen to us.[194] Over every mountain there is a path, although it may not be seen from the valley.[387] There will be times when there is no path, no road, no map, no book, no knowledge and you will just have to walk forward and leave a trail. Sometimes, taking the right path is not choosing the easiest route; some of the most beautiful paths can't be discovered without getting lost.

Spirituality

We need to always keep an open mind and acknowledge that we are more than our physical form, that within, we are the very essence of the divine.

Spiritualism is the realm inhabited by spirits, both good and evil. After death, it is said we enter the world of the spirits, which is a kind of sorting zone between Heaven and Hell, where souls become acclimatised to the new environment they find themselves in. Our souls seek out kindred spirits, because that is where they feel most at home, and so migrate to their appropriate levels within Heaven or Hell. The direction souls take is ultimately based on the decisions and choices they made whilst on Earth, either in a loving or selfish way. You are not able to hide your true nature in the spirit world; those who are truly kind and generous will be so, and those who are inherently evil will justify their bad behaviour and thereby embrace it as part of themselves. The different levels of Heaven and Hell represent the distance the soul resides from the highest point: The Lord, who is a living sun that radiates Divine good and truth throughout creation.

Souls that aren't ready to experience higher levels are forced to retreat to the lower levels until they have been properly prepared. If two people are truly of one mind on Earth, they will live together as partners in Heaven as well. If they were not happily married, they will part ways.

Souls may eventually decide to return to Earth after a period, and priority is given to those who had an untimely death. Old Souls usually have the playfulness and simplicity of children, while maintaining a certain world-weariness and deep insight.[907] Old Souls love differently; they love genuine kindness, compassion, poetry and old books, soul connection, deep conversations, chivalry, romance, love, depth and rawness.

There is a beautiful thing inside you that is thousands of years old, too old to be captured in poems, too ancient to be loved by everyone.[908] You can identify an Old Soul with young eyes, a vintage heart and a beautiful mind or voice. Some, when they sing, make angels pay attention and make us mere mortals cry. Old Souls tend to be loners as they are disinterested in the pursuits and interests of people of their age group[506]; they find it dissatisfying to make friends with people they find it hard to relate to.[909] Blessed are the Old Souls, as they feel, suffer and see more deeply. Being an Old Soul is difficult because you are not here for greed, lust, inflations, quantity, comparison, competition, nor constant experiences; you are here for solitary peace, tranquillity, wisdom, love and empathy.[910] You can tell if you are an Old Soul if you know there's another way to do things and give advice well beyond your years. You think things through and don't waste time asking why because you just know.[911] Old Souls can be social outcasts, black sheep, and can be prone to intense existential crises. They seem to have an inherent wisdom and a grounded sense of being in the world.

The history of our spiritual life is a continuing search for the unity between ourselves and the world. Religion, art and science, one and all, follow this aim. The capacities by which we can gain insights into higher worlds lie dormant with each one of us. Today, the vision of the human being is confined to the physical body. If one regards this as a reality, one cannot raise themself to what is spiritual. The souls that now look upon their own physical bodies with their eyes, and are unable to rise to what is spiritual, were incarnated among earlier peoples as Greeks, Romans and ancient Egyptians.[442]

The more you give, the more you have.[440] Condemnation before investigation is the height of all ignorance.[473] What misdeed will be set on foot if the truths of Spiritual Science are withheld? To withhold the spiritual life of goodness from men is to be no friend of humanity; whoever does this, be he Freemason or Jesuit, is no friend of humanity. Their purpose may be to confine goodness to a small circle, in order, by the help of this goodness, to dominate the helpless of humanity.

Charity

If you can help others, then you should. Not only is being charitable good for your own wellbeing, it helps make the world a better place. Charity brings to life those who are spiritually dead as it is the greatest act of grace and seeks to be useful to others with no thought of recompense. He who has no charity, deserves no mercy.

You don't need a cape to be a hero, all you need is to care.[912] The smallest act of kindness is worth more than the grandest intention,[473] and is more powerful than a thousand heads bowing in prayer.[178] When we give cheerfully and accept gratefully, everyone is blessed. Every man must decide whether he will walk in the light of creative altruism or in the darkness of destructive selfishness.[256] You have not lived today until you have done something for someone who can never repay you.[68] Beauty is not who you are on the outside, it is the wisdom and time you gave away to save another struggling soul like you.[10] To ease another's heartache is to forget one's own. Doing nothing for others is the undoing of ourselves.[913] Let's make today awesome for somebody; no act of kindness, no matter how small, is ever wasted.

Charity and love are the same; with charity you give love, so don't just give money but reach out your hand instead.[326] There is not a single person who doesn't, at times, need a helping hand to be stretched out to them. No one has ever become poor by giving, as it's not how much we give but how much love we put into it. There is no exercise better for the heart than reaching down and lifting people up.[215] The most treasured and sacred moments of our lives are those filled with the spirit of love. The greater the measure of our love, the greater our joy. In the end, the development of such love is the true measure of success in life.[504]

There are three types of people who flash cheese: the first are people who don't know any better, the second are people trying to intimidate and the third are people with honourable characters, trapped in a dishonourable world, trying to help others through charity. Giving to others in need is one of the best feelings you can ever imagine. Material things will never bring anyone deep or meaningful happiness, for everything of real value, such as love, care and sharing, is free; these are the things that money can't buy. Everything important in life is intangible.

Mindfulness

Our life is shaped by our mind, for what we think, we become.[179] Mindfulness isn't difficult – we just need to remember how to do it.[402] It is being aware of negative thoughts and discarding them before they spiral and damage us. Wherever you are, be there totally; learn to be present and enjoy the moment, happy in that moment, that it is enough.[229] The best way to capture moments is to pay attention; this is how we cultivate mindfulness.[243]

Mindfulness is an invitation to change our patterns, to become aware of where we are and how we got there.[126] The practice of mindfulness is one of the most powerful reset buttons we have. It gives us a chance to listen to the wisdom of our hearts, to notice with more clarity when we get in our own way, and shift from reacting out of habit to responding with intention. The key to keeping your balance is knowing when you've lost it.[18] Awareness is like the sun; when it shines on things, they are transformed.[199]

When we learn how to slow down internally, we begin to see our habitual reactivity, we start to understand how fear, even on subtle levels, may dictate our choices around our work.[126] Your work is going to fill a large part of your life, and the only way to be truly satisfied is to do work that you believe is great, and the only way to do great work is to love what you do. If you haven't yet found it, keep looking and don't settle.[234] As with all matters of the heart, you'll know when you find it.

Mindfulness gives you time, and time gives you choices. Choices, skilfully made, lead to freedom. If you want to conquer the anxiety of life, live in the moment, live in the breaths.[374] Meditation is the ultimate mobile device; you can use it anywhere, anytime, unobtrusively.[402] Every morning, we are born again, and it is what we do every 'today' that matters most. Value gratitude. Breathe. The only way to live is by accepting each minute as an unrepeatable miracle, so let go and remind yourself that this very moment is the only one you know you have for sure. [262 & 503] If you concentrate on finding whatever is good in every situation, you will discover life suddenly filled with gratitude: a feeling that nurtures the soul.[223]

Mindfulness means paying attention in a particular way, on purpose, in the present moment and non-judgmentally.[243] Surrender to what is and let go of what was.[315] Have faith in what will be. The present moment is filled with joy and happiness, and if you are attentive, you will see it.[199] Make the most of the day. Do not dwell in the past, do not dream of the future, but concentrate the mind on the present moment.[325] You can't stop the waves of life, but you can learn to surf.[243] The mind is the place where the soul goes to hide from the heart, and it is everything; what we think, we become.

Everything is created twice: once in the mind and then in reality.[420] Worrying is stupid, it's like walking around with an umbrella, waiting for it to rain. Your mind is your instrument; learn to be its master and not its slave.[457] Stop over-analysing; life is simple. Peace is the result of retraining your mind to process life as it is, rather than as you think it should be.[128] Look past your thoughts so you may drink the pure nectar of the present moment.[398]

Open your mind, arms and heart to new things and people; we are all united in our differences. Life is about the people you meet and the things you create with them, so go out there and start creating.[297] Ask the next person you meet what their passion is and share your inspiring dream with them; life is short, so live your dream and share your passion.[915]

There are far too many people wasting their time telling themselves that they don't have enough time, but the key is in 'finding space'. Amid movement and chaos, keep stillness inside of you. In today's rush, we all think too much, seek too much, want too much and forget the joy of just being.[457] Travel often – getting lost will help you find yourself.[639] The best way to get somewhere is to let go of trying to get anywhere at all. The journey of a thousand miles begins with a single step, but it helps if you start going in the right direction straightaway.[88] The day you decide that you are more interested in being aware of your thoughts than being in the thoughts themselves is the day you will find your way out.[427]

We like to think of ourselves and our actions as rational, well-informed and understood, when history can demonstrate that we are, in fact, irrational, impulsive, uninformed, un-awakened and misunderstood beings. The First Way of thinking and doing is largely based on instinct and the drive to survive; it is, therefore, threat-driven, emotional and fast-reacting, especially to new events and situations. Most people live much their lives in this state. The Second Way is more informed and is based on the inner mind using mindfulness, reason, logic and proactivity, and is driven by avoiding risk and learning from mistakes. However, it is often self-centric, ego driven and ignores our blind spots. People get into this state through education and maintaining an open mind and practise, but it is a difficult state to remain in forever because it takes a lot of effort and resources. It may not serve us well in emergency situations either.

The Third Way of thinking and doing considers the spiritual, the soul, caring, sharing, contemplation, the collective impact, wider perspectives, reflection. It utilises the sub-conscious mind, deals with negativity, takes a step back to fully consider things, doesn't rush into decisions you may regret later and takes a whole-world, outcomes-driven approach to the future. This is a very difficult place to live in and operate at constantly. It is similar to living on the top of a mountain where the viewpoints and experience are mind-blowing, especially the effects it has on collective societal consciousness, and its profound impacts and ethical implications for the world as a whole. It involves utilising your innate abilities that have been long suppressed to live your best life, create a better place for all people on Earth and respect everything and everyone, for we are all connected.

I hope that understanding these three states will make you think about which one is engaged when you are making decisions and performing actions, and consider that a higher state might be more beneficial. I hope this will develop your ability to periodically, and at critical crossroads moments, ask yourself which state are you in and whether or not it is serving you and others most appropriately, in this moment and with the choices and resources at your disposal.[916 & 917]

Speech

Speech is a great, magical force. Lightning makes no sound until it strikes.

The five keys to right speech are that it is spoken at the right time, in truth, affectionately, beneficially and with a mind of loving kindness. Before you speak, let your words pass through the three gates of truth, necessity and kindness.[446] Say little, but when you do speak, utter gentle words that touch the heart. Right speech is to speak truthfully, not creating harm or speaking cruelly, not exaggerating or embellishing, and in a way that relieves suffering and brings people back to themselves. Speak well of others, not of their faults. Right speech comes out of silence, and right silence comes out of speech.[49] Be truthful, express kindness and abstain from vanity.[353] This is the way.

Freedom of speech is about being able to express your opinion – however good or bad, right or wrong – and defend it. It includes the right not to speak, to say what people don't want to hear and to be able to comment on free speech.[341] It is your right to make an arse of yourself. The freedom of speech of private individuals includes the right to not agree, not to listen, and not to finance one's own antagonists.[372] Yet it is not so much freedom of speech but the right to truth that great men protect.[232] Political correctness has the potential, if inappropriately executed, to cause immense damage and destroy the fabric of society. Never before have people been so afraid to stand up against absurdity for fear of being labelled a racist, a homophobe or a bigot. Some people's idea of free speech is that they are free to say what they like but if anyone says anything back, that is an outrage.[93] The right to free speech is more important than the content of the speech. Let's get people talking again before the truth itself is labelled as hate speech.

We need to fight for our freedoms otherwise they will be taken away, one at a time, until we have none left. We need to speak out against lies and misconceptions that are being disseminated as truth. We need to speak up when we see evil, injustice, crime and corruption; these things cannot be allowed to perpetuate. We need to watch for leaders who overpromise, never deliver and are not held accountable for their words and actions, and we need to remember the names of those who say nothing yet stand by these leaders, allowing the evils, injustices, crimes and corruption to continue.

We should not be forced into making 'are you with us or are you against us?' decisions when questionable tactics are being used to obtain outcomes that undermine humanity and freedoms. We need to watch for people being hounded for expressing their opinion; passion must not overrule the law, common sense, pragmatism or the truths we hold dear. If you have an idea for change, then it should be stated, argued, challenged, modified and published in the open and not behind closed doors where secret forums act in self-interest. The truth is that hate speech is only useful to those that have something to hide.

There are times for words and there are times for tears. The people who cry when you cry, these are your people – your middle-of-the-night, no-matter-what people. It is a grave injustice to a child or adult to insist that they stop crying. One can comfort a person who is crying, which enables them to relax and makes further crying unnecessary; but to humiliate a crying child is to increase his pain and augment his rigidity. We stop other people from crying because we cannot stand the sounds and movements of their bodies; they threaten our own rigidity. It induces similar feelings in ourselves that we dare not express and evokes a resonance in our own bodies that we resist.[282] Tears are a language like no other, but one that God understands.

Do you know the lasting power of speech? The ability to exert such a potent hold and resonance with people all around the world, even down through future generations not yet born. The ability to help, heal or hinder others around you. The ability to deliver positive, unconditional love by tapping into that energising power Source, an infusion of more connectivity and creativity. It's a transformative power, not only on an individual level, but on a collective level, too. Beware what you speak, for it echoes through time like a stone hitting the water, and the ripples go well beyond the initial impact zone.

Togetherness

The sum of the parts is greater than the whole. History is a great teacher, and everyone knows that the coming together of people and workers does not diminish the strength of a nation but enlarges it.

We are stronger working together than we are fighting alone or working apart; togetherness is strength.[918] Mankind should always stay united, standing shoulder to shoulder so evil can never cheat and divide them.[247] When two brothers are busy fighting, an evil man can easily attack and rob their poor mother.[247] Nothing brings people together like a common enemy.[481] What divides us pales in comparison to what unites us! United we stand, divided we fall, so only in union can we find strength. A union only works if everyone is wishing to go in the same direction. If one suffers, we all suffer.

If you want to go quickly, go alone. If you want to go far, go together.[6] Sometimes, reaching out and taking someone's hand is the beginning of a journey.[365] At other times, it is allowing another to take yours.[331] Holding hands, for example, is a way to remember how it feels to say nothing together. As ridiculous as it may sound, sometimes all any of us needs in life is for someone to hold our hand and walk next to us.[173]

It is an absolute certainty that no one can know his own beauty or perceive a sense of his own worth until it has been reflected back to him in the mirror of another loving, caring human being.

We are all in this world together, in the same boat called Earth. We are all connected directly and indirectly. You've got to give back in this life; help others move forward and overcome their barriers so they can exceed their expectations and help others as well.

Simple

It's easy to make things more complex, sometimes simple is best. The best kind of simplicity is that which exposes the raw beauty, joy and heartbreak of life as it is.

Alignment adds to your contentment and peace of mind. When your ideal self (the image you show to others) and your actual self (the real, vulnerable you) are aligned, amazing things occur. Prioritise self-care so you are less stressed, less over-stretched and overwhelmed. You must learn to let go so you can focus on what's actually meaningful to you. Anyone can be cool, but awesome takes practice.[355]

The grandeur of the universe reveals itself through simple things. A common man marvels at uncommon things but a wise man marvels at the commonplace.[99] The magic happens when you understand that everything is impermanent and changing. Change is inevitable. Don't expect to get anything right the first time. Part of the fun of not knowing is the journey of finding out. Life is neither the start nor the destination: it is the *journey* itself, it is the putting of one step in front of another every day, whatever the circumstances. Connecting with those you know, love, like and who appreciate you restores the spirit and gives you energy to keep moving forward.[108] Sometimes it is the smallest thing that saves us. Practise doing nothing sometimes, then take full action with the intention of moving yourself in the right direction.

Cluttered environments create cluttered minds, chaos, insecurities, tensions, arguments and provoke social inequalities. A simple life is one free of clutter and complexity: remove it from your home and office space, and mentally, too; create space between things, pause and find joy in the simple things. We tend to live busy and cluttered lifestyles with unnecessary accumulations of stuff. Make the fewer things that you have beautiful things so you can cherish, use, care for and wear them with pleasure. What is the point of having lots of cheap, ugly things that take your time energy to organise, store and sift through to find the beautiful things? Make your life less cluttered so you have more room for beauty. It takes a lot of effort to make something look simple and behave effortlessly.[321] If an item brings you joy, then keep it; if it doesn't, then get rid of it or donate it.[260]

Our age of excess is destroying us and the world, but there is a simple solution. Only take what you need from the Earth and leave only a small footprint behind; leave it in a state you would like to find it. Simplicity is the prerequisite for sustainability, spirituality and social harmony.

Sometimes you are meant to be in certain places at certain times, to help others. A long time ago, I collected information from my university department that was closing down. I wasn't sure why I was doing it at the time, but I recently had the opportunity to share it, and through this I met new people, shared historical experiences and reconnected people who had been separated for many years. I really enjoyed the whole process. Take every opportunity to share what you have and spread love and care. And if you receive from another kind soul, pay it forward.

Enough

When is enough, enough? You will never get everything in life, but you can get enough. Once you begin to take note of the things you are grateful for, you begin to lose sight of the things that you lack.

The ideal amount of money is that which neither falls within the range of poverty nor far exceeds it, but enough will never be enough for some. They are always whirling in a trance of deficiency in which they equate being alone with loneliness, restraint with deprivation, and being silent with being empty. If you have what you need, it is enough; if you have what you desire or crave, it is too much. A tomb now suffices him for whom the world was not enough[14]; whoever is not in his coffin and the dark grave, let him know he has enough.

Sometimes it takes being told you're nothing—or being made to feel like you're nothing—to help you see that you are complete. You are always enough. If you understand that, you are on the right way to respecting yourself and your surroundings. Sometimes you have to realise that you've had enough to realise that you *are* enough and develop the ability to set forth into the world knowing you are enough and that this is all you need to live a healthy, happy and free lifestyle that you love.[187] Your heart is enough.[11] Love mercy, walk humbly. This is enough. Wisdom is knowing when you have just enough to keep going.

I remember the period when my father joined the 1980 national steel strike when he worked at the Velindre Tinplate Works, near Felindre. The plant was established during a wave of industrial optimism after the Second World War and offered workers a tough but secure job. However, things changed. Financial losses had occurred during the recession in the '70s, and although profitability was improving, a double whammy of 'profitability or bust' and a hardened, ideological governmental desire to pull trade unions apart proved too much for the steel industry (and the mining industry later on). Despite a victory over pay cuts and plant closures, the majority of steel workers were made redundant when the works closed in 1989, which was a significant loss to the local community and caused further hardship for the workers and their families, now supressed in the collective memory. I remember a long period during the strike when there was no income coming into our house, and a particular stage when we didn't have enough to keep going. My father took a loan from his brother to keep the roof over our heads, and to keep us fed and warm. He eventually paid back his brother, retired early on a good pension and had enough to keep him going, but something died in him that day he came home 'rationalised'.

I'm forever grateful for that family support but was too young to acknowledge it at the time. So, I am saying thank you now. That was enough for us during those dark days of struggle. A reliance on cheaper imports is such a stupid attitude; every country should ensure that it has enough basic industry, energy, food and water to survive for a significant period of time. Having an appreciation of 'enough' is very important. We all, collectively and as individual countries, need to make provisions for 'enough', for we don't know what the future will hold in terms of 'inevitable' and 'unthinkable', in this crazy world.

I was fortunate to have extended family support to help provide me with enough, but not everyone is as fortunate. I have, therefore, created a section at the end of this book called 'LiteHows', which, just like the lighthouses of old guiding ships away from hazards, is intended is to guide people into safe harbours. It is great to have powerful quotes, sensible lessons and real examples, but there are times when you need proper, professional support. 'LiteHows' focuses on UK-based advice and helplines, and has links to international equivalents.

Backdrop

This concept explores the idea that everything and everyone is part of the grand stage of our life that we ourselves orchestrate – people come into our lives and leave our lives just like actors entering and leaving the stage at just the right time in a play – and explores the profound lessons we derive from this. How would you behave differently if you understood that everything in your life – the people, the situations, the drama – is carefully chosen by you? If you are no longer a passive observer who can blame others or the Universe for your misfortunes, but an active dreamer, creator, playwright, actor and director of your own reality? We are always told we have the power to create anything we want when we tap into the immense potential of our mind. (We are fed this message every day, just look at the self-help industry, get-rich-quick schemes and the advertising sector, where nothing is impossible.)

There is some knowledge that is profoundly personal, only intended for specific individuals who are meant to receive it as a gift at the right time, to help guide them and instil trust in their journey. This information isn't for everyone, it is reserved for and accepted by only those who earnestly seek it with open hearts and minds; though, all are loved the same (both souls and those currently soulless), for everyone has the capacity to be awakened. Everything we do on Earth is geared towards learning this one fundamental lesson: manipulating energy. Earth is a school helping us master the art of energy manipulation whilst in physical form. Until we learn it and apply it to our lives, we can't graduate and are destined to continually reincarnate until we do.

Our mind is an incredibly powerful tool, but once connected to the body and soul, its ability to tap into the universal energy becomes limitless.

Our lives are not fully predetermined; although we do have soul contracts with others in this world, we are blessed with choice and have the ability to write and rewrite the script as we go along. You are not trapped by external forces in your circumstances, though you are often trapped by yourself. Everything is made up of energy, our physics has already taught us that, and as you get older and gain more insights into the true nature of existence, you will realise the boundless potential you have. We each have the ability to create, transform and manifest our desires into reality; this is the biggest secret that our leaders (soulless people, lizard-people, lowest-density-vibrational-energy people) do not want us to know.

Life is a gigantic play where we all play the lead character in our own story and wait in the wings for our next scene in someone else's story (as a backdrop person to others currently on stage). We are continually consciously creating (not unconsciously or subconsciously), and that is where the real power lies.

Backdrop people[927] fill in the background while we are centre stage. As every human being has a natural inclination to be surrounded by, connected to and interact with others, we have a rich and dynamic cast to fill out our individual experiences. There are three types of backdrop people: (1) those who have an evolutionary journey and purpose, who operate in your inner circle to help or hinder you. Yes, some people are put in place to try and stop you, but they should be seen as motivation that spurs you on; you cannot take their advice or endeavour not to be like them. (2) The ones with whom you have a soul connection. (3) The extras – those who are not real people to you, but energy individuals in your outer circle who provide a vital role in your learning and growth; their presence provides contrast and highlights lessons you need to learn.

This third category of backdrop people play supporting roles, give advice, prompt you to do things and open or close a door for you; essentially, they create the illusion of a bustling world around you. They may be people who are stuck on the same track and operating in automatic or reactive mode. They might challenge your reality and conventional thinking as they can be intriguing and thought-provoking. They may not be sentient beings with souls, but energy in human form, either holographic projections, sleepwalkers or benevolent/evil spirits, that can interact with you but that lack the depth of consciousness and energetic higher frequency that you possess. You can recognise backdrop people when you tune into their energy; they emit a lower and different frequency, and don't belong to the same energetic realm that you do. They are often energy vampires, full of negativity, hate and envy.

Backdrop people help with your spiritual and personal evolution (as they are an extension of the same Universal Source), although you may not appreciate this at the time and, rather, wish they had never appeared in your life. They can challenge you, test you and ignite growth by showing areas where you need to improve. They can act like barriers or redirectors, enabling you to shift your energy away from negativity and towards higher vibrations. Sometimes, it's 'no pain, no gain'. Hold no anger or judgement, for these tests that cross your path serve a purpose. Don't judge backdrop people or resent them; approach them with compassion, understanding that they are fulfilling their role by helping you learn from them, allowing you to move from the Old Earth (older plane of existence) to the New Earth (higher vibrational state reached via personal growth) and a better world. Practising kindness, forgiveness, respect, gratitude, supporting all life and the environment and sharing love for others are the means of entering into the New Earth.[919]

Sometimes we are not shown what to be but what *not* to be. However, you can tell people what not to do until the cows come home. Sometimes they need to experience something in order to learn from it what they now disapprove of and what not to do again.

You may be saying, at this stage, that I'm preaching to the converted, you've heard all this before. If so, I'm really happy to hear that, but take what you need for now (if anything at all) and leave the rest for another day, when you may need it.

You may be saying that I'm talking rubbish, that I don't know anything about you, your situation or circumstances. That may be so, but we all have our unique journeys, and while the human condition is very predictable, our responses can be very unpredictable. Knowing this, don't allow your life to be run by your emotions or your reactions, and don't keep blaming others; you may not think about it or consider it true, but you are the master of your own destiny. Own it. Live it. Love it.

And now a message for those who may never read it: You may not have got this far into the book. It may be sitting on your bookshelf or donated to a charity shop, destined to be read in the future, either by you or someone else. You may just be the conduit to get this information to others and may not yet be ready to accept it yourself.

Lightworking

Are you a lightworker? Agents of change and transformation, lightworkers play a pivotal role in the collective journey of human consciousness, raising the vibrational frequency of the planet and guiding humanity towards a higher state of awareness and unity. Have you received a calling, or have a burning and profound desire to [928]:

- Serve humanity? A fire inside you to go beyond the boundaries of your personal life and make a meaningful impact on the world; a resounding call that echoes through the chambers of your soul that insists you contribute to the greater good.

- Channel your gifts, wisdom and energy to create positive change and radiate positive energy? A lighthouse standing tall and firm amidst the chaos of the crashing waves below, guiding ships and the souls aboard to safety via a path of healing and transformation. Your actions, no matter how small they seem, resonate across the Universe and touch lives in ways you may not fully grasp until you ascend.

- Operate as a beacon of hope, authenticity and compassion? The very essence of your being that lies at the heart of who you are. Healing hands that mend the broken and ease the burdened, that provide a frequency and resonance that delivers relief to those in pain. This energy flows from the depths of your heart and soul to the tips of your head, fingers and toes.

- Healing modalities, fixing and building things? From a young age, and not just on a physical level, but on a deeply emotional and spiritual plane.

- Help others? A heart that overflows with compassion and boundless empathy in our harsh and unforgiving world that desperately craves and needs help. Offer comfort and guidance through the ability to walk in people's shoes and become one with them (not via ESP).

- Stand out without hesitation, illuminate the way for others, and not stand back and get lost in the shadows? Feeling like an outsider with a uniqueness and unconventional purpose, viewing the world through a different lens from others, as if you are a visitor from another realm. It may be your first time on Earth; your heart may beat to a rhythm not everyone can hear. You are not destined to follow the beaten path, so find yourself forging your own trail and breaking new ground. Your sense of otherness isn't a flaw, it is a gift and hallmark of your extraordinary, bold mission, reminiscent of Exodus 2:22 and Robert A. Heinlein's *Stranger on a Strange Land.* [138 & 205]

- Connect on a deep level? A finely tuned harmonisation of vibrations allows you to experience the unique sensitivities and symphony of energies that permeates and pulses beneath the surface of current reality across our entire Universe. Connecting with essence wherever you go, you deliver balance and serenity as you guide the ebb and flow of energies around you. You have the ability to transform chaos into tranquillity, discord into resonance and hate into love.

- Seek knowledge that transcends the mundane, toxic social media and sensational traditional news outlets? A quest for ancient wisdom: seeking hidden, profound truths within yourself; accessing the Akashic Records and timeless knowledge that spans the epochs of human existence across previous civilisations and well before the current accepted 'dawn of time'. A magnet is drawing you to these ancient whispers to help you comprehend the mysteries of the Universe and unravel the intricacies of existence. It is a journey of self-discovery and of what it means to be human, while simultaneously helping humanity. By sharing this knowledge and acting as a lantern, illuminating the path for others to follow, you inspire and uplift those who are destined to cross your path.

- Expand your horizons and those of others? An unwavering optimism, hope and positivity amidst the stormy seas of a self-obsessed, materialistic world clouded by ego, challenges and negativity. You are the light that shines into and defies the darkness. Setbacks put you on the right path; challenges are opportunities to prove to yourself what you are really capable of. You have a gift that allows you to see beyond the façade and glimpse the growth, evolution and transformative power that lies within adversity, pain and suffering. Your positivity infects those you choose to surround you, a beacon of resilience on the path we all must travel. You stand as a living embodiment of the enduring influence of hope. You call others to self-empowerment, a way of living, and to the very essence of who you are, which defies the ordinary; you are a co-creator and beacon of light in a world ready and waiting to accept the brilliance you bring.

If you resonate, connect or have an affinity with the above, then you will love the second book in this series, which continues where this one stops. In it, I question the 'jar' of knowledge in which we were brought up and conditioned, and why some of us struggle our entire lives thinking that there is something else, searching for answers outside the boundaries of the 'jar', where questions are often not encouraged.

Everything in the world is subjective, but there are some things that will resonate and activate in readers' souls. Cherish every single moment, for eternity is not that long; there is still lots of humanity in us all. I haven't lost hope in humanity, and neither should you, for we each have the power to go deeper, bringing us all closer to Source. The more the Light gives, the more is left; whatever the Light touches is awakened.[925]

Sometimes we are all so driven to get to our destinations that we forget to look out the window and appreciate the beauty that exists all around us. We are shutting our minds off from the now, getting sucked into our electronic worlds, are often too work-focused, engrossed in negative social media or dealing with a never-ending to-do list, when we should be looking after ourselves, relaxing and de-stressing so we can look after others. Don't forget to leave something in the tank for reserve, to love, care (including for yourself) and share.

For as long as I can remember, I've just wanted to do what was right, but I guess, in this crazy world, it is easy to get things confused, and I may not be sure what 'right' is anymore. All we can do is our best, and sometimes the best we can do is to start over.[926]

I've been fragile, emotional and broken, but my journey through the pain – mentally (doing the re-wiring first), physically (incrementally pushing forward, in a controlled manner, careful not to overdo it and relapse) and spiritually (wrestling with the good and bad aspects of religions) – has made me stronger, wiser and more thoughtful. I am constantly learning new things, sharing love, compassion and knowledge, knowing we are all connected to that one true Source; this is what keeps me going. I recognise that this is only the start of my journey, which I am approaching with new hope, new viewpoints and new love.

There is a superlative nature to life. It is incredibly captivating, beautiful, heart-warming, uplifting, inspiring and heart-breaking. It can give you goosebumps and priceless moments of magic, and bring you to exultation or to tears; it is an emotional roller coaster of a ride. There are times when no words can adequately describe the experiences we have; love transcends human nature to all that exists, even currently non-living creations that we bring consciousness to. Is the purpose of putting our souls in physical bodies a method of allowing us to experience, learn lessons, evolve and expand our own consciousness – that which we are unable to do in the spirit world – through suffering, cruelty and the problems only a physical body can experience (the need for food, water, air, empathy and understanding)?[305]

There are things that define generations. There was a time we were excited about the future, when times were simpler and life was good. Childhood was the best time of life for some, a time of innocence, inspiration and hope, but we seem to have reverted into a time of hate, cruelty and war. Hate is the easy path; love is hard and painful yet so rewarding; but change, now that is the real challenge. Change your mind, actions and beliefs to do a U-turn away from hate and the dark, towards love and the light, where we all truly belong.

We do not need to stay in this negativity; we have the ability to create beauty and peace, return to the good times and make good music again. It is down to me, down to you and down to all of us to make that change and difference.[925]

Dimensions of Light

If you are not a lightworker (someone with the ability to attain spiritual awakening at a rapid rate), could you be:

A Star Seed/Star Child? Someone who originally came to this Earth School to assist in elevating its consciousness and vibratory rate.

An Indigo Child/Adult? Someone who incarnated on Earth up to the year 2000, with increasing abilities in and degrees of technological and creative sophistication, about to take their place as leaders of the world.

A Crystal Child/Adult? Someone undergoing spiritual and physical transformation that awakens their 'Christ' consciousness.

An Old Soul or Empath?

Whatever role you have or take, your time is now! Awaken, my beauties, for the time of change and ascension is underway. Have a look at 'The Light' by Akiane.[929]

POSTSCRIPT

Life is not a competition; life is a blessing. Learn to really look at and love your surroundings and the little things in life. At the end of the day, we are all connected to one big wholeness and we make it through life better together than apart.

Our world is full of positive, negative and neutral energy frequencies. Life can be hauntingly gruesome, dark and painful and you may have been through difficult moments in your life, but you have survived. You will face more difficulties in the future, but as you read or listen to this, remember: you are alive, you are a survivor, you can be brave. We are all born with choices – make good ones if you can. Life wasn't designed to be easy. Keep fighting; trust in yourself; you're worth it.

I have shown you examples of lessons learnt from many different aspects of life, society and the environment. If you take one message from this whole book let it be that life is purposefully and beautifully varied, and there is no single right answer or approach that works in all scenarios. People, cultures and the world are not meant to be fully understood; they are put in place for us to experience them while we are on Earth, but we are also a species designed to experience things beyond this world. We are connected to all other people and everything else that exists where we find ourselves right now, even the inanimate objects, the place we came from before we were born and the next world we are destined to go to. Just as our head is connected to our bodies, our hands are connected to our arms and our feet are connected to our legs, we are all connected. If we can help our connected parts whilst we experience the world, and if we can leave them all a little better off than when we arrived, then that is enough. The power is in the now, not in the past or the future; experience it all fully, deeply and completely, for that is how you heal, forgive and then migrate towards peace and tranquillity. Give it a try. Allow this book to lift the veil that has been covering your eyes. What have you got to lose?

We don't see the world as it is, we see it as we are. Words, languages, the visible spectrum and our five senses are not static or limited, and they change over the generations, but the full spectrum of reality, symbols and mathematics transcend generational barriers (even if the meanings of some symbols have been temporarily lost). We have the ability to awaken and do better for ourselves and humanity in general.

Lots of people seem broken on the inside, as if nothing truly human fits anymore in this world of insanity. Most people are not really awake and let their personalities and egos run the show, perpetuating drama and pain. We all hold on to deep burdens, guilt and fury that take time to resolve, but that can only happen once you trust your intuition and get the energy flowing. We are all born gifted, but most are not yet awake or confident enough to use their gifts. Some people are gifted at awakening people, preparing them to upgrade and come out into the world doing new things (channelling, moving states, clear with Source). They can clear blockages and help people learn to deal with these new skills that are way beyond traditional teachings. We all have a stronger affinity to certain gifts (we can't be naturally good at everything); we need to discover what we are good at and use these 'superpowers' to the best of our abilities. When we bring humanity up, it is important to remember that people create their own reality (service and light), and often achieve their sacred higher self and merge with their own soul spirit. With regards to human evolution, this is not the first time humanity has tried to make the leap into the godliness of who we are; there are calibrations that have been tried but not been successful (Atlantis, Lemuria). However, this is the one where you will be successful, and it is monumental for individuals, our species and the planet, as we all ascend at the same time. Humanity will bring some missing pieces to the galactic realm through our inhabitation, incarnation and embodiment (moving beyond the angelic realm and into the creation realm). Everyone is raised up all together as a huge, connected family or brotherhood of consciousness.

This is the first book of a series covering topics associated with initial awareness. Following books will delve further into topics associated with acceptance, awakening and personal improvement and development.

The First Way. Before the atomic age, the Universe was understood through Newtonian physics, where there were clear causalities and certainties, suggesting that our Universe was logical and deterministic, and therefore knowable and understandable.[323] World War II represented a large paradigm shift in human understanding, which played out in art, culture, music, politics and psychology, providing the springboard to more radical thinking.

The Second Way. After the atomic age, the emergence of quantum physics essentially replaced certainties with the concept of probability, and the idea that there are aspects of our Universe that are not knowable and can't be quantified. It was a time of radical reinvention of the way we thought, described and understood the Universe around us; scaring off the old guard, but exciting and inspiring a new generation.

There is always a hunger for the 'new', a desire to glimpse hidden worlds, entranced by visions of a better future. The idea that we live in a 3D world, yet are driven by forces beneath our reality, even in our own subconscious, within a 5D world. The realisation that forces we thought we understood, thought we could control, are actually controlling us, imprisoning us with delusions of grandeur and self-made confinements, such as fears of and awakening to having locked ourselves into a world that we are gradually destroying, and willingly submitting ourselves to political, social and religious structures that purport to protect us but in fact entrap us.[424] The degradation of ethics, morality and rational thought, plus a willingness to throw our lot in with false prophets who promise brighter futures even though, in our hearts, we know they will never deliver. Is it the case that we project our deficiencies onto others in order to transfer our blame when we fail to deliver?

The Third Way. We stand today at the precipice of the next age; the choice between two paths awaits us. The security we thought we had is turning into anarchy. Ambition is becoming obsession and order is breaking down into all-devouring chaos. You only need to look around you to see a devolving world characterised by wars, crime, drugs, fraud and lies, and as we become slaves to them, one day they will choose to destroy us. What if there was a way to unite the opposite and opposing forces into a whole?

We approach another, even greater, transition in our modern society, as we come to realise that we have opened ourselves up to new dangers and vulnerabilities by meddling with the fabric of reality (nuclear weapons, digital dependence in an increasingly complex and fragile ecosystem, social media), with the Earth (climate change, atmospheric chemistry, nature's macro-processes) and with the Universe (barely perceivable spatial and temporal dimensions). Do we know what all these 'achievements' and developments really mean? We have created our own all-devouring Ouroboros, playing along and pretending everything will be fine, while knowing in our hearts that something is very wrong and it won't be okay. Has the real power been hiding in the shadows, directing our fate through what we perceived (or were told) was a chain reaction of coincidences, petty motivations and dumb luck?

Where once everything was neatly structured and compartmentalised – theory separated from application, noble intentions from actual outcomes – now all boundaries are breaking down and everything seems to be engulfed in an unstoppable fire as we unleash further monsters from Pandora's Box. A new, unfamiliar world also grows within us as doubt replaces certainty, horror replaces innocent joy and devastation replaces discovery. The realisation dawns that an astonishing connection exists between all matter, all human relations and even our thoughts.

Our fate may be written in raindrops, but that doesn't mean we need to get wet; we still have the choice to take an umbrella with us. No, we can't stop the rain, but we can reduce the chance of getting rained on – any fool can get wet and cold. Are we destined to relive reality over and over again? We will rebuild our world, like countless civilisations before us, and re-experience the thrill of our youth, passion and hope, but we will burn it all down again, and despair in the ashes, then start again – over and over for all eternity.

I think we can change. I think we can turn hope into humanisation. I think we can unburden the world by becoming better versions of ourselves, united, together and un-conflicted, through redemption. We need to break out of our current, fundamental concept of reality, travel through the valley of displacement, existential despair, doubt and doom, yearning for understanding, certainty and bygone days, and seek reconciliation and absolution.

What can we do to understand and prevent the existential dangers that threaten our collective survival, when we can't even understand and resolve the basic things that cause wars, famine and social unrest?

Humans are carbon-based lifeforms. Carbon exists in multiple forms, each with its own shape and structure. When we are born into the world we are akin to a piece of coal, full of energy and potential. Society turns us, out of necessity, into graphite that fills particular needs that society may have. However, graphite has the unfortunate structure of widely spaced horizontal sheets, giving us the appearance that we are dislocated and separated from each other. We are slowly beginning to realise that we, our societies and our environment are not individual layers or entities, but part of the same whole, just in different forms. Just look around and you will see this connectedness in the little things of our day-to-day lives, our experiences and our world itself. We are, in fact, all part of the same beautiful, strong diamond, with a connected, crystallised tetrahedral structure. Proudly bear your diamond inside you, and let your rebellious, unique soul shine from it; pulled from the dust, bright, clear and flawless. We just need to open our eyes, raise our awareness and let the beauty out.

Remember:

People don't realise how a person's whole life can be changed by one book.[292]

It's not enough to have lived. We should be determined to live for something.[93]

When we put God first, all other things fall into their proper place or drop out of our lives.[39]

LiteHows

*Providing **light** at the end of the tunnel to help guide you to a safe place and showing you **how** you can get expert help by pointing you in the right direction.*

What are the UK advice and helpline contact details?

- Call NHS **111** (for when you need help but are not in immediate danger).

- Contact your GP and ask for an emergency appointment.

- Contact the Samaritans – **116 123**, **08457 90 90 90** or email jo@samaritans.org (24-hour response).

- Use the 'Shout' 24/7 crisis text line – text 'SHOUT' to **85258**.

- Text 'HOME' to **741741** to connect with a crisis counsellor.

- For a mental health crisis call **0300 123 3393** or email: info@mind.org.uk

- Text 'CONNECT' to **685868** to chat to a trained volunteer crisis responder.

- 'Childline' – **0800 1111** or email from the website https://www.childline.org.uk/get-support/contacting-childline/

- Family Lives (Parent Line) **0808 800 2222**

- Runaway Helpline **116 000**

- 'The Mix' (Under 25s) **0800 808 4994** or text 'THEMIX' to **85258**

- Citizens Advice

- Al-Anon (Alcohol Issues) **020 7404 0888** (10am - 10pm)

- Cruse Bereavement Care **0808 808 1677**

- Bullying UK **0808 800 2222**

- Carers UK **0808 808 7777**

- Victim Support **0845 30 30 900**

- Scope (Disability) **0808 800 3333**

- 24-Hour National Domestic Violence **0808 20000 247**

- Refuge (Help for Teenage Girls) **0808 2000 247**

- Survivors UK (Rape or Sexual Abuse) Chat via SMS **020 3322 1860**

- Women and Girls Network (WGN Violence/Abuse) **0808 801 0660**

- Men's Advice (Violence/Abuse) **0808 801 0327**

- Talk to Frank (Drug Issues) **0300 123 6600**

- ACAS (Employment Issues) **0300 123 1100**

- Equality Advisory Support Service **0808 800 0082**

- Big Deal (Gambling issues) **0808 800 4444**

- Switchboard (LGBTQ+) **0300 330 0630**

- Coram Voice (Support for Young Children) **0808 800 5792**

- National Youth Advocacy Service **0808 808 1001**

- Family Rights Group **0808 801 0366**

- Young Minds (Mental Health) **0808 802 5544**

- Community Advice & Listening Service (Wales)
  0800 132 737 Text **81066**

- Step Change (Money and Debt) **0800 138 1111**

- 'The Money Advice Service' (Money and Debt) **0800 138 7777**

- 'The National Debt Line' (Money and Debt) **0808 808 4000**

- Woman's Self-Injury Support (Self-harm) **0800 800 8088**

- 'Beat' Helpline (Eating Disorders) **0345 634 7650**

- Migrant Children's Project (Asylum-seekers and Refugees)
  0207 636 8505

- Mumsnet (By parents for parents) https://www.mumsnet.com

In emergency situations, call:

- Emergency Services (Police, Fire, Ambulance and Coast Guard) **999**

- SMS messages can be sent after texting 'Register' to **999**

- Non-emergency Police **101**

- Power Outages **105**

- Gas Leaks **0800 111 999**

Each country has their own set of emergency numbers that can be found here:

- https://en.wikipedia.org/wiki/List_of_emergency_telephone_numbers

The UK Government has set up a website in case you are affected by a crisis abroad:

- https://www.gov.uk/guidance/how-to-deal-with-a-crisis-overseas

If any of the information I have provided is out of date or no longer accurate, then please contact me to let me know. The latest information will be published and updated regularly on 'The Third Way' website:

- thethirdwaybook.com

If you want to provide any feedback, please email me at:

- karl@thethirdwaybook.com

Listen to my podcasts on YouTube. Example versions are listed below:

- https://www.youtube.com/watch?v=wdgq_eueuHo
- https://www.youtube.com/watch?v=RQwbH3mO3xE
- https://www.youtube.com/watch?v=5q21iDkPiHQ

Although the UK advice and help contact details are UK focused, many have websites that you can look up and find multiple resources, however whatever advice you read, it will be never as good as consulting an expert. Please consult experts when at all possible, as they can define the complete picture and best approach understanding your specific needs and the overall context.

REFERENCES

1   1 Corinthians 15:32 (The Bible)
2   1 Timothy 6:7 (The Bible)
3   Abbott, John
4   Abraham, Lalachan
5   Adler, Mortimer
6   AFRICAN PROVERB
7   Agyei, Steve
8   Ajina, Sara
9   Alan, Nicky
10 Alder, Shannon L.
11 Alderton, Dolly
12 Aleichem, Sholom
13 Aleo, Toni
14 Alexander the Great
15 Anderson, Marian
16 Angelou, Maya
17 Anna, Kofi
18 Anon.
19 Anthony, Robert
20 Arabella, Machika Kaye
21 Aral, Sinan
22 Aristotle
23 Aronofsky, Darren
24 Asevedo, Sasha
25 Asimov, Isaac
26 Attenborough, David
27 Aurelius, Marcus
28 Balan, Vidya
29 Barrymore, Ethel
30 Bartlett, Steven
31 Baum, Frank
32 Bay, Holly A.
33 Beak, Sera J.
34 Bedford, Michael
35 Beggs, Jim
36 Belfort, Jordan
37 Bell, Rob
38 Bennett, Roy, T.
39 Benson, Ezra Taft
40 Bergson, Henri
41 Berkun, Scott
42 Berra, Lawrence Peter 'Yogi'
43 Berstein, Gabrielle
44 Beyoncé (Singer)
45 Bhagavad Gita
46 Blake, William
47 Bohr, Neils
48 Bolano, Roberto
49 Bonhoeffer, Dietrich
50 Bono (Paul David Hewson)
51 Brautigan, Richard
52 Brilliant, Ashleigh
53 Brinkley, Christie
54 Brite, Poppy Z.
55 Brockway, Connie
56 Brown Jr, H. Jackson
57 Brown, Brené
58 Brown, Chris
59 Brown, Eleanor
60 Brown, Joel
62 Bryant, Caroll
63 Bucchianeri, E. A.
64 Buehner, Carl W. (Not Bucher or Angelou)
65 Bueller, Ferris (Screenplay by John Hughes)
66 Buffet, Warren
67 Bulwer Lytton, Edward

236 Johnson, Hiram Warren (Former US Senator)
237 Johnson, Michael Bassey
238 Johnson, Spencer
239 Jolie, Angelina
240 Jones, David
241 Jones, Matthew
242 K. L. de Ville
243 Kabat-Zinn, Jon
244 Kalwar, Santosh
245 Kant, Immanuel
246 Kanter, Rosabeth Moss
247 Kassem, Suzy
248 Kassorela, Irene C.
249 Kawasaki, Guy
250 Kayarize
251 Keen, Sam
252 Keller, Helen
253 Kennedy, John F. (Former US President)
254 Kettering, Charles
255 Kierkegaard, Soren
256 King Jr, Martin Luther
257 Kingsolver, Barbara
258 Knight, Tim
259 Knox, Dr William F.
260 Kondo, Marie
261 Kong, Francis
262 Kornfield, Jack
263 Koulouris, Melanie
264 Kram, Olivia
265 Kushner, Harold
266 Lacocca, Lee
267 Landes, Les
268 Laozi
269 Larkin, Michelle
270 Lauren, Ash
271 Laurence, J. M.
272 Lee, Bruce
273 Leik, McLaine
274 Leoni, Tea
275 Lewis, C. S.
276 Lewis, Christin
277 Lim, Wyatt Mingji

278 Lincoln, Abraham
279 London, Jack
280 Lord Tennyson, Alfred
281 Louv, Richard
282 Lowen, Alexander
283 Lozoff, Bob
284 Lui, Herbert
285 Luke 9:24 (The Bible)
286 Macauley, Thomas
287 MacDonald, George
288 MacLaren, Ian (not Plato)
289 Macy, Joanna R.
290 Madonna
291 Majumdar, Suparna
292 Malcolm X (Malcolm Little)
293 Malee, Alison
294 Man, Horace
295 Mandela, Nelson
296 Mandino, Og
297 Manifesto, Holstee
298 Maraboli, Dr Steve
299 Maroutian, Emily
300 Márquez, Gabriel García
301 Martin, Daryl
302 Martini, Angela
303 Marx, Karl
304 Marzo, Paula
305 Mason, John
306 Maynard, Joyce
307 McConaughey, Matthew
308 McCormack, Beth
309 McGill, Bryant H.
310 Mead, Margaret
311 Mejer, Dionne
312 Mencken, Henry Louis
313 Meurer, Dave
314 Meye, Joyce
315 Michel, Andréa A.
316 Miller, Alice
317 Miller, Russ
318 Millman, Dan
319 Milne, A. A.

320 Mishima, Yukio
321 Mitchell, Ben
322 Mitchell, David
323 Mooney, Darren
324 Moore, Alan
325 Morrissey, Mary Manin
326 Mother Teresa
327 Murat ildan, Mehmet
328 Musashi, Miyamoto
329 Myss, Caroline
330 Nappo, Stephane
331 Nazarian, Vera
332 Neustroev, Dmitry
333 Nicole, Brigitte
334 Nietzsche, Friedrich
335 Nin, Anaïs
336 Obama, Barack
(Former US President)
337 Obama, Michelle
338 Olson, Jeff
339 Ono, Yoko
340 Orlick, Terry
341 Orwell, George
342 Osborn, Ronald E.
343 Paine, Thomas
344 Parish, Sarah
345 Parkes, Dr Colin Murray
346 Parton, Dolly
347 Patrick, Pat
348 Paul Wiese
349 Pauling, Linus
350 Pearce, Dan

351 Peguy, Charles
352 Peirce, Penney
353 Perino, Dana
354 Peter, Steve (Prof)
355 Peterson, Lorraine
356 Phillips, Bill
357 Phillpotts, Eden
358 Picoult, Jodi
359 Pierson, Rita
360 Pinto, Freida
361 Plato
362 Pliszka, Jodi

363 Poetry, Atticus
364 Pope, Alexander
365 Powell, John Joseph
366 Proust, Marcel
367 PROVERB
368 Purcell, Veronica
369 Pye, Reece
370 Rajneesh, Osho
371 Raktivist
372 Rand, Ayn
373 Randolf. G. (Modified Quote)
374 Ray, Amit
375 Ray, John
376 Raymond, J.
377 Reagan, Ronald
378 Rhys, Jean
379 Richardson, Cheryl

380 Rien, Andre
381 Rilke, Rainer Maria
382 Rinpoche, Mingyur
383 Riordan, Rick
384 Robbins, Tony
385 Roberts, Donna
386 Robin, Dr Michelle
387 Roethke, Theodore
388 Roger, Carl R.
389 Rogers, Rikki
390 Rohn, Jim
391 Rooney, Andy
392 Roosevelt, Eleanor
393 Roosevelt, Theodore
(Former US President)
394 Roth, Veronica
395 Rove, Karl
396 Rowling, J. K.
397 Rufus, Allan
398 Rumi
399 Russell, Bertrand
400 Ruth, Babe
401 Sakthivel, Adhithya
402 Salzberg, Sharon
403 Sandberg, Sheryl
404 Sarton, May
405 Satyarthi, Kailash

496 Whipple, Edwin Percy
497 Wilcox, Ella Wheeler
498 Wilde, Oscar
499 Wilder, Laura Ingalls
500 Williams, Tennessee
501 Williamson, Marianne
502 Wilson, Tom
503 Winfrey, Oprah
504 Wirthlin, Joseph B.
505 Wolchin, Rachel
506 Wolfe, David
507 Wolfe, Thomas
508 Ali, Muhammad.
509 Woolf, Virginia
510 Wordsworth, William
511 Writes, Mariza
512 Yogananda, Paramahansa
513 Young, Brigham
514 Ziglar, Zig
515 Meurisse, Thibaut
516 Adams, Douglas

600 https://www.relationshiphub.net/what-did-you-learn-too-late-in-life/
601 https://alyjuma.com/dokkodo-the-path-of-aloneness/
602 https://www.momsoulsoothers.com/beautiful-moments-seen-through-soul/
603 https://www.huffpost.com/entry/12-universal-truths-that-will-change-your-life-for-the-better_b_5998144
604 https://www.inc.com/matthew-jones/20-brutal-truths-about-life-no-one-wants-to-admit.html
605 https://www.lifehack.org/articles/lifestyle/life-truths-17-universal-truths-all-share.html
606 https://tinybuddha.com
607 https://screencraft.org/blog/screenwriting-lessons-denzel-washington/
608 https://cac.org/daily-meditations/every-viewpoint-view-point-2015-02-25/
609 https://themindsjournal.com/its-all-in-your-mind/
610 https://www.goodreads.com
611 http://statusmind.com/cool-facebook-status-57/
612 https://www.nbcnews.com/think/opinion/why-humans-believe-most-people-are-telling-truth-even-when-ncna1259456
613 https://www.mikeveny.com/blog/stop-worrying-about-small-things
614 https://www.youtube.com/watch?v=kzFvPVOpbhM
615 https://focus3.com/the-power-of-belief/
616 https://www.linkedin.com/pulse/dust-diamonds-dr-karl-phillips
617 https://www.sermoncentral.com/sermon-illustrations/58428/success-is-a-little-like-wrestling-a-gorilla-by-sermon-central

618 https://www.andalusiastarnews.com/2018/05/19/life-is-a-marathon-not-a-sprint/

619 https://www.trendingus.com/most-important-things-in-life/

620 https://www.iliketoquote.com/the-best-things-in-life-are-worth-waiting-for-fighting-for-believing-in-and-just-never-letting-go-of/

621 https://medium.com/@eric.klimowich/shortcuts-are-for-the-lazy-and-the-efficient-8631d90f3870

622 https://www.pinterest.co.uk

623 https://ihearts143quotes.com/note-to-self-you-cant-control-how-other-people-receive-your-energy-anything-you-do-or-say-gets-filtered-through-the-lens-of-whatever-they-are-going-through-at-the-moment-which-is-not-a/

624 https://pennbookcenter.com/your-why-quotes/

625 https://en.wikipedia.org/wiki/The_Social_Dilemma

626 https://www.childpsychiatryuk.com/news/the-technology-that-connects-us-also-controls-us/

627 https://sites.google.com/site/baldimirmesh/Downhome/Week-5/therealproblemisnotwhethermachinesthinkbutwhethermendo

628 https://www.eyerys.com/articles/people/1367632976/opinions/changing-way-web-works-we-can-make-it-better-place

629 https://theconversation.com/after-75-years-isaac-asimovs-three-laws-of-robotics-need-updating-74501

630 https://www.masterstudies.com/article/why-study-digital-management/

631 https://www.wickedlocal.com/story/marblehead-reporter/2015/08/28/new-isnt-always-improved/33616501007/

632 https://www.theguardian.com/science/2016/jan/19/stephen-hawking-warns-threats-to-humans-science-technology-bbc-reith-lecture

633 https://thoughtcatalog.com/ash-lauren/2016/12/what-did-your-last-relationship-teach-you/

634 https://www.inthespiritoflife.com/blank-2

635 https://www.lifehack.org/articles/lifestyle/life-truths-17-universal-truths-all-share.html

636 https://quoteinvestigator.com/2010/06/29/be-kind/

637 https://www.droudi.com/dont-raise-your-kids-to-have-more-than-you-had-raise-them-to-be-more-than-you-were/

638 https://www.marcandangel.com/2015/10/25/17-quotes-every-struggling-parent-should-read/

639 https://www.bartleby.com/essay/Every-Child-Deserves-A-Champion-An-Adult-FKUUZCT398E7W

640 https://sourcesofinsight.com/friendship-quotes/

641 https://www.skiptomylou.org/friendship-quotes/

642 https://sourcesofinsight.com/friendship-quotes/

643 https://thehabitstacker.com/surround-yourself-with-people/

644 https://wealthygorilla.com/best-friend-quotes/

645 https://www.goalcast.com/true-friendship-quotes/

646 https://sourcesofinsight.com/friendship-quotes/

647 https://travishellstrom.com/articles/win
648 https://sourcesofinsight.com/friendship-quotes/
649 https://www.smitcreation.com/a-good-friend-knows-all-your-best-stories/
650 https://www.riddlester.co/quotes-about-friends/
651 https://en.wikipedia.org/wiki/War_Is_a_Force_That_Gives_Us_Meaning
652 https://www.lovesove.com/best-friends-are-people-who-make-your-problems/
653 https://www.lifehack.org/articles/communication/grow-realize-becomes-less-important-have-ton-friends.html
654 https://getchip.com/night-out-captions/
655 https://quotabulary.com/troubled-relationship-quotes
656 https://www.youtube.com/watch?v=b1iIpml0bD8
657 https://www.trendingus.com/most-important-things-in-life/
658 https://livestreaminghd.medium.com/wherever-you-are-in-life-and-based-on-who-is-around-you-and-based-on-your-current-aspirations-447ba60883e7
659 https://bemorewithless.com/extraordinary/
660 https://www.inc.com/benjamin-p-hardy/why-most-people-will-never-be-successful.html
661 https://www.youtube.com/watch?v=OmG9bfA1jww
662 https://easyorganizedhomes.com/organization-quotes/
663 https://www.randomterrain.com/favorite-quotes-success.html
664 https://www.pinterest.ca/pin/82331499582826806/
665 https://tinybuddha.com/wisdom-quotes/allow-yourself-to-be-proud-of-yourself-and-all-the-progress-youve-made/
666 https://unfoldandbegin.com/the-first-step-towards-change/
667 https://parade.com/975999/marynliles/quotes-about-change/
668 https://www.goodreads.com/quotes/643995-rather-than-being-your-thoughts-and-emotions-be-the-awareness
669 https://www.selfgrowth.com/articles/GITEN1.html
670 https://avisionforgod.wordpress.com/page/2/
671 http://www.gymquotes.co/motivational-quotes/believe-in-your-vision-turn-it-into-reality/
672 https://www.linkedin.com/pulse/make-your-vision-so-clear-fears-become-irrelevant-ify-okafor
673 https://www.searchquotes.com/search/The_Best_Way_To_Succeed_Is_To_Have_A_Specific/
674 https://www.leadershipfirst.net/post/maturity
675 https://elevationrecovery.com/compelling-visions-for-addiction-recovery/
676 https://www.mi6-hq.com/sections/movies/qos_quotes#:~:text=Mathis%3A%20When%20one%20is%20young,heroes%20get%20all%20mixed%20up.
677 https://www.youtube.com/watch?v=mNEUkkoUoIA
678 https://www.healthylifestylesliving.com/liberate-the-mind/personal-development/in-times-of-great-stress-or-adversity/
679 https://www.manufacturedhomepronews.com/wordsofwisdom/its-not-stress-that-kills-us-it-is-our-reaction-to-it/

680 https://www.themindsetjourney.com/overcoming-challenges/the-people-in-your-life-should-be-a-source-of-reducing-stress-not-causing-more-of-it/

681 https://mindzip.net/fl/@johnstan/quotes/when-you-find-yourself-stressed-ask-yourself-one-question-will-this-matter-in-5-years-from-now-if-yes-then-do-something-about-the-situation-if-no-then-let-it-go-22b69975-b740-4169-8de1-885296115cc3

682 https://www.lifehack.org/articles/communication/grow-realize-becomes-less-important-have-ton-friends.html

683 https://medium.com/positivity-post/25-quotes-to-bring-out-your-personal-greatness-2944418e0bd2

684 https://www.goodreads.com/quotes/612549-worrying-does-not-take-away-tomorrow-s-troubles-it-takes-away

685 https://psychcentral.com/anxiety/quotes-about-anxiety

686 https://m1psychology.com/your-relationship-with-yourself-sets-the-tone/

687 https://lessonslearnedinlife.com/dont-stress-yourself-life-is-too-short/

688 https://www.themindsetjourney.com/mindset-quotes/stress-anxiety-and-depression-are-caused-when-we-are-living-to-please-others-paulo-coelho/

689 https://lessonslearnedinlife.com/take-life-day-by-day/

690 https://psycatgames.com/magazine/quotes/finding-peace-quotes/

691 http://www.quotationspage.com/quote/30962.html

692 https://www.pinterest.com/pin/470555861060408770/

693 https://medium.com/@davidgonyo/the-one-hard-truth-about-success-i-finally-accepted-d282f7b99235

694 https://psychcentral.com/anxiety/quotes-about-anxiety

695 https://www.reddit.com/r/Showerthoughts/comments/c1t02v/the_more_people_you_meet_the_more_you_realise_and/

696 https://www.lifehack.org/articles/lifestyle/life-truths-17-universal-truths-all-share.html

697 https://digitalcommons.slc.edu/cgi/viewcontent.cgi?article=1068&context=dmt_etd

698 https://medium.com/live-your-life-on-purpose/are-we-more-connected-now-5324f7fd5950

699 https://www.invajy.com/relationship-quotes/

700 https://www.lovethispic.com/image/227262/sometimes-you-fall-in-love-with-the-most-unexpected-person-at-the-most-unexpected-time

701 https://ponbee.com/quotes-about-meeting-someone-for-the-first-time/

702 https://ponbee.com/quotes-about-meeting-someone-for-the-first-time/

703 https://www.coursehero.com/file/pjg4vg5/Communication-the-human-connection-is-the-key-to-personal-and-career-success/

704 https://www.lovethispic.com/image/348972/you-can't-give-up-on-someone-because-the-situation's-not-ideal

705 http://www.wittyprofiles.com/q/4528042

706 https://lingoties.com/en/quote/6322

707 https://themindsjournal.com/finding-someone-you-can-really-connect-with-is-like-winning-the-lottery

708 https://www.cincinnati.com/story/opinion/contributors/2017/09/04/there-only-one-race-human-race/607985001/

709 https://dissertationsexperts.com/education/education-is-the-passport-to-the-future.html

710 https://www.goodreads.com/quotes/tag/peace

711 https://libquotes.com/kofi-annan/quote/lbq4m4o

712 http://thequotesmaster.com/2015/11/45-religious-quotes-about-life/

713 https://www.theindianpanorama.news/featured/essence-ramadan-may-traceable-faith/

714 https://www.universalmedicine.com.au/blog/science-without-religion-lame-religion-without-science-blind

715 https://en.wikiquote.org/wiki/Kofi_Annan

716 https://www.passiton.com/inspirational-quotes/3597-religions-are-many-and-diverse-but-reason-and

717 https://hackingchristianity.net/2010/02/it-is-our-light-not-our-darkness-that-frightens-us.html

718 https://www.aliomyoga.com/blog/selflove

719 http://sfcfoundations.com/learning-to-ignore-things-is-one-of-the-greatest-paths-to-inner-peace/

720 https://www.goodreads.com/quotes/741506-never-be-in-a-hurry-do-everything-quietly-and-in

721 https://www.goodreads.com/quotes/tag/peace

722 https://www.youtube.com/watch?v=_FbcIpjde40

723 https://thestartupfactory.tech/take-a-walk-on-the-wild-side%E2%80%8B/

724 https://www.lifehack.org/articles/lifestyle/life-truths-17-universal-truths-all-share.html

725 https://www.youtube.com/watch?v=D00TKEMQOHE

726 https://cbd-consultancy.co.uk/blog/page/2/

727 https://oceanrecoverycentre.com/2019/03/20-of-the-absolute-best-addiction-recovery-quotes-of-all-time-top-5/

728 https://www.alcoholsayings.com/a-shot-to-kill-the-pain-a-pill-to-drain-the-shame-a-purge-to-end-the-gain/

729 https://en.wikipedia.org/wiki/The_Prestige_(film)

730 https://www.goodreads.com/quotes/tag/livelihood

731 https://www.mindtools.com/pages/article/newTED_85.htm

732 https://gnews.org/1299469/

733 https://www.trendingus.com/most-important-things-in-life/

734 https://textappeal.com/cultureshocks/insightful-quotes-about-culture/

735 https://www.bartleby.com/essay/A-Nation-s-Culture-Of-The-Heart-FKRK6D929BWW

736 https://www.independent.ie/regionals/wicklowpeople/opinion/the-answer-to-difference-is-to-respect-it-39867754.html

737 https://www.coursehero.com/file/p2op6hl/Culture-is-the-name-for-what-people-are-interested-in-their-thoughts-their/

738 https://www.goodreads.com/quotes/21953-culture-is-the-widening-of-the-mind-and-of-the

739 https://www.northpass.com/blog/the-50-most-inspirational-company-culture-quotes-of-all-time

740 https://hbr.org/2012/05/culture-takes-over-when-the-ce

741 https://blog.vantagecircle.com/company-culture-quotes/

742 https://www.bornleadership.com/leadership-lessons/employee-engagement-2/

743 https://en.wikipedia.ord/wiki/Culture

744 https://isaccurate.com/blog/cultures-around-the-world

745 https://www.youtube.com/watch?v=9cz4ikFcwMY

746 https://www.goodreads.com/quotes/tag/cycle-of-life

747 https://www.animalsinourhearts.com/articles/death-afterlife/reincarnation-reunions.html

748 https://hackingchristianity.net/2010/02/it-is-our-light-not-our-darkness-that-frightens-us.html

749 https://www.lifehack.org/articles/lifestyle/life-truths-17-universal-truths-all-share.html

750 https://examples.yourdictionary.com/articles/yearbook-catch-phrases.html

751 https://www.betterhelp.com/advice/love/30-love-quotes-that-depict-true-love/

752 https://www.trendingus.com/most-important-things-in-life/

753 https://www.lifehack.org/articles/lifestyle/life-truths-17-universal-truths-all-share.html

754 https://lawandsocietymagazine.com/why-do-people-hate/

755 https://www.lifehack.org/321085/these-9-amazing-things-will-happen-when-you-show-people-who-you-really-are

756 https://www.city-data.com/forum/parenting/202241-parents-enabling-adult-children-opinions-wanted-3.html

757 https://discover.hubpages.com/education/How-to-stage-a-coupand-how-not

758 https://www.youtube.com/watch?v=n66mXOQPUnM

759 https://jeopardylabs.com/play/ctc-jeopardy-e

760 https://www.bustle.com/articles/151446-7-things-youre-doing-that-you-dont-realize-make-you-less-likable

761 https://www.embraceyourdifference.com/testimonials/

762 https://www.youtube.com/watch?v=J5dfcvmXAyM

763 https://www.theodysseyonline.com/your-life-is-only-as-good-as-your-mindset

764 https://www.youtube.com/watch?v=sSLj-fQJrO8

765 https://www.selfimprovementdailytips.com/podcast/look-for-something-positive-in-each-day-even-if-some-days-you-have-to-look-a-little-harder

766 https://www.goodreads.com/quotes/tag/life?page=13

767 https://tinybuddha.com/wisdom-quotes/key-happy-knowing-power-choose-accept-let-go/

768 https://saltsworldwide.com/success-is-what-happens-after-you-have-survived-all-of-your-disappointments-unknown-4/

769 https://www.quotemaster.org/energy+and+life

770 https://jimokina.wordpress.com/2015/05/29/the-law-of-attraction/

771 https://bobbeliveau.wordpress.com/2017/07/21/why-are-you-inspired-to-vibrate-higher/

772 http://www.inspirelove.net/collection-of-wisdom.html

773 https://aminoapps.com/c/thewitchescav179/page/item/universal-law/pkpg_jEspInoP7P2dx3b1BbnYgXvVRQDva

774 https://bridget-publishmylove.blogspot.com/2015/03/your-emotions-are-indication-of-what.html

775 https://christinabreault.wordpress.com/2012/12/05/your-energy-stream-a-sua-corrente-de-energia/

776 https://iamfearlesssoul.com/dandapani-quotes-change-your-life/

777 https://www.quotemaster.org/energy+and+life

778 https://www.reddit.com/r/quotes/comments/fcb87z/the_universe_doesnt_recognize_the_difference/

779 https://themindsjournal.com/you-can-care-about-someone-without-letting-them-drain-you/

780 https://funzumo.com/top-quotes-inspirational-for-success-inspire-you/

781 https://www.youtube.com/watch?v=PZVq3zSkqIY

782 https://blog.mtparanschool.com/understanding-god-why-does-god-allow-evil#:~:text=If%20the%20free%20will%20solution,relationships%20anchored%20in%20genuine%20love.

783 https://www.gotquestions.org/God-allow-evil.html

784 Romans 5:3-5 (The Bible)

785 James 1:2-4 (The Bible)

786 https://swabjockeysrumblings.wordpress.com/

787 https://www.smallstepsguide.co.uk/take-small-steps/

788 https://bible.org/seriespage/appendix-need-hour

789 https://www.goodreads.com/quotes/7014741-we-are-all-in-the-same-game-just-different-levels

790 https://wellbeing.gmu.edu/famous-quotes-on-confidence-and-well-being/

791 https://positlive.com/every-next-level-of-your-life-will-demand-a-different-you/

792 https://staymotivatedwithpramesh.wordpress.com/2018/09/30/stop-explaining-yourself-when-you-realize-other-people-only-understand-from-their-level-of-perception/

793 https://www.askideas.com/dont-dumb-yourself-down-for-the-comfort-levels-of-others/

794 https://quotefancy.com/quote/1463302/Ai-Weiwei-Life-is-much-more-interesting-when-you-make-a-little-bit-of-effort

795 https://themindsjournal.com/material-things-doesnt-impress-much/

796 https://www.lifehack.org/articles/communication/respect-people-who-find-time-for-you-their-busy-schedule.html

797 https://www.reddit.com/r/Buddhism/comments/7p707o/please_can_you_explain_the_greatest_effort_is_not/

798 https://www.makingsenseofcents.com/2016/05/money-and-life-lessons.html

799 https://www.morganseniorliving.com/

800 https://www.huffpost.com/entry/12-universal-truths-that-will-change-your-life-for-the-better_b_5998144

801 https://ineedmotivation.com/45-unforgettable-quotes-about-ideas/

802 https://www.therandomvibez.com/imagination-quotes-imagining/

803 https://www.locusresearch.com/think/blog/2017/01/ideas-wont-keep/

804 https://ineedmotivation.com/45-unforgettable-quotes-about-ideas/

805 https://www.therandomvibez.com/imagination-quotes-imagining/

806 https://philosiblog.com/2012/08/30/ones-mind-once-stretched-by-a-new-idea-never-regains-its-original-dimensions/

807 https://ineedmotivation.com/45-unforgettable-quotes-about-ideas/

808 https://malecare.org/you-do-things-when-the-opportunities-come-along-ive-had-periods-in-my-life-when-ive-had-a-bundle-of-ideas-come-along-and-ive-had-long-dry-spells-if-i-get-an-idea-next-week-ill-do-somethi/

809 https://dxinnovationinstitute.com/you-can-have-brilliant-ideas-but-if-you-cant-get-them-across-your-ideas-wont-get-you-anywhere/

810 https://www.educationindex.com/essay/Relevance-Of-The-Communication-Cycle-For-Effective-PKZZ3TH44Z

811 https://libquotes.com/tom-peters/quote/lbd2m9f

812 https://www.goodreads.com/quotes/133314-daring-ideas-are-like-chessmen-moved-forward-they-may-be

813 https://thoughtcatalog.com/sam-marinelli/2017/12/what-making-space-in-your-life-really-means-because-its-not-just-cleaning-out-your-closet/

814 https://medium.com/@nulfogernaquijoyjr/try-not-to-become-a-man-of-success-but-rather-try-to-become-a-man-of-value-35bb36518bee

815 https://soulgardenpathway.com/the-mystery-of-human-existence/

816 https://www.quoteambition.com/purpose-quotes/

817 https://www.themindsetjourney.com/inspirational-quotes/appreciate-where-you-are-in-your-journey-even-if-its-not-where-you-want-to-be-every-season-serves-a-purpose/

818 https://www.goodreads.com/quotes/9943740-the-things-that-excite-you-are-not-random-they-are

819 https://lifecharger.org/the-meaning-of-life-is-to-find-your-gift-the-purpose-of-life-is-to-give-it-away/

820 https://www.finerminds.com/whats-the-purpose-of-life-16-possible-answers-from-16-inspirational-people/

821 https://mot.global/2019/11/there-is-only-one-thing-that-makes-a-dream-impossible-to-achieve-the-fear-of-failure/

822 https://www.youtube.com/watch?v=pJGCAWTgbn0

823 https://quoteinvestigator.com/2017/09/08/new-dream/

824 https://www.reellifewisdom.com/when_you_get_old_in_life_things_get_taken_from_you_i_mean_that_39_s_a_part_of_life_but_you_only_learn_that_when_you_start_losing

825 https://en.wikipedia.org/wiki/Incident_at_Pristina_airport

826 https://www.youtube.com/watch?v=pxBQLFLei70

827 https://www.huffpost.com/entry/12-universal-truths-that-will-change-your-life-for-the-better_b_5998144

828 https://thisisryanrough.blogspot.com/

829 https://www.speakingtree.in/allslides/how-people-treat-you-is-their-karma-how-you-react-is-yours

830 https://dr.library.brocku.ca/bitstream/handle/10464/4997/Brock_Levac_Dylan_Edward_Ryan_2013.pdf

831 https://www.itsnevertoolatetomarry.com/the-art-of-letting-go-in-relationships/

832 https://medium.com/@jpdacres/you-have-to-make-sacrifices-to-get-what-you-want-d5da1c3985a4

833 https://medium.com/@TheValuesWeShare/values-57-sacrifice-55985ad064b3

834 https://www.myartofvision.com/post/understanding-the-value-of-sacrifice-can-you-make-necessary-sacrifices

835 https://www.geckoandfly.com/25219/quotes-about-life-lessons-disappointments/

836 https://www.quoteambition.com/feelings-quotes/

837 https://celebrateyoga.org/47-quotes-about-shutting-down-emotionally/

838 https://blog.gratefulness.me/gratitude-quotes/

839 https://ponbee.com/life-is-too-short-quotes/

840 https://fakebuddhaquotes.com/holding-onto-anger-is-like-drinking-poison/

841 https://www.goodreads.com/quotes/tag/life-lesson?page=2

842 https://www.howhabit.com/life-quotes/

843 https://kidadl.com/quotes/best-preparation-quotes-to-be-ready-for-anything

844 https://kidadl.com/quotes/best-preparation-quotes-to-be-ready-for-anything

845 https://www.amazon.com/Always-Plan-Sometimes-Breathe-Happens/dp/1797090623

846 https://www.goodreads.com/quotes/tag/under-pressure

847 https://www.goodreads.com/quotes/tag/focus-on-positive

848 https://www.dreamsquote.com/33-stay-positive-quotes-life-inspire-words-wisdom/

849 https://www.improvemyworld.com/blog/control-how-you-respond-to-whats-happening

905 https://medium.com/beyond-lucid-technologies/death-is-what-gives-life-meaning-c9eb0e629522#.

906 https://tfiglobalnews.com/2022/02/27/best-deep-soul-quotes/

907 https://kidadl.com/quotes/old-soul-quotes-for-people-who-are-wise-beyond-their-years

908 https://nomadrs.com/signs-you-are-wise-beyond-your-years/

909 https://themindsjournal.com/old-soul-2/

910 https://themindsjournal.com/being-an-old-soul-is-difficult/

911 https://countryheartandhome.com/do-you-believe-in-past-lives-reincarnation-and-ten-signs-you-are-an-old-soul-collaboration/

912 https://www.leadershipnow.com/leadingblog/2022/04/you_dont_need_a_cape_to_be_a_h.html

913 https://dinyarbharucha.wordpress.com/2016/02/19/lend-a-helping-hand/

914 https://www.goodreads.com/quotes/tag/livelihood
915 https://www.youtube.com/watch?v=pShvlq7vT38
916 https://www.youtube.com/watch?v=_OwoCu9y06w
917 https://www.youtube.com/watch?v=Iu8B0_LV5oE
918 https://www.stern.nyu.edu/experience-stern/news-events/message-nyu-stern-leadership-stern-community-regarding-recent-events
919 https://www.bookey.app/quote-book/master-your-emotions
920 https://www.quora.com/What-causes-so-many-people-to-lack-the-ability-to-self-reflect
921 https://www.youtube.com/watch?v=o3exSWWlDjk
922 https://www.amazon.co.uk/Its-All-About-Sex-Insight-ebook/dp/B019017LX8
923 https://en.wikipedia.org/wiki/Masaru_Emoto
924 https://www.ids.ac.uk/news/new-insights-on-global-sex-education-in-our-digital-era/
925 https://www.youtube.com/watch?v=DvyCbevQbtI
926 https://www.youtube.com/watch?v=daV3T2biCfA
927 https://www.youtube.com/watch?v=LpZOVJeyvGo
928 https://www.youtube.com/watch?v=l4Tw9_VGOEw
929 https://www.youtube.com/watch?v=MqjGLFNmorg
930 https://www.finerminds.com/whats-the-purpose-of-life-16-possible-answers-from-16-inspirational-people/

Notes

1. All website links were correct, working and valid at the time this book was written. Websites have been our digital footprints for decades, but they change and get modified, and with the relentless march of technology, will they become extinct? This information has thus been provided to the readers as the best available to the author and should be taken as snapshot in time. The author cannot be held responsible for maintaining these websites, keeping them active, or for any content changes that may or will occur on these websites in the future, especially where user-generated content is ubiquitous, or erroneously reproduced/copied or altered. As the information is considered 'in the public domain' and freely accessible on the internet, the author has listed these references to identify the source of the information provided in this book, but it is not known if these websites are the originators of this material or if it has been reproduced in violation of copyright law, or with liability for direct, contributory or vicarious infringement. If this is the case, and where these cases are brought to the attention of the author, corrections will be made in future editions.

   The author cannot verify the validity, truth or authenticity of website content.

2. All references are provided based on the best information available to the author. There are multiple cases where quotes' origins are vague, especially when the internet cites multiple people as the source. Every effort has been made to cite the correct references, but some may be missing, incorrect or wrong. This is the world we live in, where it can be very difficult to get to the truth with so much information that is readily and publicly available.

3. The internet is one of the most powerful agents of freedom in terms of free access to knowledge, but it is vulnerable to agents who seek to misinform, fake and copy information, damage a sharing and learning culture, and push their own agendas. We should never be afraid to share information that seeks to improve, benefit, help, educate and inform others; it should not be hidden behind commercial/government barriers, laws or cultures, just

because it makes people think. We need to think right now, our collective survival depends upon it as we face future challenges, the likes of which we have never seen before. For all solutions start with a thought.

INDEX OF TOPICS

Loving	115	Success	19
Loyalty	196	Teachers	52
Mental	11	Things	1
Mindfulness	250	Time	230
Movement	207	Togetherness	255
Music	91	Touch	215
Negativity	125	Trusting	27
Opportunities	25	Truth	14
Organising	170	Untaught	66
Peace	90	Urgency	161
People	47	Vibrations	131
Perseverance	28	Viewpoints	13
Planning	167	Vision	78
Positivity	127	Wealth	234
Purpose	146	Willpower	218
Race	85	Winning	165
Reacting	175	Work	98
Reflections	198	Yourself	205
Regrets	191		
Religion	87		
Resolve	31		
Respect	204		
Sacrificing	159		
Sadness	120		
Self-Help	31		
Sex	56		
Simple	256		
Smile	186		
Social	50		
Speech	253		
Spirituality	247		
Starting	157		
Stay Real	42		
Stress	79		

TOPICS BY
'THIRD WAY' CATEGORIES

MIND

Acceptance, Achievements, Addictions, Adversity, Anger, Belief, Change, Choosing, Confidence, Dreams, Education, Failing, Fear, Focus, Grieving, Hate, Influencing, Innovation, Jealousy, Knowledge, Learning, Lessons, Loyalty, Mental, Negativity, Opportunities, Positivity, Reacting, Regrets, Resolve, Sadness, Self-Help, Starting, Stress, Success, Time, Untaught, Urgency, Willpower.

BODY

Aging, Art, Artificial Intelligence, Boundaries, Ceilings (Glass), Confrontation, Consistency, Controlling, Culture, Cycles, Death, Dishwashing, Doing, Effectiveness, Effort, Family, Fighting, Food, Friends, Health, Here Be Dragons, Imperfect, Kids, Levels, Lifecycles, Limitations, Livelihood, Movement, Organising, People, Perseverance, Planning, Race, Sex, Social, Teachers, Trusting, Winning, Work.

SOUL

Awareness, Backdrop, Beauty, Charity, Conditioning, Connections, Enough, Faith, Good and Evil, Happiness, Helping, Home, Hope, Intimate Relationships, Intuition, Joyful, Kindness, Lightworking, Less, Lifecycles, Loving, Mindfulness, Music, Peace, Purpose, Reflections, Religions, Respect, Sacrificing, Simple, Smile, Speech, Spirituality, Stay Real, Things, Togetherness, Touch, Truth, Vibrations, Viewpoints, Vision, Wealth, Yourself.

ABOUT THE AUTHOR

Dr Karl Phillips completed his doctorate in Mining Engineering from Cardiff University before working in many different sectors and for a wide variety of organisations. Karl is a self-professed life learner and is always seeking to be at the cutting edge of technology, data, knowledge. He is now a consultant, an educator and a winner of multiple awards, including the international InnoCentive award. He has been fortunate enough to write many technical and management papers, present at worldwide conferences, and work and travel all over the world.

He has always been willing to try new things, push the boundaries and tries to keep an open mind on things as well, whilst recognising that 'doing nothing is so under-rated' because it allows the mind and body to rest, and for the soul to speak, if you listen ever so carefully.

Karl believes that everyone can change the world, and he uses this philosophy to inspire and empower people through everything he does.

Website: https://60bc8b72d0748.site123.me

Facebook: https://www.facebook.com/karl.phillips.5074644/

What Did You Think of '*The Third Way*'?

A big thank you for purchasing this book. It means a lot that you chose this book specifically from such a wide range on offer. I do hope you enjoyed it, the vast majority of it, or took something away that you didn't appreciate beforehand. The world is so vast, human experience so strange with everyone being unique, our journey takes us to high mountains and through deep valleys. We can often feel incredible small, yet we have the potential to all achieve great things if we put our mind, body and soul to it. We all have a wonderful tale to tell, so join me when we continue the journey in Book 2.

Book reviews are incredibly important for an author. All feedback helps them improve our writing for future projects, subjects and topics for the follow-on books in this series and for developing additional materials to complement this edition. If you are able to spare a few minutes to post a review on Amazon, that would be much appreciated.

Publisher Information

Rowanvale Books provides publishing services to independent authors, writers and poets all over the globe. We deliver a personal, honest and efficient service that allows authors to see their work published, while remaining in control of the process and retaining their creativity. By making publishing services available to authors in a cost-effective and ethical way, we at Rowanvale Books hope to ensure that the local, national and international community benefits from a steady stream of good quality literature.

For more information about us, our authors or our publications, please get in touch.

www.rowanvalebooks.com
info@rowanvalebooks.com

Milton Keynes UK
Ingram Content Group UK Ltd.
UKHW051914180724
445692UK00007B/87